Foreword

by Gary Jobson

The great thing about sailing is that there is something in it for everyone — of any age. Whether it is competing for the America's Cup or just day sailing on an inland lake, the common denominator is simple — having fun.

Over the past few years, thanks to my America's Cup television commentary with ESPN and hundreds of lectures throughout the country, I have sensed a tremendous surge of enthusiasm for our sport. Leisure time is a precious commodity in today's busy world, and sailing is a reward many people seek.

Start Sailing Right is a fantastic primer for anyone with an urge to get out on the water — and a reference guide for a lifetime. It offers one practical, usable tip after another and the profuse use of large, clear diagrams and humorous illustrations makes sailing quickly understandable and puts the new sailor at ease.

But sailing can also be a challenging sport. A good sailor is always aware of changing wind and weather, and develops a healthy respect for Mother Nature and the safety of everyone on board. It's called seamanship, and it's a message that comes through loud and clear in this book.

Start Sailing Right goes a long way toward giving sailors a faster start, and a chance to be better, safer sailors than ever before.

Acknowledgements

S ailors are special people. Their love of the sport and their willingness to contribute time and effort for the good of their fellow sailors is unique. That feeling of commitment and purpose was present in virtually everyone who worked on *Start Sailing Right*, and I feel privileged to have worked with them all.

I would like to thank the United States Yacht Racing Union and the American Red Cross for the opportunity to be associated with such a fine project. Without the vision and support of the USYRU, USYRU Executive Director Steve Black, his successor John Bonds and John Malatak, Officer of Health and Safety for the American Red Cross, this book would have never become a reality. They are, in a sense, the founding fathers of *Start Sailing Right*.

Supervising the project from start to finish was Timmy Larr, who also worked with the author in refining the content and organization of the book. Timmy was Chairman of the USYRU Training Committee when this project was initiated, and her efforts have been instrumental in the rapid expansion of training programs within USYRU.

Current Training Committee Chairman Jim Muldoon provided valuable assistance in the drafting of agreements and contracts between USYRU and American Red Cross, and fellow Training Committee member Mike Thompson, who was project coordinator on the USYRU/Red Cross *Learn to Sail Videos*. The videos, in consort with *Start Sailing Right* and on-the-water instruction with Red Cross/USYRU trained instructors, form the most effective learn-to-sail teaching system in the world.

The primary editing of *Start Sailing Right* was performed by Ron Dwelle, a professor of communications at Grand Valley State University, well-known marine journalist and dedicated sailor, who worked diligently to refine and polish the text.

Dr. Jane Kent, who has served as Director of the Sports Medicine Program for the U.S. Sailing Team, assisted with recommendations for the sections on exercise and nutrition. As an avid sailor, Jane has contributed significantly to the advancement of the physical and mechanical aspects of the sport.

Finally, to Emmett McNamara Inc. of Warren, Michigan, who also produced the award-winning *Learn to Sail Videos* for USYRU and the American Red Cross, we all wish to extend thanks and appreciation for their outstanding work in the typesetting, illustration and graphic production of this book.

Derrick Fries

START SAILING RIGHT!

The national standard of quality instruction for anyone learning how to sail using the S.T.A.R. method — a proven system for becoming a confident, safe sailor. . .*fast!*

BY DERRICK FRIES

DESIGNED BY MARK SMITH

Published by the United States
Yacht Racing Union and The American National Red Cross

This participant's textbook is an integral part of the
American Red Cross/United States Yacht Racing Union Basic
Sailing Course. By itself, it does not constitute complete
and comprehensive training in sailing. Please contact your
local Red Cross or the United States Yacht Racing Union for
further information on the Basic Sailing course.

ISBN: 0-86536-144-4

The Author

Since 1979 Derrick Fries has been a regular contributor to several national sailing magazines and has written two books; *Successful Sunfish Racing* and *Single-Handed Racing: High Performance Sailing Techniques*. In 1986, he served as technical advisor and performed in USYRU/ARC's *Learn to Sail Videos*.

In 1985, he was selected as a finalist for the NASA Teacher-in-Space Program and is currently a certified NASA Space Ambassador, lecturing on the program to school districts throughout the Great Lakes area. Derrick has his master's degree from Oakland University and is a school administrator for Birmingham Public Schools in Birmingham, Michigan.

Derrick has been teaching sailing and been director of sailing at various programs since 1973. As an active USYRU Clinic Director, he is involved in the training and certification of instructors for junior sailing and learn-to-sail programs in the Great Lakes area. He lives with his wife Denise in Drayton Plains, Michigan.

In addition to his teaching experience, Derrick was a collegiate All-American sailor at Michigan State University in 1973 and '74 and has won national and world championship titles in several dinghy classes.

Derrick Fries

The Designer

Mark Smith began sailing at age six on Long Island Sound and has been an active one-design and offshore sailor ever since.

Mark is a graduate of the Rhode Island School of Design, where he majored in architecture. He was Art Director of *Yacht Racing/Cruising* magazine (now *Sailing World*) from 1970-1983. In 1984 he teamed up with author John Rousmaniere to design and illustrate *The Annapolis Book of Seamanship*, published by Simon & Schuster. Mark was editor and publisher of *Sailor* Magazine from 1984-1986.

Currently Mark is Editor and Art Director of *American Sailor*, USYRU's monthly newsmagazine, and a free-lance creative consultant. He lives in Rowayton, CT with his wife Tina and daughters Stephanie, Natalie and Cristina.

Mark Smith

Dedication

The spirit and soul of this book is former USYRU Training Committee Chairman Timmy Larr, who has been truly dedicated to helping all learn-to-sail students—young and old— discover the rewards of sailing. Her enthusiasm and sensitivity to the human side of the learning process have been an important force in shaping the character of *Start Sailing Right*. Her unselfishness and untiring effort have been an inspiration to us all.

— *Derrick Fries.*

Contents

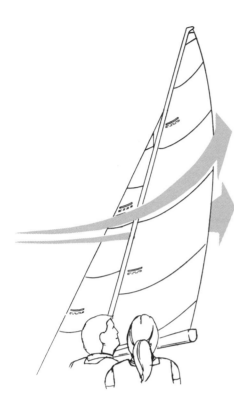

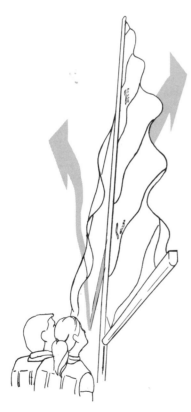

Contents *continued*

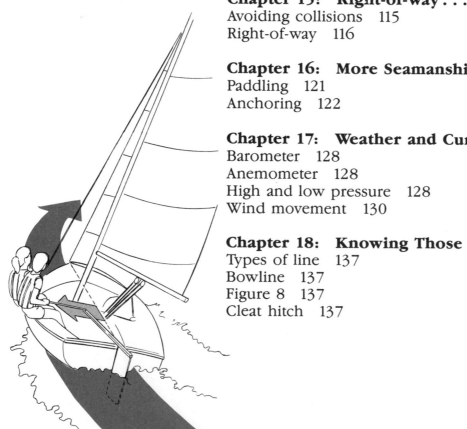

An Introduction

The United States Yacht Racing Union (USYRU) is our country's governing body for the sport of sailing. The American Red Cross is responsible for teaching water safety in many aquatic activities, including canoeing, kayaking, swimming and sailing. With *Start Sailing Right,* these organizations have joined together to provide unprecedented support for sailors on all levels of sailing in all kinds of sailboats.

One of the primary objectives of this historic alliance is to provide an effective standard of quality instruction for all students learning to sail. The USYRU/Red Cross program includes *Start Sailing Right,* a series of video tapes designed to work with the book, a program of student certification and an extensive educational and training program for instructors themselves. It is one of the most highly developed and effective national training systems for students and sailing instructors in the world.

This program is conducted at a professional level to ensure a high degree of continuity and success for its students. Our hope is that you will become not only a successful sailor but also a safe sailor who knows how to have *fun* on the water.

Start Sailing Right is intended as a supplement to your first sailing lessons, rather than as a substitute for them. It is designed to work well with a wide variety of basic courses offered in different regional sailing communities. It was created to help build your enthusiasm and make your introduction to the fantastic sport of sailing a positive experience that you can carry far into the future.

What is the S.T.A.R. Method?

S.T.A.R., or Standards for Training with Accelerated Results, is a national instructional system for instructors and students that is recognized by the American Red Cross and the United States Yacht Racing Union. This learning and teaching process is designed to develop safe, confident and responsible sailors. Learning is accelerated by using a building-block approach and emphasizing active on-the-water participation by the student. As new skills are introduced, previously learned skills are reviewed and consolidated by a carefully designed system of chapter and course reviews.

USYRU/Red Cross Video Tapes

These award-winning *Learn to Sail* video tapes, available in both instructor and student versions, are a valuable supplement to *Start Sailing Right.* To help them work better together, the book is cross referenced to the tapes with symbols that correspond to segments in the tapes. Like the book, the *Learn to Sail* tapes are intended as support for an on-the-water course with an instructor or as a post-course refresher.

The three-tape instructor/student version of the *Learn to Sail* tapes is available from the American Red Cross and the United States Yacht Racing Union. The two-tape student version is available from Sea TV, P.O. Box 8969, New Haven, CT 065632.

How to Use This Resource Book

Start Sailing Right was created to help you become a more confident and accomplished sailor at the end of your learn-to-sail experience. Visualize it as a tool that will accelerate your learning curve and clarify your understanding of the principles of sailing.

Sailing language and terminology have traditionally been emphasized as a first step in sailing instruction. This book places more emphasis on getting on the water quickly and learning sailing skills "by doing." It makes your learning experience more exciting and immediately satisfying. To use the book most effectively, we encourage you to follow these steps:

1. Be committed and enthusiastic toward learning how to sail.
2. Learn to sail with a *qualified* sailing instructor.
3. Read each chapter thoroughly.
4. Examine each of the illustrations. They have been carefully designed to help you visualize concepts and procedures clearly and simply.
5. Practice each sailing maneuver on-shore and then on-the-water.
6. Review each chapter and be sure you understand it before moving on to the next one. Review questions are listed at the end of each chapter for this purpose.

Remember, your own learning rate may be different from other students based on a number of factors, the most important being your commitment to becoming a good sailor. Also remember — a good sailor (even a great one) never stops learning.

Swimming

To be a safe and accomplished sailor does require one prior skill — swimming. In the interest of safety *and* confidence, we recommend that everybody acquire this skill before learning to sail. You should be able to swim at least 25 yards unassisted. In addition, you should be able to tread water while fully clothed for at least five minutes without assistance and without the use of a life jacket, and be able to put on an approved life jacket in water that is six feet deep or more. While learning to sail, there will be times when you will have to enter the water to practice various boat handling skills and techniques. Such things as capsize and man-overboard recovery are an integral part of sailing and require swimming skills by the sailor.

The American Red Cross and local YMCA's and YWCA's offer many excellent swimming courses.

What Makes Sailing Special?

Within the past 20 years, the advent of fiberglass boatbuilding and other new technologies has opened up the sport of sailing to people of all ages, incomes and abilities. Sailing offers virtually limitless choices in boat types and designs, each with its own unique characteristics. This book has been designed to standardize the learn-to-sail process for many different boat types.

Most sailors will acquire entry-level skills quite rapidly. However, mastering them is an experience that will be rewarding, mentally stimulating and pleasurable for a lifetime.

As you learn to sail, you will find that sailing is more than simply being pushed and pulled by the wind. For most people, sailing is meeting new friends, enjoying nature's beauty and challenge, and sharing a unique fellowship with all boaters. A tremendous camaraderie exists among sailors, particularly on the water, which makes sailing — and the people who do it — very special.

Start Sailing Right **is designed as part of a learn-to-sail system that includes the award-winning video series** *Learn to Sail.* **Throughout this book, symbols adjoining select passages serve as a key to coordinate the videos with the book for instructors and students. The black symbols with white numbers indicate corresponding segments in the student (two-tape) version. The white symbols with black numbers indicate corresponding segments in the instructor/student (three-tape) version of the videos.**

Chapter 1

You as a Sailor

"Bill, why don't you just break down and take some lessons?"

KEY CONCEPTS

- **The sailing environment**
- **The self-reliant sailor**
- **Personal sailing gear**
- **Sun protection**
- **Exercise and nutrition**

Sailing a boat is a unique and rewarding experience. If you asked experienced sailors why they sail, you would get a tremendous variety of answers. In part, the variety comes from the great versatility in the sport. Few hobbies offer as much choice and freedom as sailing.

You can choose to sail in a small high-performance dinghy or you can relax in a day sailer. Later on, you might wish to race or cruise along a scenic coast. Sailing can be enjoyed in so many different ways that it is truly a lifelong sport.

Environmental Awareness

What should you bring to your first sailing experience? Besides your personal sailing gear, you should have an appreciation for the forces of the wind and water. Developing your sensitivity to wind and the water will make it easier for you to anticipate and "see" their changes.

The sailing environment has many different moods. It can be peaceful and serene, making it thoroughly enjoyable for any sailor. But as a new sailor, you must be aware that it can change, often quickly. A beautiful sunny day with a warm sea breeze can rapidly turn into poor weather with strong winds.

Sailors learn to develop their awareness of the sailing environment so they can anticipate these changes. This **environmental awareness** calls for continuous observation of the wind, weather, sea conditions, current, and distance from the shore. By always watching these factors, you will become a **self-reliant** sailor. Being self-reliant will allow you to sail confidently and safely in different weather conditions without having to call for assistance.

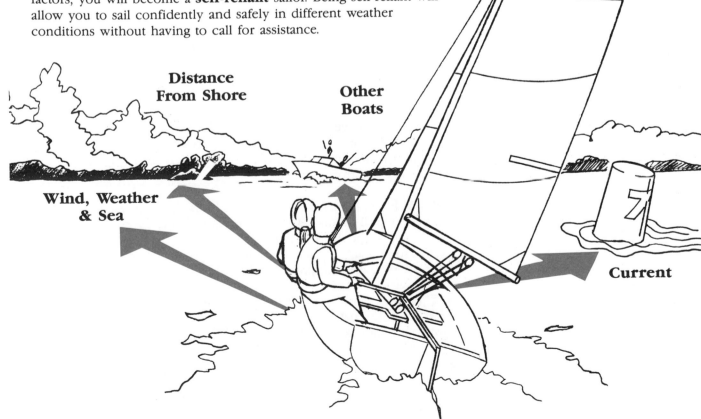

Distance From Shore

Other Boats

Wind, Weather & Sea

Current

Dressing For Sailing

Often it is cooler on the water than ashore, and nothing takes the fun out of sailing more than being cold. On the other hand, the sailor must also deal with the heat and the rays of the sun.

The marine clothing industry now offers a wide variety of choices in sailing clothes. You should select your clothes by keeping in mind the season of the year and by listening to daily weather forecasts. Handling a sailboat involves lots of twisting and moving about, so it is important that your clothes allow a full range of motion. A duffel bag of extra clothing will allow you to add more layers or to change into dry clothes.

THE BODY. During warmer days, you should wear light clothing to keep your body cool and reflect the sunlight. If you are prone to sunburn, a high collared shirt will protect your neck, and long sleeves will protect your arms. Dark clothing absorbs the sun and makes your body heat up quickly.

On cooler days, you should dress in layers. Lightweight jackets, sweaters, and long underwear are a good idea for keeping your body warm. Wool or some of the new synthetic materials retain your body's warmth and protect you against the cold. Smart sailors overdress on cooler days.

THE HEAD. Your head, face, and eyes have to be protected from the ultraviolet rays of the sun, and you should always use a sunscreen to protect your skin. This sunblock protects you not only from direct sunlight but also from the sunlight reflecting off the water. Even on cloudy days some ultraviolet rays penetrate the clouds. Coating your exposed skin with a high numbered sunblock will keep you from being sunburned.

On hot days you should wear a visor or light-colored hat to protect your head and forehead. The visor is often better since it shields the face but allows heat to escape. On cold days, body heat escapes through the head, just like a chimney, and a hat or hood will help keep you warm and dry.

To protect your eyes, you should use good quality sunglasses that have ultraviolet protection. They will reduce the chance of developing an eye disease caused by exposure to the sun and aggravated by salt water. (It rarely occurs around fresh water.) Since most sunglasses won't float, wearing a cord around your neck will keep them from falling overboard. On windy days, sunglasses can also help keep the salt and water out of your eyes.

FOOTWEAR. Nonskid shoes are necessary for firm traction. Tennis shoes work well as long as they have a good nonskid sole. They should be comfortable but tight enough to keep your foot from sliding around, and should dry quickly if you get them wet. In wet and cold weather, waterproof boots will keep your feet warm and dry.

GLOVES. Because you will be working with ropes or lines that must slip through the palms of your hands, gloves are desirable, at least until your hands get toughened up. Gloves also provide you with better grip for holding the lines. During cooler days, you might wear gloves for added warmth, and during the coldest weather you may even want a pair of waterproof gloves.

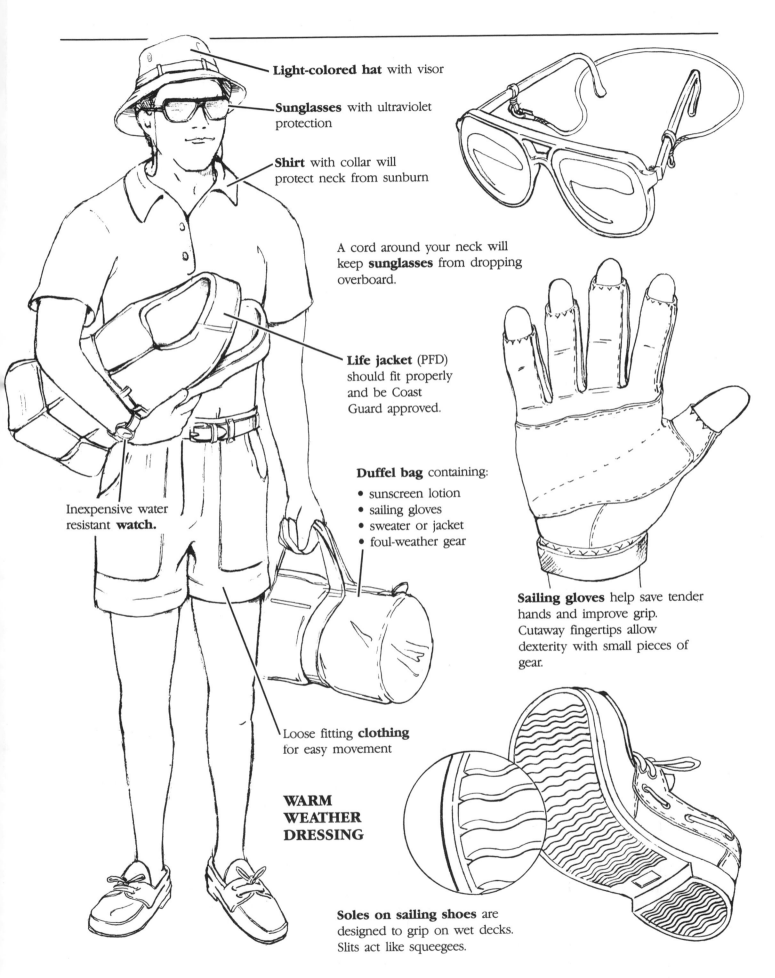

Light-colored hat with visor

Sunglasses with ultraviolet protection

Shirt with collar will protect neck from sunburn

A cord around your neck will keep **sunglasses** from dropping overboard.

Life jacket (PFD) should fit properly and be Coast Guard approved.

Duffel bag containing:
- sunscreen lotion
- sailing gloves
- sweater or jacket
- foul-weather gear

Inexpensive water resistant **watch.**

Sailing gloves help save tender hands and improve grip. Cutaway fingertips allow dexterity with small pieces of gear.

Loose fitting **clothing** for easy movement

WARM WEATHER DRESSING

Soles on sailing shoes are designed to grip on wet decks. Slits act like squeegees.

5

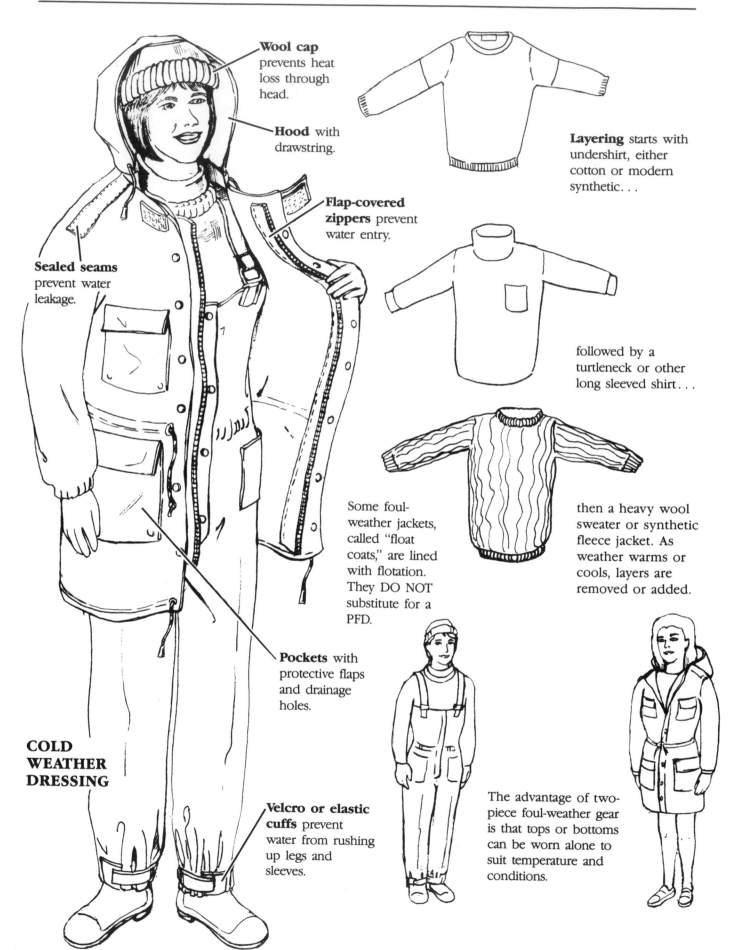

Wool cap prevents heat loss through head.

Hood with drawstring.

Flap-covered zippers prevent water entry.

Sealed seams prevent water leakage.

Pockets with protective flaps and drainage holes.

COLD WEATHER DRESSING

Velcro or elastic cuffs prevent water from rushing up legs and sleeves.

Layering starts with undershirt, either cotton or modern synthetic . . .

followed by a turtleneck or other long sleeved shirt . . .

Some foul-weather jackets, called "float coats," are lined with flotation. They DO NOT substitute for a PFD.

then a heavy wool sweater or synthetic fleece jacket. As weather warms or cools, layers are removed or added.

The advantage of two-piece foul-weather gear is that tops or bottoms can be worn alone to suit temperature and conditions.

6

FOUL-WEATHER GEAR. You should choose foul-weather gear for warmth, comfort, and durability. Typical gear includes a waterproof jacket with a hood, and waterproof pants with suspenders. Other possibilities are one-piece dinghy suits which offer excellent protection. During cold or wet weather, the sailor may choose a wet suit or even a dry suit. The wet suit provides protection by allowing some water to filter in and be heated up by the body, whereas the dry suit keeps the body perfectly dry and free of water. Some people think that a wet or dry suit provides adequate flotation should you end up in the water, but they do not. Both must be worn with a life jacket, for safety.

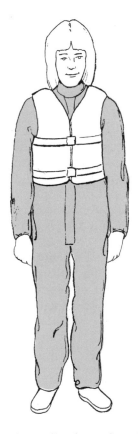

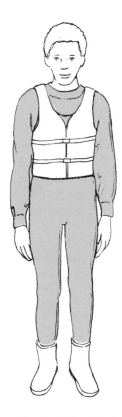

One-piece dinghy suits offer convenience and good water protection, but top or bottom can't be removed to cool off, as with a two-piece suit.

Wet suits, initially developed for skin divers, allow water to filter in and be heated by the body. In colder weather, they are often worn under outer clothing and PFD's. They are available as complete, one-piece suits, tops or bottoms. Boots and hoods are also available in wet-suit material.

Dry suits are insulated one-piece outfits that are tightly sealed at neck, wrists and ankles. They provide water protection AND warmth.

Physical Fitness

EXERCISE. Being in good condition will add to your enjoyment of sailing. To a beginning sailor, the power of the wind can be easily underestimated. In medium and heavy air, sailing can sometimes require strength and endurance. Hiking out, sheeting sails, and moving in the boat call for flexibility as well as strength. To prepare for this type of movement in the boat, you can do **aerobic** and **anaerobic** exercises.

Aerobic exercise involves active motion that will increase your heartbeat, such as running or playing fast-moving games like tennis or volleyball. Anaerobic exercise results from lifting or pulling to help build strength and muscles. Weight lifting and certain types of flexing and stretching exercises are anaerobic. Your exercise should also include warm-up and cool-down activities.

The exercise program should be tailored to your needs and physical condition. The accompanying illustrations show some flexibility exercises for sailors.

NUTRITION. Along with proper exercise, a balanced diet is very helpful, particularly for younger sailors. Energy and concentration are directly related to nutritional intake. An active sailor may need more than 3,000 calories per day just to perform the tasks of sailing. Often a change in diet will cause an improvement in performance.

A good diet will have a balance of protein, carbohydrate, fat, vitamins, minerals, and water. Nutrition for sailing is similar to other active sports.

A careful diet, coordinated with your periods of activity, is smart. It will allow you to learn and understand new sailing concepts and techniques and increase your physical performance and endurance. It will also help you recover from a vigorous day on the water and prepare yourself better for the next day.

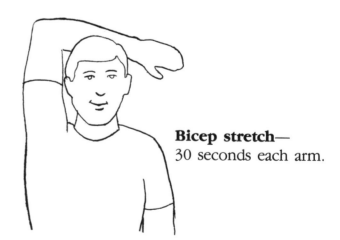

Bicep stretch—
30 seconds each arm.

Sailing requires movements in many atypical positions. It is helpful to do several simple stretching exercises before AND AFTER you sail to help minimize stiffness or discomfort.

Lower leg stretch —
30 seconds each leg.

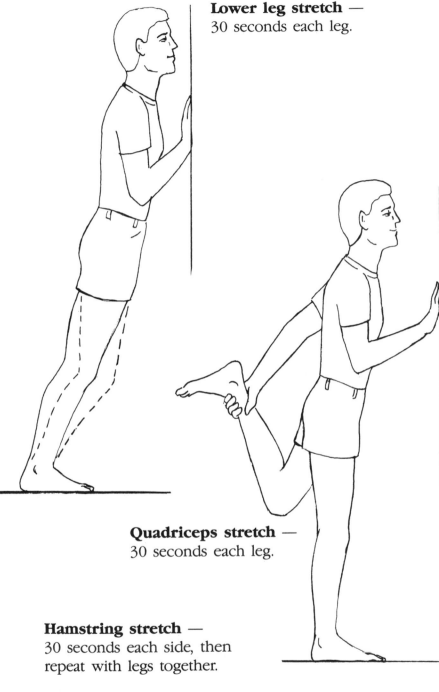

Quadriceps stretch —
30 seconds each leg.

Hamstring stretch —
30 seconds each side, then
repeat with legs together.

Review Exercises

I. Multiple Choice

1. In sailing, the term "self-reliant" means
   a. watching the weather and clouds around you.
   b. being able to take care of yourself in different weather conditions without needing assistance.
   c. always wearing your life jacket around the sailing site.
   d. sailing by yourself.

2. To protect yourself from the sun, you should use
   a. light-colored clothing, sunblock, sunglasses, and visor.
   b. a light-colored life jacket, sunblock, sunglasses, and sweater.
   c. dark-colored clothing, hat, sunglasses, and sunscreen.
   d. a dry suit, sun oil, sunglasses, and foul-weather gear.

3. It is best to over-dress for sailing because
   a. sailors like to look fashionable.
   b. it is often cooler and windier on the water.
   c. it will prevent injuries.
   d. it will keep you from being sunburned.

II. Matching

1. Environmental awareness
2. Sailing gloves
3. Sun and cold
4. Light-colored clothes
5. Proteins and carbohydrates

a. Hand protection from lines and sheets
b. Used for very hot weather
c. Elements of a balanced diet
d. Always knowing the conditions around you
e. Two common concerns of a sailor

III. Exploring Sailing
(discussion or writing)

1. What are some particular environmental awareness problems that you have at your sailing site?
2. Why are exercise and nutrition important to the sport of sailing?
3. What kinds of special sailing gear do you need for your location and boat type?

Chapter 2

Safety and You

"There's one in every crowd."

KEY CONCEPTS

- **Sailor's code**
- **Life jackets (PFDs)**
- **Hypothermia**
- **Heat emergencies**
- **Electrical hazards**
- **Control signals**
- **Safety equipment**

There is an unwritten code for sailors that has been passed down over centuries. It includes courtesy, consideration, and respect for fellow boaters. The water must be shared by people who wish to enjoy its rewards — fellow sailors and power boaters, fishermen, swimmers, and water skiers, as well as many who make their living in commercial shipping.

The attitude displayed by the helmsman sets an example for the crew, so the helmsman needs to be considerate and thoughtful at all times.

You should also avoid littering the water and always observe local laws and regulations — observing scuba-diving areas, water-skiing areas, and swimming markers. Because your boat has underwater appendages such as the centerboard and rudder, it is best to avoid fisherman and stay clear of their lines and hooks.

Sailboats usually have the right-of-way over powerboats. However it is not polite to ask a huge power boat to alter its course around you when it may be easier for you to stay clear. This is particularly important in small areas where bigger boats have little room to maneuver. It is also best to stay clear of shipping channels or areas used by commercial vessels such as freighters or barges.

Another tradition that has been honored since the first days of sail is always to come to the aid of a boat in need of help. The biggest single courtesy that you can demonstrate, however, is to be in control of yourself and your boat.

All of these courtesies are called **the sailor's code**. It's one of the things that makes sailing so special, and you should do your part in keeping it that way.

Life Jackets `1` `1`

Another term for a life jacket is a **PFD**, or **Personal Flotation Device**. The PFD is key equipment for safe sailing and should become your best friend. Just as the snow skier cannot ski without safety bindings, the sailor cannot sail safely without the PFD.

It is smart to wear your PFD at all times around the waterfront. Accidents can happen at any time, and the PFD is a great protector. After a while it will become second nature to wear your life jacket at all times.

In choosing your own PFD, make sure that it is Coast Guard approved. You will find the Coast Guard approval and classification sewn or stamped on the vest where it is easy to see. Select a PFD that will be visible when you are in the water. Yellow and orange are good, while blue or white are hard to spot, especially in waves. Since many PFDs look alike, it is a good idea to write your name in the jacket with a waterproof marker. The vest-style flotation aid (Type III) is often used for sailing in protected waters. If used in rough seas, it may not hold your head above the waves.

The PFD will do a number of things for you:
1. It adds buoyancy to your body.
2. It holds your head and body higher in the water for better visibility.
3. It helps keep your body warm.

Offshore Life jacket
(Type I)

Near-shore Buoyant Vest
(Type II)

Flotation Aid
(Type III)

4. It helps build confidence when you are just beginning to sail.
5. When worn over clothing, it allows for easy identification by instructors or other sailors.
6. It helps you to enter and exit the boat.

The PFD should become a natural part of your sailing wardrobe. If you have just purchased your PFD or been issued one by your instructor, spend some time getting familiar with it. Try it out both on land and in the water. Before long, you will be very comfortable with it at all times.

You must *never* underestimate the worth of your life jacket around the waterfront. Make your PFD your best friend.

The Safety Factor

Safety on the water is a state of mind. In this story, reprinted from USYRU's monthly newsmagazine AMERICAN SAILOR, an experienced sailor describes an incident that brought home the message clearly.

Most overboard incidents we read about involve offshore sailors, but the situation can be just as serious for small boat sailors close to shore. The following is the personal account of dinghy racer Pam Baxter, of Phoenixville, PA, who fell over the side of her Thistle dinghy during a race on a blustery day.

"At the East Coast Fall Series Regatta at Nyack this past year, we griped a bit because, due to light rain, the race committee ruled that everyone had to wear life jackets. It wasn't blowing hard, but they insisted, "You can't swim in foul-weather gear!" We put on the life jackets, but felt the decision to wear them should have been left to our own discretion.

I found out several weeks later at Lake Hopatcong that it's true: you can't swim in foul-weather gear. In fact, it's darn hard to stay afloat — period!"

No big deal. "It was cool and windy on Saturday, and very puffy. At least three Thistles capsized that day. We've capsized before, and it's no big deal — you climb to the high side, right the boat, and sail it dry.

"This weekend we were all wearing full foul-weather gear, but not life jackets. About a third of the way up the first windward leg of the second race, I heard a "ping" and then realized I was falling backward out of the boat. I was in the water, and then, very quickly, under the water. Suddenly I became very much afraid that I would not come to the surface — my boots seemed to weigh 25 pounds each. I did surface,

however, in time to see the transom of our boat sliding away from me faster than I would have thought possible. I thought briefly about trying to pull off my boots but was having so much difficulty just trying to keep my head above water that I didn't want to 'go below' to work on my footgear. I wasn't at all sure just then that I would not sink if I stopped treading water. And that act in itself, in an alarmingly short time, was becoming very difficult.

> **❝ I wasn't at all sure just then that I would not sink if I stopped treading water. And that act in itself, in an alarmingly short time, was becoming difficult. ❞**

Thoughts in fear. "Lincoln and Carl came about and picked me up — they say — in something less than a minute, but that minute was almost too long. Long enough to make me think I might drown. The weight of my wet clothes and the resistance of my foul-weather gear and boots made it feel like I was swimming in lead soup. I was dismayed at how exhausted I felt, and I consider myself a fairly strong (if not great) swimmer. I couldn't even reach my hand up to the gunwale when the boat came by.

"To put it simply, I was terrified. I suddenly realized I was screaming for Linc to hurry up, afraid he wouldn't know how critical the situation was. In the midst of my panic, the thought

occurred to me how completely ridiculous it would be to drown in the middle of a lake, boats all around, on a beautiful sunny day — all because I couldn't stay afloat for a minute or so. I thought of my three-year-old son back on shore trying to understand why Mommy hadn't come back . . .

"The experience also gave me cause for serious concern because I had gone overboard under the best possible conditions — the water was not very cold, there was no chop, I hadn't inhaled any water on my way in, and Linc and Carl got back to me very quickly. What might have happened if any of these conditions had been different?

"We consider ourselves to be good sailors, but with all our boat and rigging preparations, have we forgotten to look out for ourselves?

"Personal safety is, of course, just that: personal safety — something we must decide for ourselves. I'm lucky that I was not the first Thistling casualty, and I'd like the count to remain 0."

Pam and Lincoln Baxter, of Phoenixville, PA, are active in Thistle dinghy class racing. They wrote this account so others could raise their safety awareness from their experience.

Hypothermia

When sailing in cold weather, the combination of cold temperatures and cold water can cause a life-threatening condition if you are not dressed properly. **Hypothermia** occurs when the body is subjected to prolonged cold temperatures. The most common cause of hypothermia is exposure to cold water, though long exposure to cold air can cause it as well.

There are a number of important signals for the onset of hypothermia, listed in the accompanying chart. Look for these whenever a person has been in chilly water, such as during a capsize or in a man-overboard situation.

Physical symptoms may vary with individuals as they react to the cold temperatures, since age, body size, and clothing will cause individual differences. Medical assistance should be given to anyone with hypothermia. Until medical assistance arrives, these steps should be taken:

- Move the person to a warm place and handle gently.
- Remove all wet clothing.
- Warm the body temperature gradually.
- Cover with blankets or sleeping bags and insulate from cold.
- If the person is fully conscious and can swallow, give him/her something warm, such as warm soup broth or warm gelatin. If the person is not fully conscious, don't give any food or drinks.

Five Stages of Hypothermia

- Stage 1 — Shivering
- Stage 2 — Apathy
- Stage 3 — Loss of consciousness
- Stage 4 — Decreasing heart rate and breathing rate
- Stage 5 — Death

Hypothermia Signals
include:
- Shivering
- Dizziness
- Numbness
- Confusion
- Weakness
- Impaired judgement
- Impaired vision
- Drowsiness

Heat Emergencies

Although most sailors do not think of heat emergencies as common conditions, they do occur. On hot humid days with no breeze, anyone may be affected by the heat. People who are especially susceptible to extreme heat are the very young, very old, chronically ill, overweight, those who work in hot places, and athletes. They may suffer heat stroke, heat exhaustion, or heat cramps.

Heat Stroke is life threatening. The signals for heat stroke are listed in the accompanying chart. Anyone afflicted with heat stroke needs to be cooled down. First aid for it includes:

- Move the person to a cool environment.
- Cool the person rapidly by immersing the person in a cold bath or wrapping wet towels or sheets around the body.
- Contact EMS (Emergency Medical Services) personnel.
- Do not give the person anything to eat or drink.

Heat Exhaustion is less dangerous than heat stroke. The signals for heat exhaustion are listed in the accompanying chart. First aid for it includes:

- Move the person to a cool environment.
- Care for shock by placing the person on his/her back with the feet elevated 8 to 12 inches.
- Remove or loosen the person's clothing.
- Apply wet towels or sheets.
- Give the person a ½ full glass of cool water every 15 minutes, if fully conscious and can tolerate it.

Heat Cramps are muscular pains and spasms due to heavy exertion. First aid includes removing the person to a cool environment, and if the person has no other injuries and can tolerate it, giving him/her a ½ full glass of cool water.

Drinking water at regular intervals is the primary defense, along with cooling off through supervised swimming activities. This might be a good time to practice capsize procedures. Wearing light, airy clothing with a hat and sunglasses can also help prevent heat emergencies.

Heat Stroke Signals
include:
- Hot, red skin
- Constricted pupils
- Very high body temperature
- Skin may be wet, if the person was sweating from heavy work or exercise, otherwise skin will feel dry.

Heat Exhaustion Signals
include:
- Cool, pale, moist\skin
- Heavy sweating
- Dilated pupils
- Headache
- Dizziness
- Nausea
- Vomiting

▮1▮ ☐1   Electrical Hazards — *Heads Up For Safety*

One danger often overlooked around sailing facilities is overhead electrical wires. When rigging and de-rigging a boat and even when sailing, sailors often forget to look overhead. But a metal mast on a boat can be a conductor for electricity and cause electrocution.

It is important that you become familiar with your sailing site and identify all **electrical hazards**. Also be careful when using electrical power tools around the waterfront. Electricity and water can be a dangerous mix.

Other areas of danger are overhead power cables that may be strung between docks or from the shore to islands. In addition, there are submerged power cables around docks that must be avoided.

Metal masts and their rigging can act as lightning rods. During threatening weather, the tip of the mast is a natural target for lightning. When bad weather approaches, particularly thunderstorms, it is important that you head for shore immediately and remove yourself from danger.

Communication ☐15☐

While learning to sail, you will need to communicate with your instructor. The sound of waves against the boat, the noise of the wind, and sails luffing often make communication difficult. Normally, arm and hand motions — called **control signals** — are used.

There are many different hand and arm signs that sailors can use. The most basic are **safety position, come closer, slow down, pull sheet in, let sheet out, I need assistance,** and **I'm OK**. Although these control signals may look funny at times, they are a good way to communicate safely on the water. They will certainly help reduce confusion.

Safety Equipment

Whenever you go sailing, you should make sure that your boat has basic safety equipment on board. The equipment may vary a bit, depending on regional and state laws, but a basic list usually includes:

a. PFDs for everyone on board
b. anchor with plenty of extra line
c. paddle
d. bailers
e. horn
f. compass
g. tools, such as knife, pliers, screwdriver, and tape
h. first aid kit
i. supply of water

First Aid for the Sailor

Although accidents seldom happen while sailing, it is always a good idea to be able to help people who may need first aid. Taking Red Cross courses to learn first aid and CPR (Cardiopulmonary Resuscitation) skills will improve your safety as well as your ability to give aid to anyone who needs it.

SAILING IS SAFE!

Sailing is a very safe sport. All these safety considerations may seem overwhelming at first, but with time and experience they will become a natural part of your sailing.

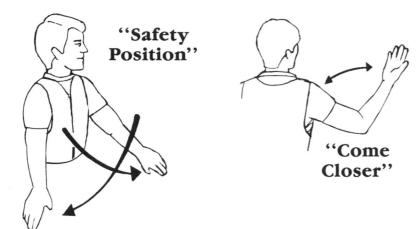

"Safety Position"

"Come Closer"

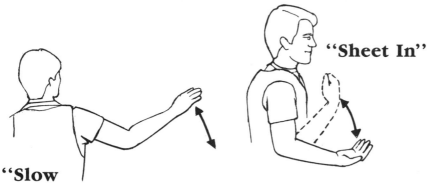

"Sheet In"

"Slow Down"

"Sheet Out"

"I Need Assistance"

"I'm OK!"

Review Exercises

I. True or False

1. The sailor's code involves only the written laws of the sailing community.
2. Covering a victim with blankets helps to relieve heat exhaustion.
3. Removing all wet clothing is a step in treating a victim of hypothermia.
4. Electrical hazards pose a threat to sailors only when the boat is on the trailer.
5. Control signals are effective ways to communicate on the water.
6. PFD stands for Personal Flotation Device.
7. Sailboats usually have right-of-way over powerboats.

II. Exploring Sailing
(discussion or writing)

1. Why are control signals so important for sailing?
2. List all the safety equipment needed for your sailboat.
3. Name all the electrical hazards around your sailing community.

III. Mastery Activities

1. Be able to list recommended treatments for
   a. Hypothermia
   b. Heat emergencies
2. Know the sailor's code for your sailing site.
3. Know and identify all the control signals.

Chapter 3

The Sailboat

"And what do you call the nut holding the tiller?"

KEY CONCEPTS

- **Monohull**
- **Multihull**
- **Centerboard**
- **Keel**

- **Rig**
- **Port**
- **Starboard**
- **Boat and sail parts**

Like any sport, sailing has its own language. This new language can seem a little overwhelming at first, but as you use the new terms, they will quickly become familiar.

It is not important that you know all of the vocabulary of sailing by your first sail. But, by the end of this course you should have a good understanding of the special names. We will focus on the different boat parts of small sailboats, since learning on small boats is the best way to develop the basics for lifelong sailing skills.

The Hull

The body of the boat is called the **hull**. The hull carries all the boat parts and equipment as well as the sailors.

There are two types of hulls: **monohulls** and **multihulls**. The most common — monohull — has a single hull, while the multihull will have either two hulls connected together called a **catamaran**, or three hulls connected together, which is a **trimaran**. Generally multihulls sail faster then monohulls.

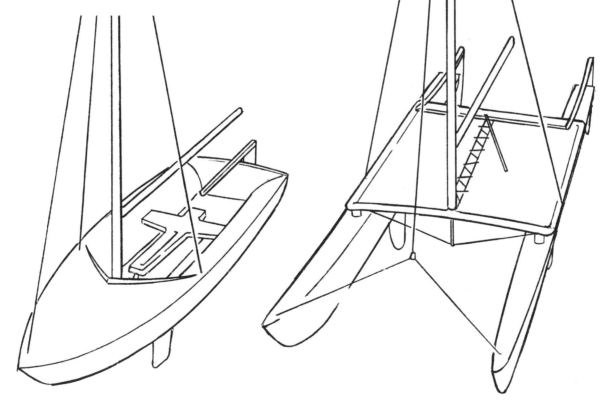

A monohull has a single hull.

A multihull has two hulls (a catamaran) or three hulls (a trimaran).

The front end of the hull, the **bow**, is usually pointed, while the back end, the **stern**, is wider and has a flat, vertical surface called the **transom**. Sailboats less than 10 feet long sometimes have a square, flat bow and are called **prams**. Two typical prams are the Optimist and the Sabot. They are often used as learn-to-sail boats for young people.

When a boat floats in the water, it will displace a volume of water equal to the weight of the boat, so the boat's weight is often called its **displacement**. As the boat sits in the water, there is a line where the water surface meets the hull, called the **waterline**. The waterline is sometimes marked by a stripe on the hull.

To travel forward without being pushed sideways by the wind, most boats have an underwater fin, such as a **centerboard** or **keel**. The centerboard can be lowered and raised while the keel is fixed. Some sailboats have a **daggerboard**, similar to a centerboard but designed to be raised and lowered vertically rather than by pivoting up and down. If the centerboard is attached to the side of the boat, instead of the center, it is called a **leeboard**. The Optimist and Laser have a daggerboard, while the Sabot has a leeboard.

A keel is different because it usually cannot be moved and it is made of iron or lead. This fixed **ballast** helps to keep the boat upright by counteracting the wind pressure on the sails. On a centerboard or daggerboard boat, the weight of the sailors is used like movable ballast, to stabilize the boat.

Daggerboard, centerboard, and keel all act to keep the boat moving straight through the water. Without these underwater fins, the boat could not make progress sailing toward the wind.

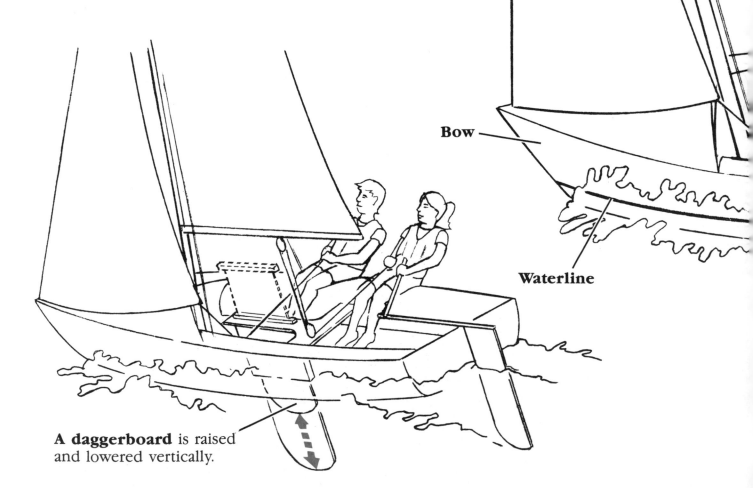

Bow

Waterline

A daggerboard is raised and lowered vertically.

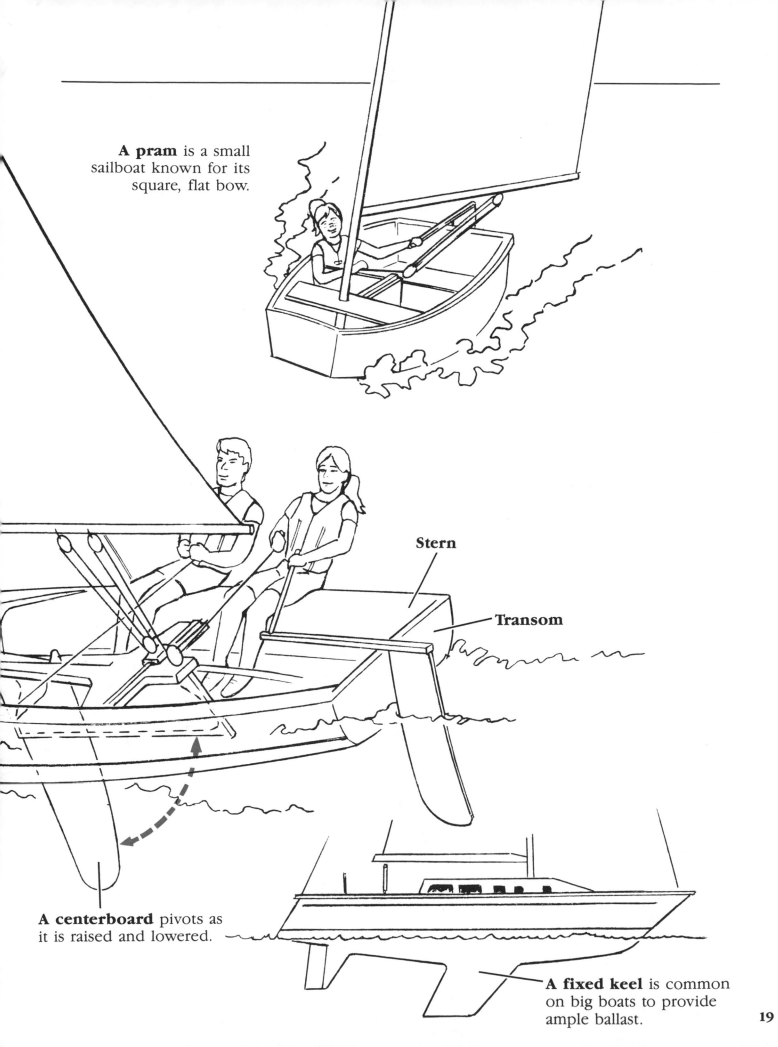

A pram is a small sailboat known for its square, flat bow.

Stern

Transom

A centerboard pivots as it is raised and lowered.

A fixed keel is common on big boats to provide ample ballast.

19

The Rig 2 2

Above the hull is the **rig**, consisting of sails, mast, and rigging. Most sailboats have only one **mast**, which holds up the sails to the wind. Boats with a single mast have either one sail called a **mainsail**, or two sails, a mainsail and a smaller forward sail, called a **jib**. A popular single-sail boat is the Laser. A boat with a mainsail and a jib is called a **sloop**, and a typical example is shown. Big sailboats may have two masts which can carry more sail. The Appendix shows examples of these rigs.

The mast on many single-sail boats is strong enough to stand upright by itself without additional support. Some single-sail boats and most sloops need supporting wires to keep the mast standing upright. These supporting wires are called **standing rigging**. The wires connecting the mast to the sides of the hull are **shrouds**, and the wire connecting the front of the mast to the bow is the **forestay**.

The control lines that move and adjust the sail are often referred to as **running rigging**. Typical control lines are main sheet, jib sheet, outhaul, halyard, cunningham, and boom vang, shown in the accompanying illustration.

A single-sail boat like the popular Laser (shown) often has a mast that can stand by itself without additional support.

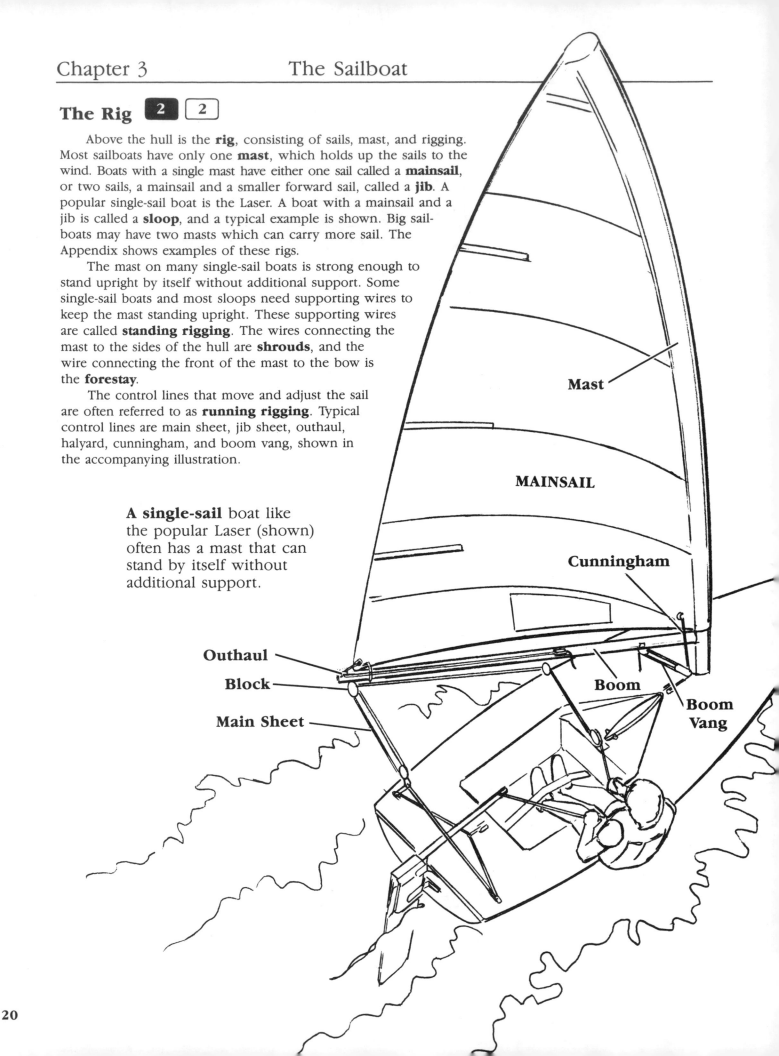

Mast

MAINSAIL

Cunningham

Outhaul

Block

Main Sheet

Boom

Boom Vang

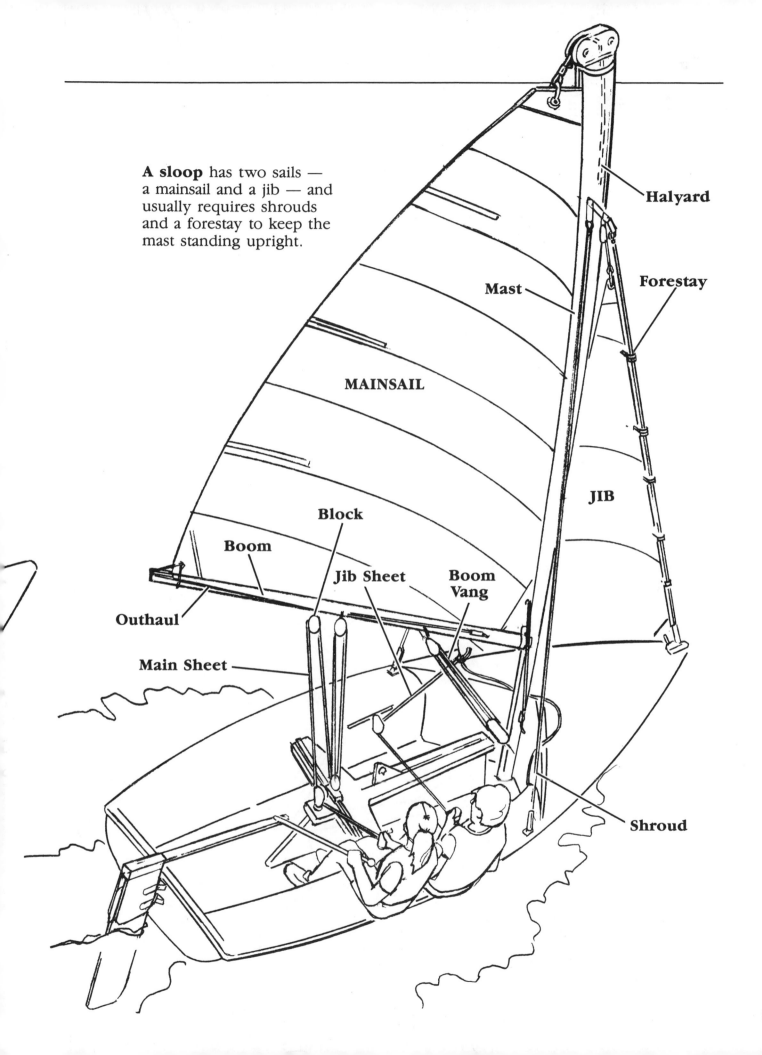

A sloop has two sails — a mainsail and a jib — and usually requires shrouds and a forestay to keep the mast standing upright.

Halyard

Mast

Forestay

MAINSAIL

JIB

Block

Boom

Jib Sheet

Boom Vang

Outhaul

Main Sheet

Shroud

Steering 2 2

A **rudder** is used to steer the boat. This rudder is controlled by a **tiller** which gives the **helmsman** (the person who steers the boat) leverage to move the rudder. Often, a **tiller extension** is attached to the forward end of the tiller, to let the helmsman move more freely around the boat. Tiller extensions are common in smaller boats. In bigger boats, you often steer with a wheel, as you would in an automobile. The wheel uses cable or gears to control the boat's rudder.

Directions 2 2

The two sides of the boat have different names. The left side is **port** and the right side is **starboard**. Colors are used to help identify port and starboard — red being associated with port and green with starboard. An easy way to remember these: **port, left,** and, **red** are short words and **starboard, right** and **green** are the long words. Some beginning sailors find it helpful to put green tape in a visible location on the deck on the starboard side, and red tape on the port side, as a reminder.

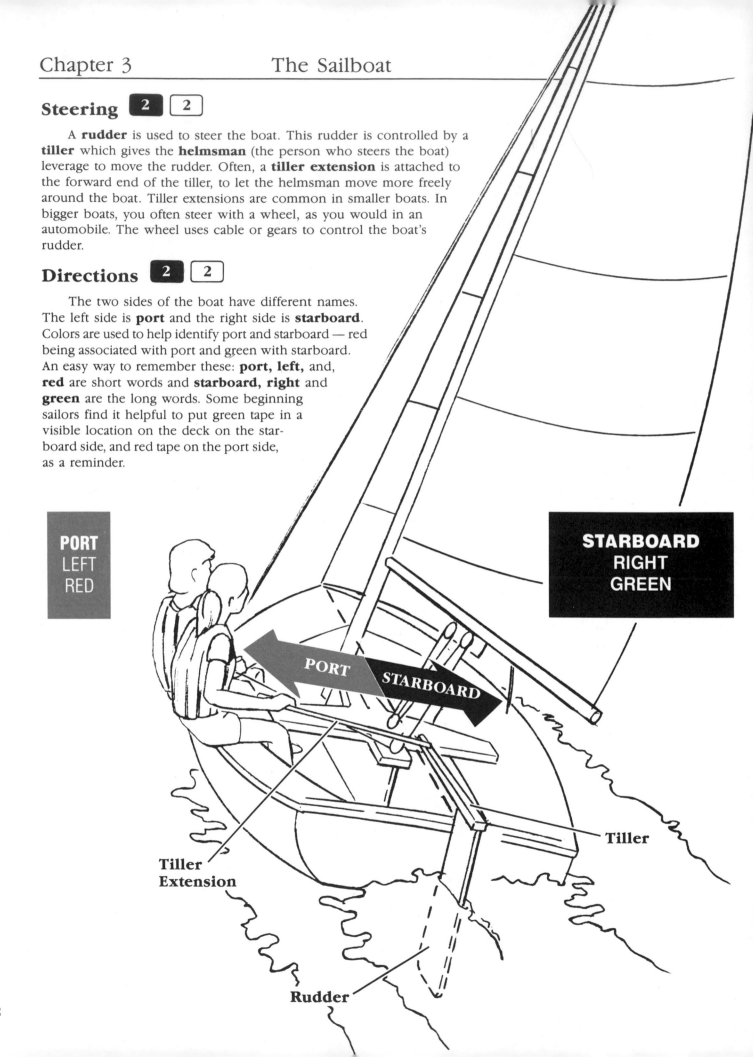

PORT
LEFT
RED

STARBOARD
RIGHT
GREEN

PORT   STARBOARD

Tiller

Tiller
Extension

Rudder

Review Exercises

I. True or False

1. Catamarans have one hull.
2. One mast can only hold up one sail.
3. The weight of the crew can be used as ballast for the boat.
4. The daggerboard is an underwater fin on a sailboat which pivots as it is raised.
5. The centerboard keeps the boat from sliding sideways when sailing upwind.
6. The forward sail on a sloop is called the mainsail.
7. The tiller extension is used to control the centerboard.

II. Matching

(match the words to the correct illustration)

1. Waterline
2. Port
3. Halyard
4. Jib
5. Daggerboard
6. Mainsail
7. Catamaran
8. Rigging
9. Monohull
10. Rudder
11. Starboard
12. Mast
13. Boom vang
14. Main sheet
15. Outhaul
16. Boom

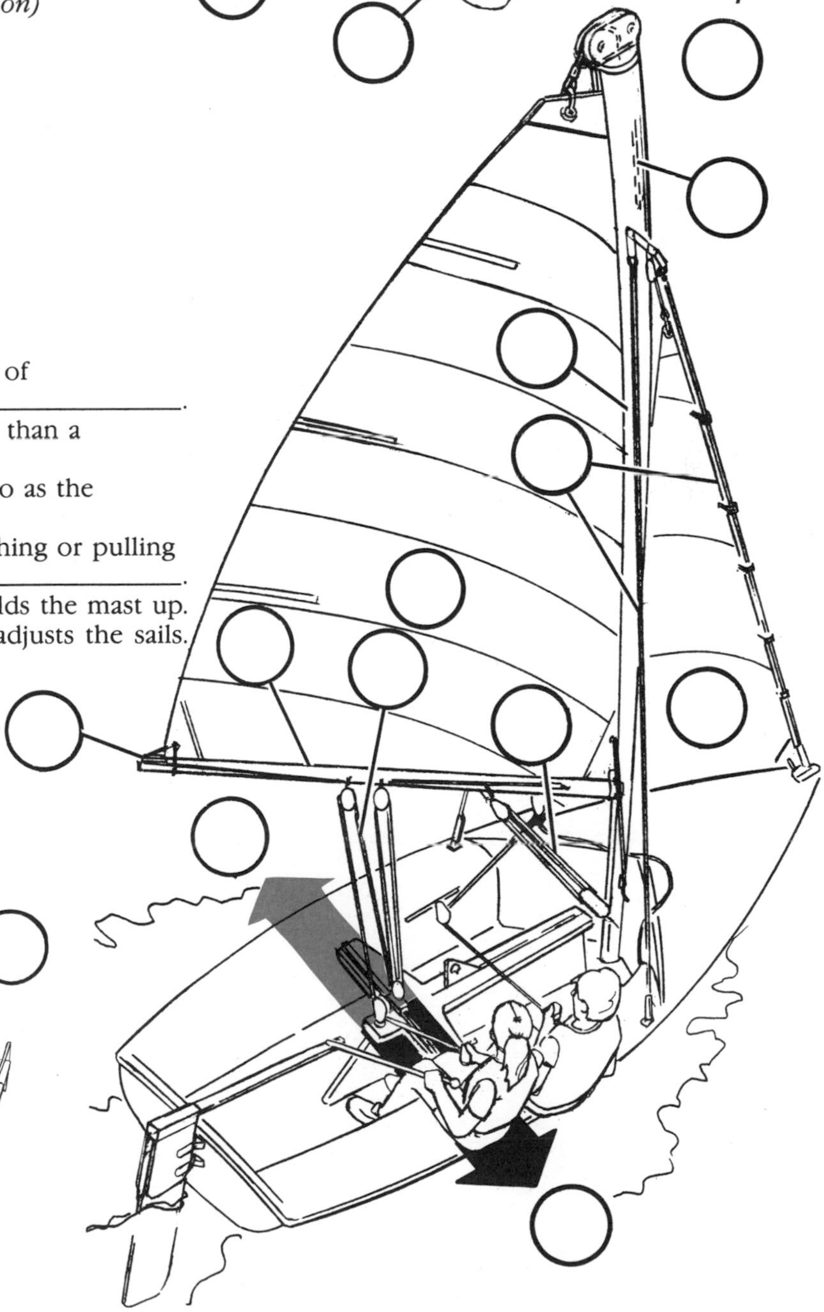

III. Fill in the Blanks

1. The keel in a sailboat is usually made of _____ or _____.
2. A _____ is usually much faster than a monohull.
3. The left side of a sailboat is referred to as the _____ side.
4. The helmsman steers the boat by pushing or pulling the _____.
5. The _____ rigging holds the mast up.
6. The _____ rigging adjusts the sails.

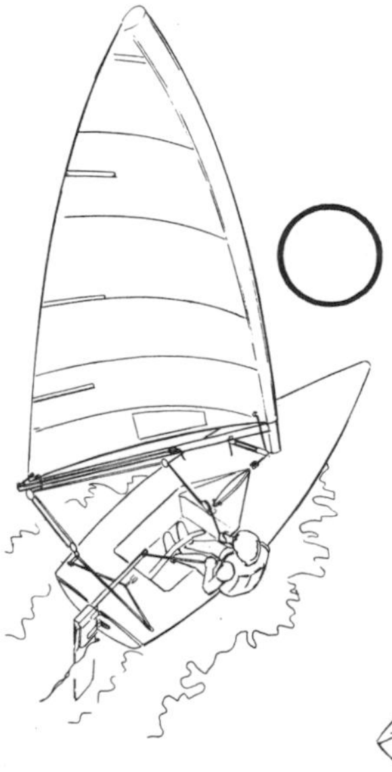

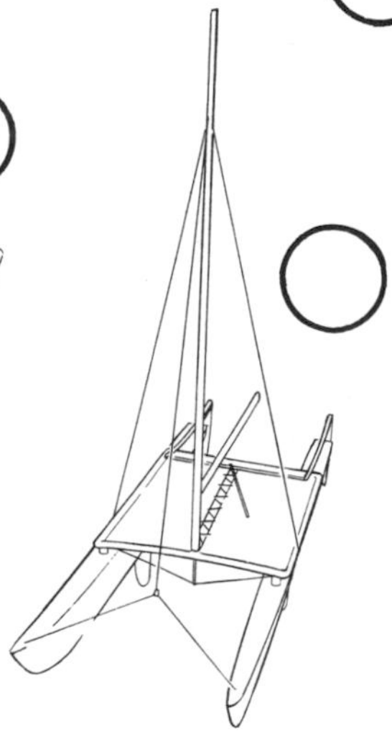

Chapter 4

Understanding Wind

"What do you mean, you THINK you left the bathtub running?"

KEY CONCEPTS

- **Wind sensing**
- **Wind direction**
- **Points of a compass**
- **Puffs and lulls**
- **Apparent wind**
- **True wind**

The wind is a fascinating challenge for both beginning and experienced sailors. Its direction and speed are always changing. These changes can be so small that you hardly notice them or large enough to make you steer a different course or change the trim of your sails. Part of the fun in sailing is learning to anticipate and react to these changes — this is called **wind sensing**.

Sailing a boat depends on knowing where the wind is coming from. Before you go for your first sail, check the wind direction with your instructor and review the methods of determining wind direction and speed.

11 **9** **12**

How can you tell which direction the wind is blowing from? There are many ways to do it, and they involve your senses of feel, sight, hearing, and sometimes even smell. As you approach the water-front, you will feel the wind on your face, hands, and neck. You will see it on the water. The wind causes waves or ripples on the surface, blowing perpendicular — at right angles — to the ripples.

Wind sensing is determining the direction of the wind, and whether it is building or decreasing in strength. Visual wind indicators for this are flags, smoke, trees, telltales, and flapping sails. Often the clouds will be moving in the same direction as the wind on the water. But don't use flags on other boats that are moving fast, like a motor-boat. Their flags do not show the true wind direction. The best way is to feel the wind on your skin or see the ripples on the water.

Once you have determined the direction that the wind is blowing from, you can figure out the best way to rig your boat, leave a dock, sail around a harbor or out to the channel entrance.

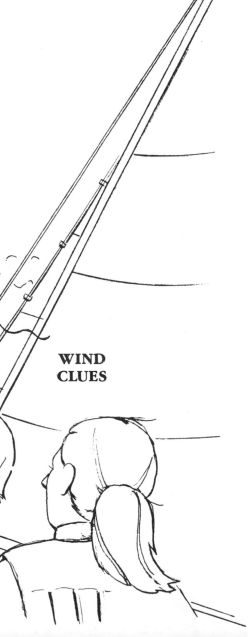

Smoke

Boats on moorings

Flags

WIND CLUES

Ripples on Water

Wind Identification

The direction the wind is blowing **from** (not blowing **to**) is the assigned direction of the wind. The direction can be described by referring to the points on a map or chart — such as North, East, South, and West — or to the degree numbers on a compass — 0, 90, 180, and 270. If the wind is blowing from the North, you would say, "We are sailing in a Northerly wind," or "The wind is at zero degrees."

If you have a compass on your boat, you can determine the wind direction by pointing your boat into the wind and reading the number on the compass.

Changes in wind speed are usually called puffs or lulls. A **puff** is an increase in speed for a short duration, and a **lull** is a decrease in speed. A lull is sometimes called a "hole" in the wind. It is common to sail in and out of many puffs and lulls.

You can see and feel these puffs and lulls. A puff usually makes the water surface look darker. A lull is a little more difficult to see, but it's usually lighter in color then the surrounding water. Always watch the water for puffs and lulls.

In describing the speed or strength of the wind, a nautical term, **knots**, is frequently used. One knot is slightly more than one mile-per-hour (1 knot = 1.2 mph, or 10 knots = 12 mph).

Changes in the speed and direction of wind can be caused by rising warm air over land or water (called "thermals"), by the height and shape of the surrounding land, and by general weather systems which will be covered in Chapter 17, "Weather and Currents."

To the experienced sailor, the wind is always a subject of dicussion and fun. For the less experienced, learning to sense the wind speed and direction is a fascinating new challenge.

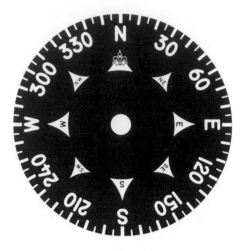

The face of a compass is divided into 360 degrees, with North, South, East, West and other major points usually marked with large numbers or letters.

A puff usually makes the water look darker, allowing you to see it coming

Apparent Wind and True Wind

To understand the interaction between a sailboat and the wind, it is helpful to know the difference between true wind and apparent wind. **True wind** is the wind speed and direction at a stationary position. The wind blowing by a boat that is not moving would be the true wind. Weather reports always give the true wind. **Apparent wind** is the true wind altered by the motion of the boat. An example would be if you were riding in a convertible car with the top down. If it was calm with no wind at all, the true wind would be 0 miles per hour. But you would feel **apparent** wind when the car was moving. If the car moved 20 miles per hour, you would feel an apparent wind of 20 miles per hour from directly ahead of the car. If the true wind was blowing 20 mph from behind you, you would feel no apparent wind. If the true wind was blowing 20 mph from ahead of you, you would feel 40 mph of apparent wind. If the true wind was blowing at right angles to you, the apparent wind would be a mixture of the true wind and the "wind" made by the car's motion.

The same thing occurs when you are sailing. In fact, whenever your boat is moving you are sailing in an apparent wind and sheeting your sails to this wind. When sailing with the wind coming from behind the boat, the boat will move almost at the same speed as the wind and you will feel almost no wind. If you turn and sail toward the wind, the speed of the boat will be added to the true wind, and the apparent wind will feel much stronger. The difference between the directions of the true wind and apparent wind are usually small, and are of no great concern to most sailors.

Sails are always sheeted to the apparent wind direction.

I. Matching

1. Wind sensing
2. Lull
3. 90 degrees
4. Southerly
5. Puff
6. 270 degrees
7. Visual aids
8. Apparent wind

a. East
b. Decrease in wind speed
c. Wind blowing from the south
d. Increase in wind speed
e. Wind speed affected by the boat's motion
f. Sailor's sensitivity to wind speed and direction
g. West
h. Smoke and flags

II. True or False

1. Puffs and lulls are unusual when sailing.
2. A flag on a flagpole indicates true wind direction.
3. All sailboats which are moving have an apparent wind.
4. The compass has a total of 360 degrees.
5. Knots are used to describe wind speed.

III. Mastery Activities

1. Be able to match the different wind directions with compass degrees and points.
2. Determine wind changes, like puffs and lulls, whenever you go outside, for one week.
3. Determine the wind direction by looking at the water surface only.
4. Determine wind direction, while sailing, by using a compass.

Wind created by motion of boat.

TRUE WIND
The actual wind that is blowing.

APPARENT WIND
Combination of true wind and wind created by motion of boat.

Chapter 5

Introduction to Sails

"Boy, that Bill really knows how to trim!"

KEY CONCEPTS

- **Push-pull principle**
- **Lift**
- **Windward**
- **Leeward**
- **Luffing**
- **Sheeting**
- **Constant angle to the wind**
- **Sail telltales**

The sails interact with the wind to propel the boat through the water, using the **push-pull principle**. Nowadays sails are made from panels of synthetic fabric such as dacron, mylar, or kevlar. The fabric panels are cut and sewn together in such a way that the sail forms a curved shape when it is hit by the wind. Most of the time, the curved shape of the sail works much like an airplane wing to generate power and lift.

Lift is created by changing the speed and direction of the wind as it travels along the sail's surface. This lift pulls the boat forward and sideways.

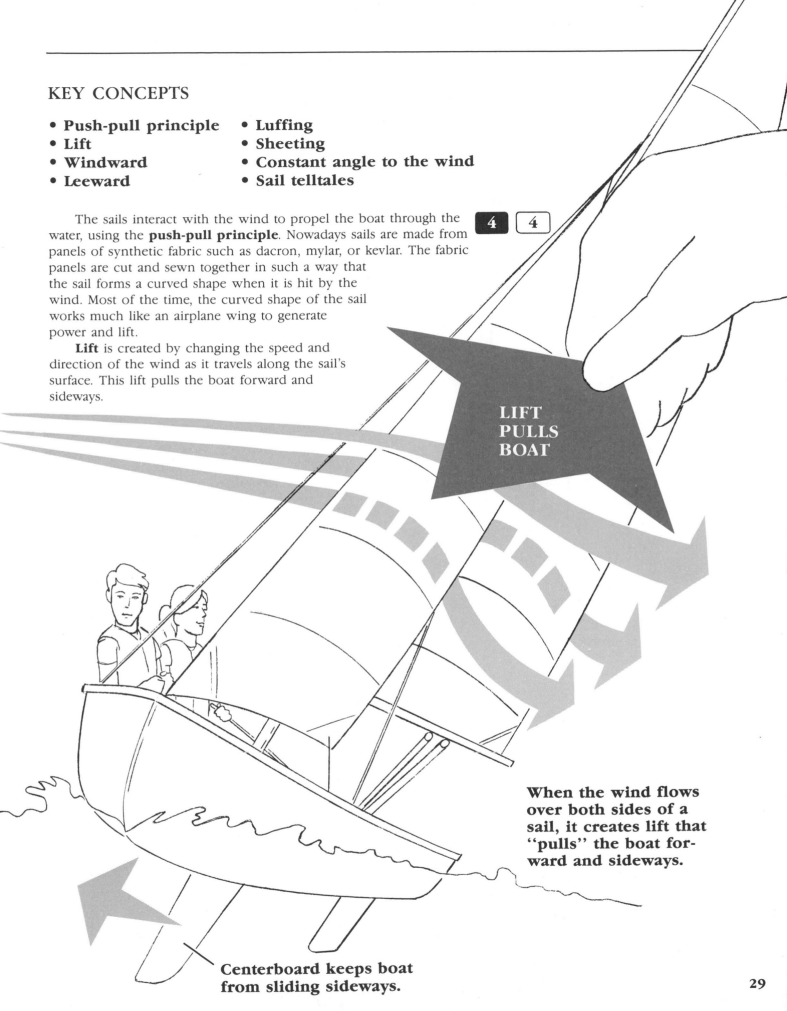

4 4

LIFT PULLS BOAT

When the wind flows over both sides of a sail, it creates lift that "pulls" the boat forward and sideways.

Centerboard keeps boat from sliding sideways.

An underwater fin such as the centerboard prevents the boat from moving sideways but lets it move forward. Other times the sail blocks or captures the wind, which pushes the boat forward and sideways through the water.

4 ⬜ 4

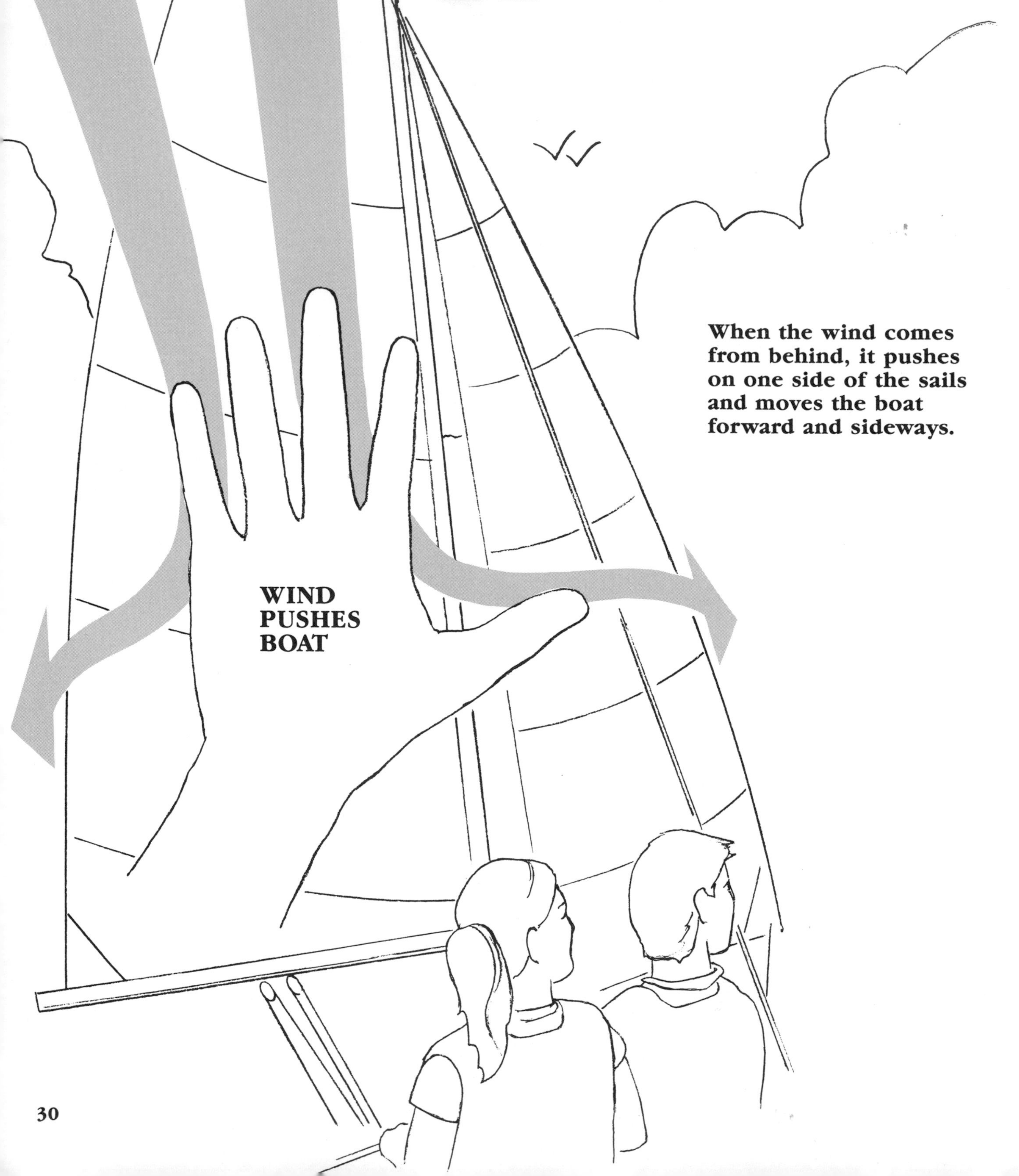

When the wind comes from behind, it pushes on one side of the sails and moves the boat forward and sideways.

WIND PUSHES BOAT

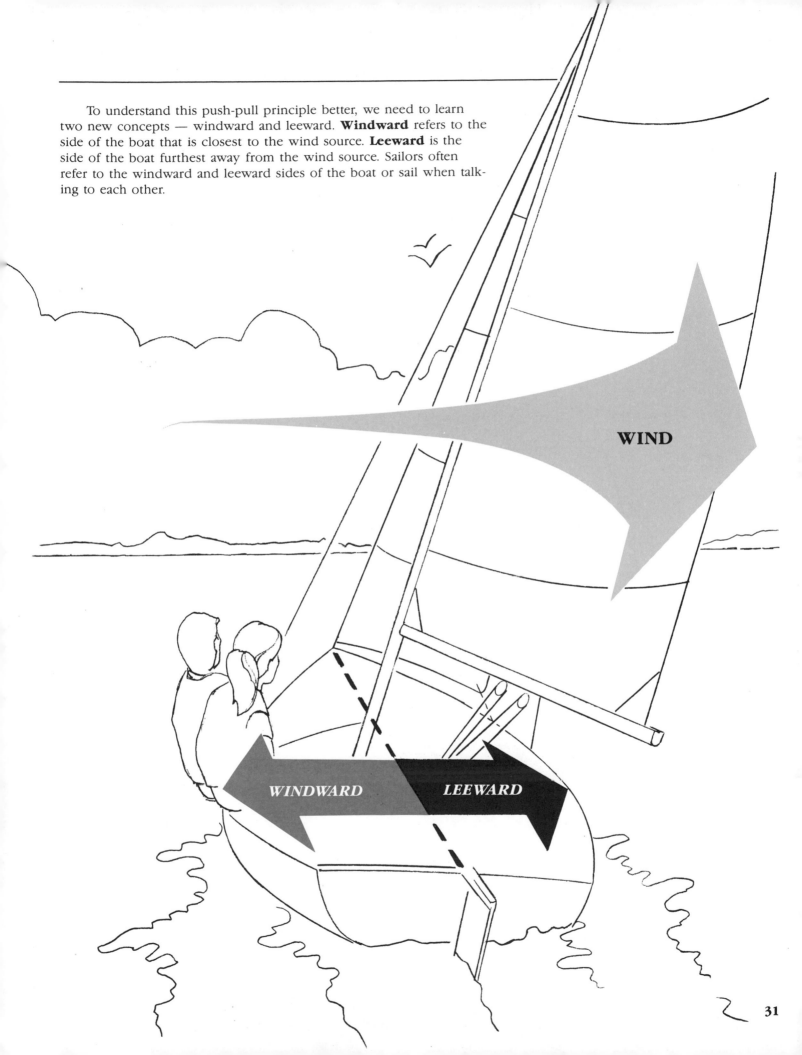

To understand this push-pull principle better, we need to learn two new concepts — windward and leeward. **Windward** refers to the side of the boat that is closest to the wind source. **Leeward** is the side of the boat furthest away from the wind source. Sailors often refer to the windward and leeward sides of the boat or sail when talking to each other.

WIND

WINDWARD

LEEWARD

8 **8**

The efficiency of the sails, and the speed of the boat, can be controlled by altering the air flow over the sails. Maximum pull, and consequently maximum speed, are obtained when the air flows smoothly across both the windward and leeward side of the sail. However, to slow or stop the boat, you can make the air turbulent rather than smooth, thus decreasing the pull and making the sails inefficient. You can do this by adjusting the sails or by turning the boat.

When the sail is flapping in the wind and there is no curvature at all in the sail, the sail has no power and is **luffing**. Luffing is a normal part of sailing, mostly used as a way of controlling boat speed, particularly to stop the boat. When a sail luffs, it can make a lot of noise, but this noise is natural and necessary to allow the boat to be controlled.

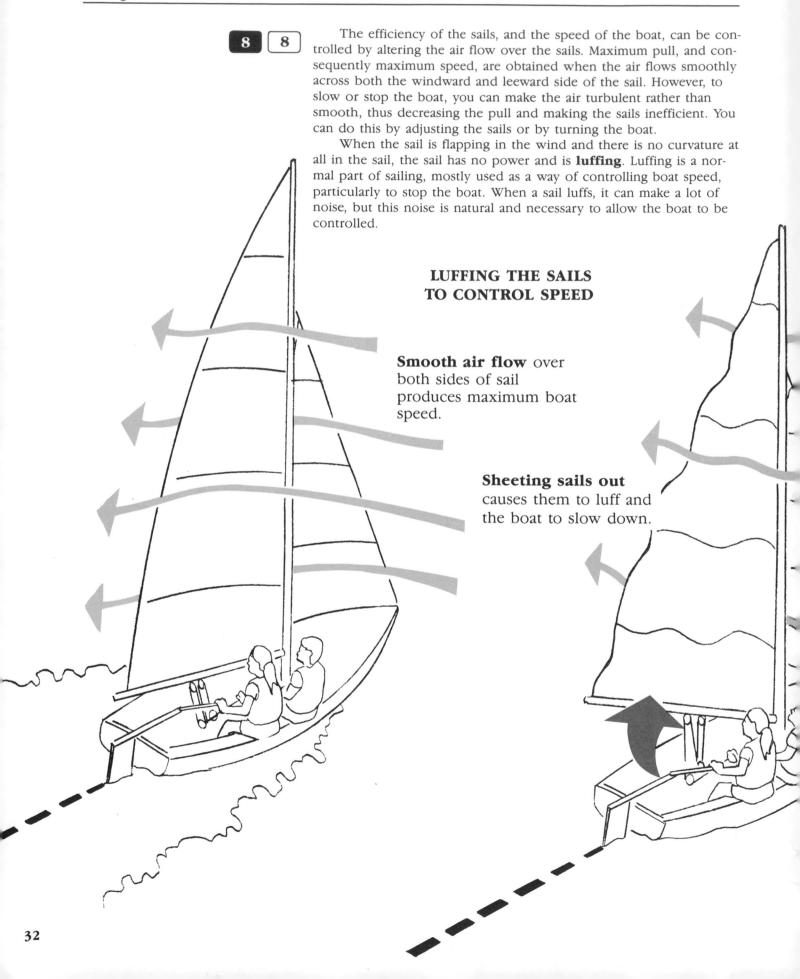

**LUFFING THE SAILS
TO CONTROL SPEED**

Smooth air flow over both sides of sail produces maximum boat speed.

Sheeting sails out causes them to luff and the boat to slow down.

To make the sail efficient, you need to adjust the sail so that it has the proper curve and the best angle to the wind. Altering the angle of the sails to the wind can be done either by using the sheets to adjust the sail or by changing the direction of the boat.

Adjusting the tension of the main sheet or jib sheet is called **sheeting**. Pulling in the sails is called **"sheeting in."** Letting the sails out is called **"sheeting out."** Sailors sometimes refer to sheeting in as "trimming" and to sheeting out as "easing."

When sheeting for maximum speed, the sail will keep a constant **angle to the wind**. This constant angle is controlled by steering and sheeting the sails.

Steering into the wind will also cause sails to luff and the boat to slow down.

Sail Telltales 8   8

Using a **telltale** on a sail, to "show" the invisible wind flow over the sails, can help you to sheet the sails properly. Telltales are made of yarn, thread, computer tape, or any other material that blows easily in the wind. They are normally placed on the forward one-third of the jib and near the center of the mainsail. Some sailors like to place a telltale on the leech (back edge) of the sail to show the air flow as it leaves the sail's surface.

Both telltales back — smooth air flow on both sides of sail.

Windward telltale fluttering — sail sheeted too far out. Air flow turbulent on windward side of sail.

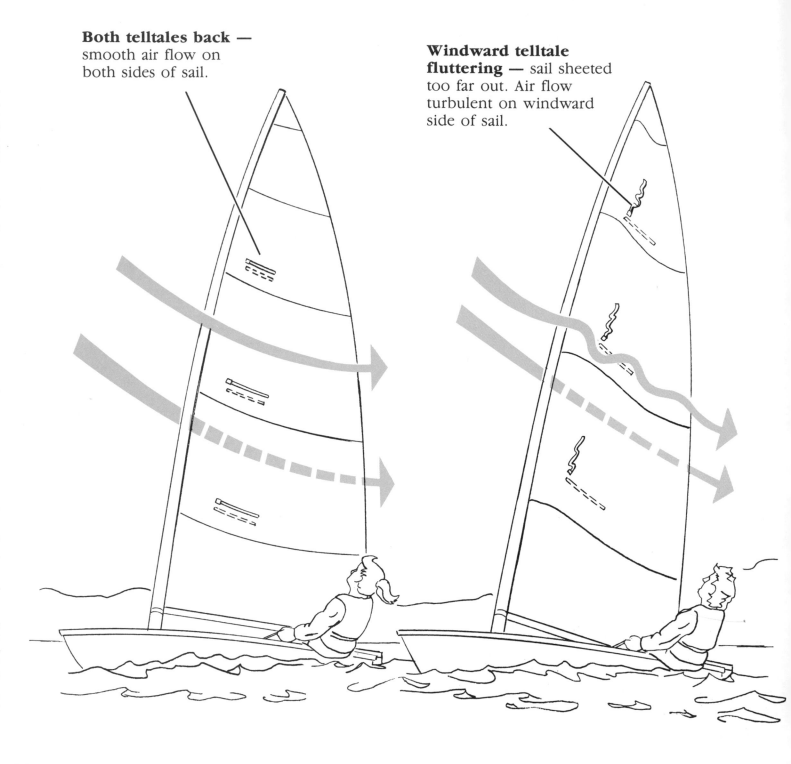

Wherever they are located, the telltales show whether the air flow along the sails is smooth or turbulent. When the windward and leeward telltales on the jib and the main are flowing horizontally to the water, the wind flow is smooth and the sails are correctly sheeted. When the telltales bounce around and flutter erratically, the air flow is turbulent and the sails are inefficient.

The telltales are easy to use, but the helmsman should look at more than just telltales. Don't forget to keep your wind sensing operating and to anticipate changes in the wind and air flow by looking at other boats and at the surface of the water.

Leeward telltale fluttering — sail sheeted too tight. Air flow turbulent on leeward side of sail.

Review Exercises

I. True or False

1. Sheeting out the sails can also be called "easing."
2. In the pull mode, a sail creates lift as an airplane wing does.
3. A boat can be stopped by luffing.
4. Telltales on a sail can be used to determine the true wind direction.
5. Boat speed can be changed only by sheeting the sails in or out.

II. Matching

1. Push-pull principle
2. Telltales
3. Sheeting in
4. Sheeting out
5. Windward
6. Leeward
7. Centerboard

a. Detect the invisible wind
b. Easing the sails
c. Result of wind acting on sails
d. Away from the wind
e. Underwater fin
f. Toward the wind
g. Pulling in the sails

III. Mastery Activities

1. While sailing on a reach, set the tiller and, without moving it, practice sheeting the sail(s) to make the telltales flow smoothly.
2. While sailing on a reach, cleat the sail(s) and steer the boat to make the telltales flow smoothly.

Chapter 6

Rigging and De-rigging Your Sailboat

"Oops!"

KEY CONCEPTS

- **Rigging the hull**
- **Rigging the mainsail**
- **Rigging the jib**
- **Raising the sails**
- **De-rigging**
- **Handling/folding sails**
- **Lifting**

Before you can go sailing, the sailboat must be rigged. Rigging each boat will be a little different, but you should follow a definite order in rigging and de-rigging. Knowing the right method will make things easier and save you time.

To **rig** the boat, the procedure is usually:

1. Collect the sails which match the boat.
2. Collect the rudder, tiller, extension, and daggerboard.
3. Make sure the boat is pointed into the wind.
4. Rig the hull.
5. Rig the mainsail.
6. Rig the jib.
7. Check your safety equipment.

To **de-rig** the boat:

1. Point the boat into the wind.
2. De-rig the jib.
3. De-rig the main.
4. De-rig the hull.
5. Fold and store sails.
6. Rinse the boat, if fresh water is available.
7. Tie down the boat to the trailer or dock.

Following these patterns will allow the best use of your time and ensure safety.

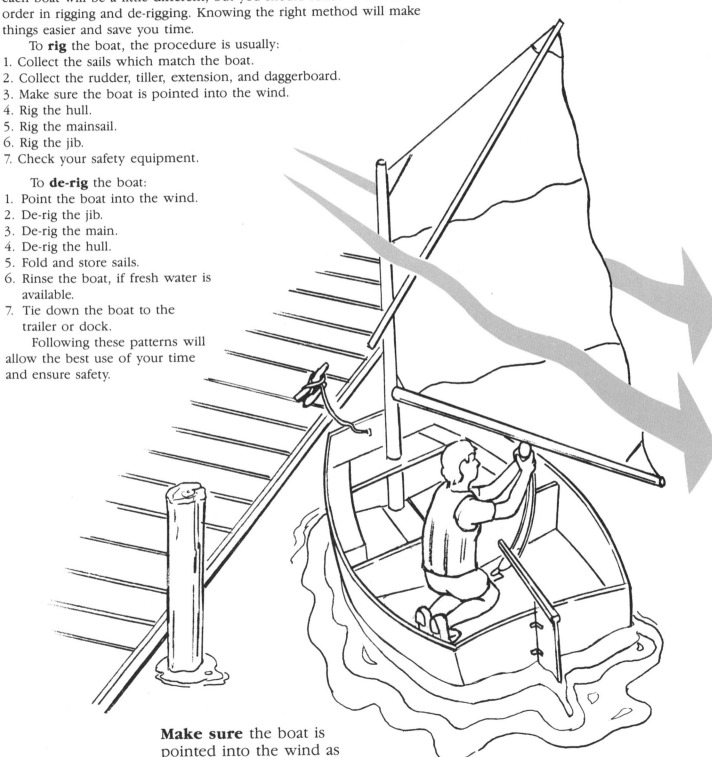

Make sure the boat is pointed into the wind as you rig the sails.

Rigging the Hull

After collecting the sails and all the necessary boat parts like the rudder and tiller, you are ready to begin. It is best to start with the boat pointed into the wind, to keep the sails from blowing over the side of the boat.

Rigging the hull requires only a few simple tasks. First, attach the rudder with the tiller and the tiller extension to the boat. The centerboard or daggerboard then needs to be positioned in the boat properly. If necessary, you should remove any water from the boat and close any drain plugs. If the boat has a cover, it should be folded and stowed in a safe place.

Head

Leech

Luff

Tack

Foot

Clew

1. **Insert head** into groove on mast and attach halyard.

2. **Attach tack** to gooseneck.

3. **Insert clew** into groove on boom at gooseneck and pull out to end. Attach outhaul.

Rigging the Mainsail 7 8 7 8

A neatly folded sail in a sail bag can be small and easily handled, but when opened up can be large and awkward. It is best to take the sails aboard the boat in a sail bag before removing them.

Start by rigging the mainsail. The mainsail has three corners, and it is important that you keep track of all three corners as you take the mainsail out of the bag. Don't let the sail get twisted as you unfold and rig it. The best procedure is to find the top corner and run your hand down the front edge of the sail, the **luff**, to make sure the sail is not twisted.

First start by inserting the **head** (top) of the sail into the groove or track on the mast. Next attach the **halyard**. Tighten and cleat the halyard to keep the sail from dropping out of the track. The second step is to attach the **tack** (front corner) at the bottom of the sail to the **gooseneck** (a fitting) that connects the **boom** to the mast. Third, uncleat the control line for the **outhaul** and insert the **clew** (back corner) in the groove or track on the boom. Pull the clew to the end of the boom and attach it to the outhaul. Tighten and cleat the outhaul control line.

Most learn-to-sail boats have the **battens** pre-sewn into the mainsail. If you have a boat with battens that are removable, now is the time to insert them. Careful. Don't drop them in the water. Many battens sink.

Some mainsails may have cunningham and boom vang controls. Their use will be covered after you learn the basics of sailing. At this point, you only need to know how to rig them. There are several different ways, and your instructor will show you the best way for your boat.

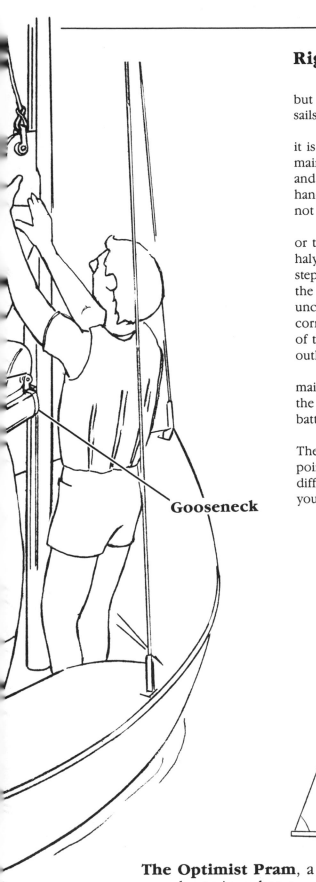

Gooseneck

Review Steps

1. Locate three corners of the sail.
2. Attach the head to the mast track.
3. Attach halyard to the head.
4. Attach tack to gooseneck fitting.
5. Pull clew to end of boom and attach outhaul.
6. Tighten the outhaul.

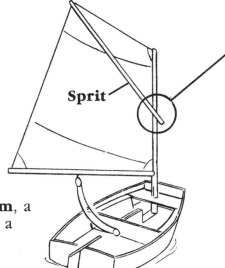

Sprit

After rigging the Optimist, the tension on the sprit is adjusted to remove wrinkles from the sail.

The Optimist Pram, a popular trainer, has a "sprit rig."

Rigging the Jib

The procedure for rigging the jib varies somewhat for different boats. Usually, you first attach the **halyard** to the **head** (top) of the sail. Then attach the **tack** (bottom front corner) to the fitting on the bow. The sheets for trimming the jib are usually attached to the **clew** (back corner) of the sail and are fed through the **jib blocks**.

Some jibs may have fasteners or clips on the **luff** (front edge) of the sail. They are attached to the **forestay** (the wire that connects the mast to the bow of the boat). Start by attaching the fastener at the bottom of the luff first, and continue up the luff to the fastener at the top of the sail.

Review Steps

1. Locate the three corners of the sail.
2. Attach halyard to the head.
3. Attach tack to bow clip.
4. Run jib sheets through the fairleads or blocks.
5. Secure sail.

Raising the Sails

Once the jib and main are rigged, you are ready to raise the sails. But before you do it, double check to make sure
1. the main sheet and jib sheet are not cleated and will run freely.
2. the outhaul control line has been adjusted and cleated.
3. the cunningham or downhaul and the boom vang are not cleated.
4. the centerboard or daggerboard are in the "down" position.
5. the boat is pointed into the wind.

Forestay

1. Attach the halyard to the head of the jib.

Jib Sheet Block

3. Attach (or tie) sheets to the jib clew and feed through jib blocks on each side of cockpit.

2. Attach the tack to the fitting on the bow.

Different ways of attaching the jib to the forestay include sleeves (left) and metal or plastic clips (right).

When raising the jib, be sure to pull the halyard very tight before cleating it. The mainsail is raised by hoisting the halyard hand over hand, with the crew helping to guide and feed the sail into the mast groove as it is being raised.

Once the mainsail is up, the sail will luff and shake in the breeze. Be careful of the boom moving about. It is perfectly acceptable to allow the boom and sails to shake or luff until you're ready to sail. If the mainsail has a downhaul or cunningham control line, or a boom vang, now is the time to tighten and cleat them.

Which sail you raise first depends on where your boat is. If your boat is attached to a mooring, normally you will raise the mainsail first because it helps to keep the boat pointed into the wind until you have the jib up and are ready to leave the mooring. If your boat is tied to a dock or you are sailing off a beach, often the jib will be raised first. Your instructor will help you decide what best suits your situation.

De-rigging

After sailing, you normally de-rig in the reverse order of rigging. Lowering the main first helps to stabilize the boat and stops the boom from flogging in the wind, but when picking up a mooring it is best to lower the jib first. With the sails down, you can de-rig the hull, removing the rudder and other hardware.

Before raising sails make sure mainsheet, boom vang and cunningham are eased. Be careful of the boom swinging in the breeze.

Cunningham

Boom Vang

Mainsheet

Centerboard down

Folding the Sails 7 7

If possible, the sails should be laid out on a lawn. Sails used around salt water will need to be rinsed to keep the sail in good condition, and then dried.

The sails should be folded in a zig-zag pattern like a road map, with the first fold taken parallel to the **foot** (bottom) of the sail. Once the zig-zag is complete, you then fold the sail starting at the luff and roll it to the clew. Wrapping the jib sheets around the outside of the folded jib will secure it. Normally the mainsail goes into the sail bag first, then the jib.

If the battens are sewn into the sail, the same folding method can be used, except that during the zig-zag you should make sure that the **leech** (back edge) of the sail lines up on each fold. If you make the width of the fold larger at the back of the sail than at the front side when you start, the leech and the battens will line up.

On small sailboats that have only a mainsail, the sail is often rolled around the mast, which is then removed from the boat and stored inside on a rack.

On some boats, especially bigger sailboats, the main is stowed on the boom, with a covering to protect it. Each boat will vary slightly in the way sails are folded and stored.

Before folding, rinse and dry sails (if they have gotten wet), and stretch out on lawn.

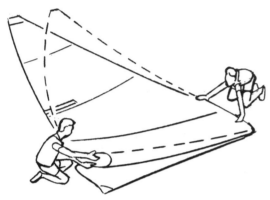

When folding sails with battens, make the folds along the leech larger than the luff to start. Then the battens will line up on the end.

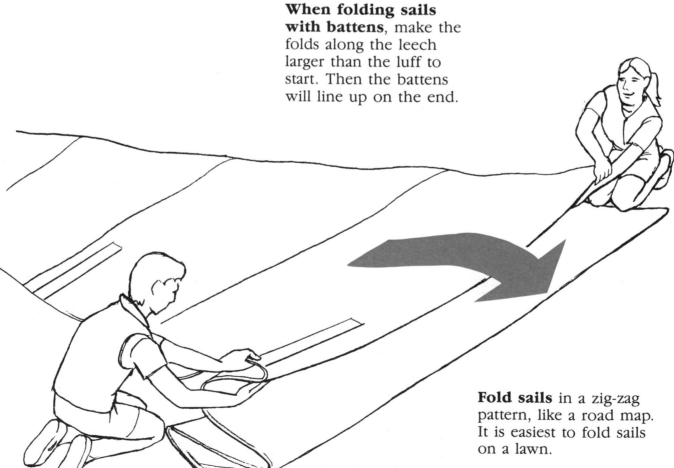

Fold sails in a zig-zag pattern, like a road map. It is easiest to fold sails on a lawn.

Storage, Maintenance, and Lifting 1 1

Like the sails, the boat too should be rinsed off with fresh water to remove dirt and salt. Rinsing is particularly important for the fittings and blocks on the boat. If the boat is kept on a trailer, try to store it on an incline so that rinse water and rain will drain readily. A boat cover is often used to keep the boat clean and dry.

Leaving the mast in the boat increases the chance of the boat moving when stored on a trailer or dock. Tie a safety line over the hull to keep it from moving.

If you have to lift a boat to move it, do not use your back, but lift with your legs to reduce the chance of injury. Lifting a boat is a team effort. Don't do it alone.

A sailing center will usually have special areas for storing boats and trailers, and a building for storing equipment, such as sails, masts and booms, rudders and tillers, daggerboards, life jackets and so forth. This equipment is often stored on moveable racks which can be rolled to the boats when they are rigged on land or at the dock.

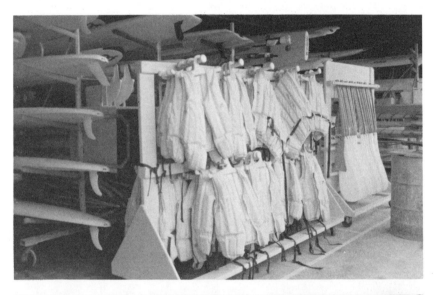

Review Exercises

I. True or False

1. Before raising the jib, you must attach the halyard.
2. It is best to take the sail bag into the boat before removing sails.
3. Sails can be raised safely without pointing the boat into the wind.
4. Always lift a boat with your legs.
5. Rigging the hull is the last step before going sailing.
6. The jib halyard needs to be tight for proper sailing.

II. Exploring Sailing
(discussion or writing)

1. Explain how to raise the main on your sailboat.

III. Mastery Activities

1. Rig and de-rig a boat, including folding sails, in the correct order without any mistakes.
2. Show your instructor how you fold a sail.

Sailing centers have developed special storage techniques which allow sailors to get on and off the water quicker.

Chapter 7

Your First Sail

"Next time, let's remember to close the drain plugs before launching."

KEY CONCEPTS

- **Getting into a boat**
- **Helmsman and crew**
- **Steering with the tiller**
- **Steering with weight**
- **Steering with sails**
- **Safety position**
- **Starting and stopping**

During your first sail you will find out why so many people love this marvelous sport. Your instructor will show you how to use the sails to start and stop and how to steer the boat. You will begin to see how the wind direction affects the way the boat is sailed, and you'll get a chance to steer and adjust the sails. Relax and enjoy it.

Boarding a Boat 9

When you enter and leave a boat, step into or from the center of the boat to keep it from tipping too much. Also make sure that you have a firm hold on some part of the boat when you are boarding. If a person is already in the boat, he or she should also be near the center. The centerboard should be lowered to keep the boat more stable. For your first sail, you can keep the centerboard lowered the whole time.

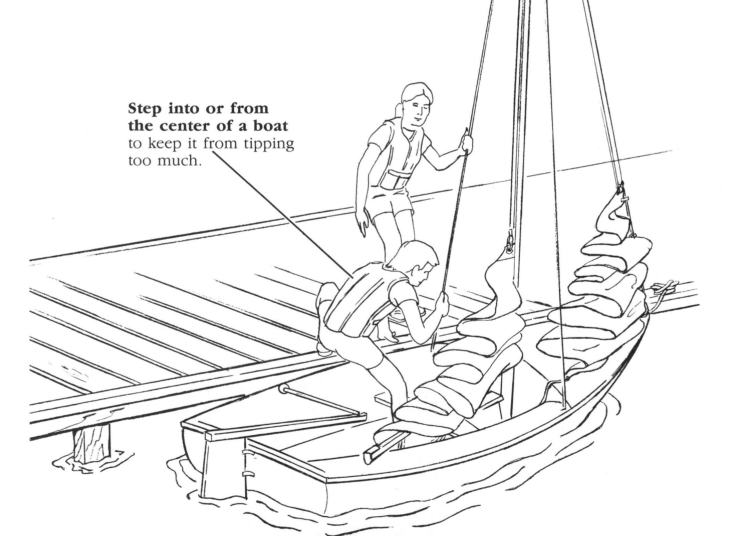

Step into or from the center of a boat to keep it from tipping too much.

Helmsman

The person who steers the boat and controls the mainsheet is the **helmsman**. The helmsman should always sit on the windward side of the boat, opposite the boom, and at the front end of the tiller. This position gives a better view of the sails and of the approaching wind and waves. The helmsman is responsible for making sure everyone on-board is wearing a life jacket and following safe procedures. The helmsman is a partner with the crew in sailing the boat properly.

Crew **9** **10**

The crew position on a sailboat is also very important. The crew is responsible for balancing the boat and keeping a lookout for other boats and obstacles.

The crew should sit in line with the centerboard so the boat will float evenly, with neither the bow nor the stern too low in the water. If the wind is light, the crew will sit on the leeward side of the boat to keep the boat level or slightly heeled. If the wind increases, the crew will move to the windward side to counteract the tipping and maintain the correct angle of heel. Moving about should be done smoothly, with no jerky motions.

**Helmsman and
Crew Position**

WIND

If the boat has a jib, the crew will be in charge of trimming it. He or she should be able to adjust it quickly and easily. This is best done by hand, holding the sheet and not cleating it. Many boats will have the jib sheets coming through a fitting on each side of the cockpit so the crew can sit in different positions and have the sheet led to them. Eventually, the crew may also have to adjust the boom vang, outhaul, and cunningham for the mainsail. But the crew's main tasks are keeping the boat balanced properly and maintaining a lookout.

If you are sailing a single-handed boat, you must be responsible for all the controls including the main, centerboard, boom vang, and boat balance. This may seem like a lot to do at first, but it soon becomes very easy. In light air you will sit in the center of the boat facing the boom.

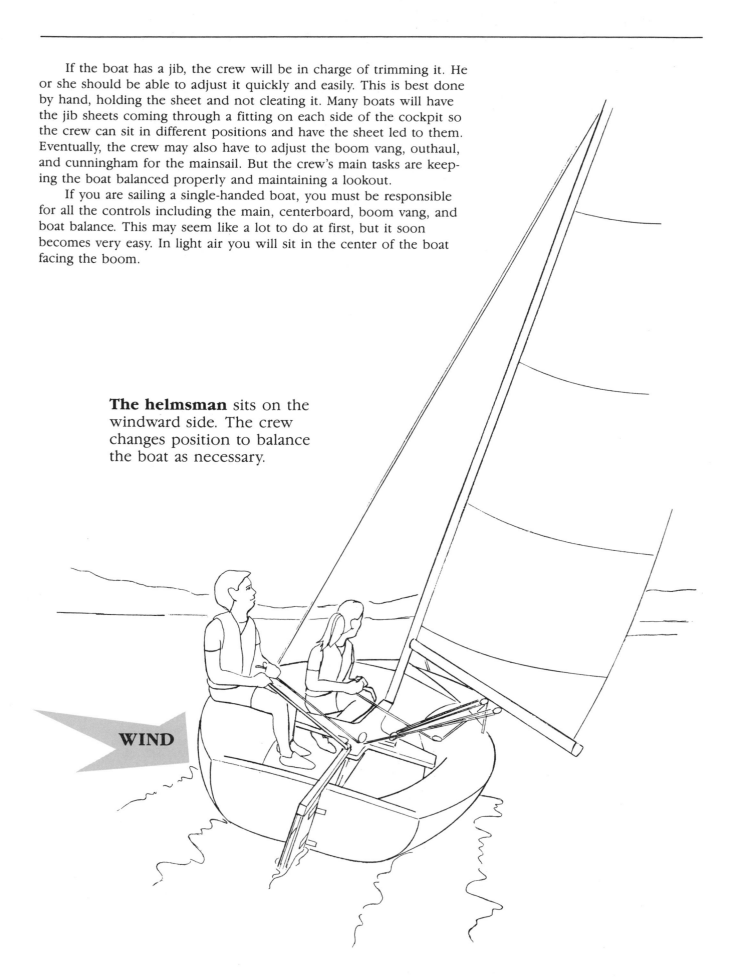

The helmsman sits on the windward side. The crew changes position to balance the boat as necessary.

WIND

Steering

Steering a sailboat takes a little practice. Steering with a tiller is different than steering a car. The tiller works by moving it in the direction opposite to the direction you want the boat to go. To turn a car to the right, you turn the wheel to the right, but to turn a boat to the right (starboard), you move the tiller to the left (port).

Usually on a boat you are steering in relation to the wind. To turn the boat toward the wind, push the tiller toward the sail. To turn the boat away from the wind, pull the tiller away from the sail.

To stop, you turn the boat toward the wind until the sail luffs like a flag flapping in the wind, and to start the boat you turn it away from the wind until the sail stops luffing. Turning towards the wind is sometimes called "heading up." Turning away from the wind is sometimes called "heading down" or "falling off." Your instructor will also show you how to slow the boat or stop and start it by adjusting only the sails.

To steer a boat, move the tiller opposite the direction you want to go.

WIND

Turning away from the wind is sometimes called "**heading down**" or "**falling off**."

The Mechanics of Steering 9 10

To steer properly, the helmsman should sit at right angles to the boat, facing the leeward side, the back hand holding the tiller and the front hand holding the mainsheet. The hands should be close together, with the palms facing downward. Your head will be turned to look forward at the sails, the approaching wind, and the water in front of the boat. Your eyes should be constantly watching these three things. And don't forget to look under the boom to leeward, to check for boats approaching from that side.

You may want to learn to steer holding only the tiller, but using a tiller extension can let you move about more freely.

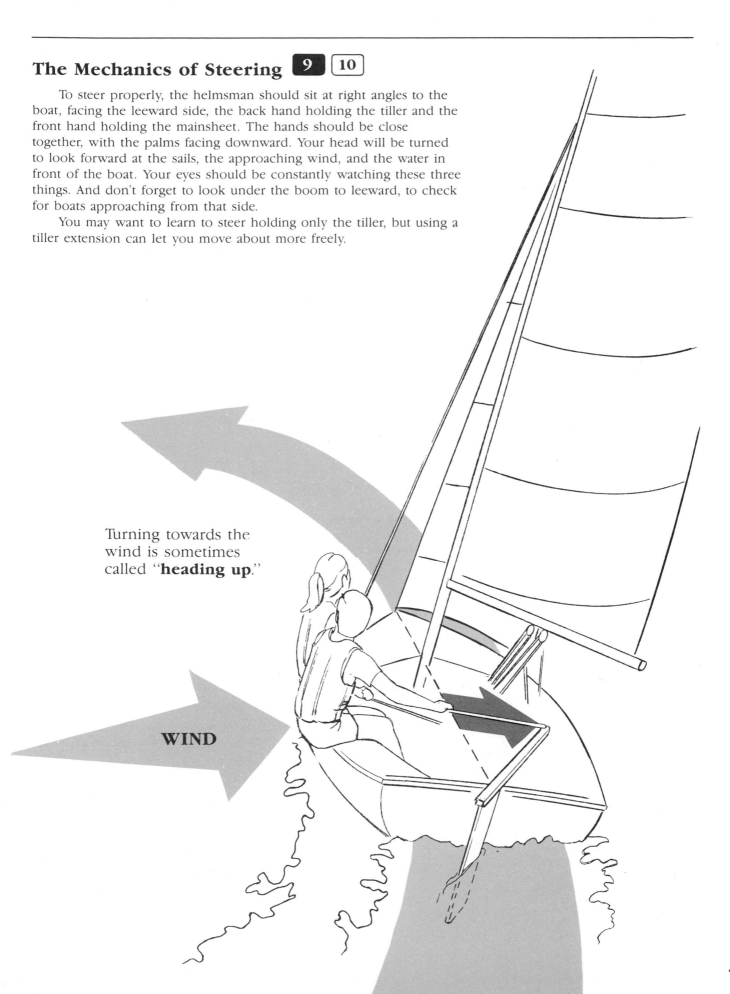

Turning towards the wind is sometimes called "**heading up**."

WIND

Steering with Sails and Body Weight

Besides the rudder, the boat can also be steered using the sails and your body weight. When the boat is heeled to leeward (toward the sail) the boat turns toward the wind. When the boat is heeled to windward (away from the sail) the boat turns away from the wind. Try sailing with the rudder fixed on the centerline, turning the boat by heeling it first to windward and then to leeward.

You can also use the sails to turn the boat. Sheeting in the main sail will make the boat slowly turn toward the wind. Sheeting out the jib at the same time, so that it completely flaps, will make the boat turn more quickly toward the wind.

Sheeting out the mainsail will make the boat turn away from the wind. It will be very difficult to turn the boat away from the wind if the mainsail is not eased, especially in medium or heavy winds.

During your first sail, you will probably sail most of the time on a reach. This is the easiest point of sail for a beginner. The boat will be level and easy to steer. You will be able to concentrate on trying the various methods of turning the boat, stopping and starting it, and using the telltales on the sail. You should also try the safety position.

Heeling to windward turns the boat away from the wind.

Heeling to leeward turns the boat toward the wind.

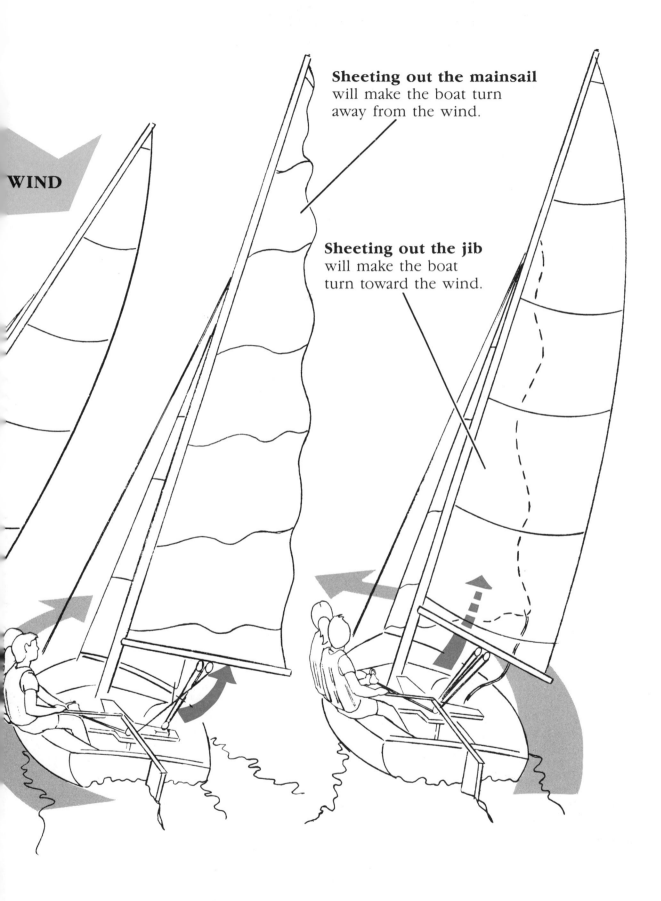

WIND

Sheeting out the mainsail will make the boat turn away from the wind.

Sheeting out the jib will make the boat turn toward the wind.

Safety Position   `9` `9` `10`

The safety position is easy to do. Sail with the wind coming on the side of the boat (a **beam reach** — see points of sail in Chapter 8), then sheet out your sails until they flap in the wind like a flag; push your tiller a little toward the flapping sail to keep the boat heading straight ahead. The boat will slow down and stop — you are in the safety position. Sheet in your sails and you are on your way again. Try it several times until you feel comfortable doing it.

Stopping and Starting Your Boat   `9` `9` `10`

A basic factor in sailing safely is knowing how to start and stop your boat. Getting started is really very easy. Your centerboard must be down and the sails must be sheeted in only enough to allow the air to start flowing evenly on both sides of the sails. If you are sheeting your sails properly, the telltales on the windward and leeward

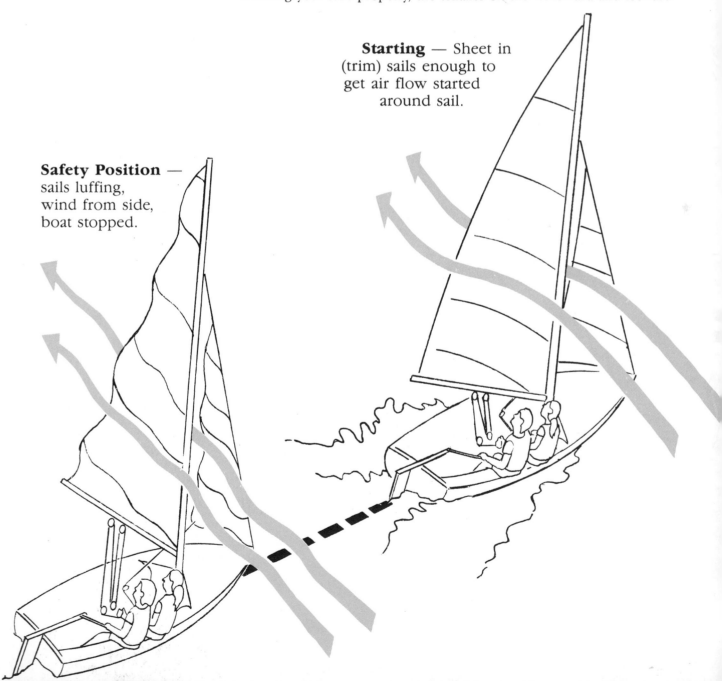

Starting — Sheet in (trim) sails enough to get air flow started around sail.

Safety Position — sails luffing, wind from side, boat stopped.

sides will flow smoothly back. Getting started means sheeting in the sails to a point that uniform air flow is established. The tiller should be centered and the centerboard down.

Stopping the boat is just as easy as starting. You can stop the boat in two ways. By turning the boat into the wind, or **no-go zone**, you will stop. This is often the preferred way when coming up to a dock. You can also stop by easing the sails until they flap. When the wind is coming over the side, letting the sails luff completely will put you in the safety position. Once in the safety position, you can make crew changes, adjust equipment, or simply stop and rest.

Stopping — Sheet out sails until they luff completely, or. . .

. . .head up into the **no-go zone.**

Review Exercises

I. Multiple Choice

1. The best place to step aboard a dinghy is
   a. the seat.
   b. the bow.
   c. the center of the cockpit.
2. To turn the boat toward the wind, you must
   a. pull the tiller away from the sail.
   b. push the tiller toward the sail.
   c. pull up the centerboard.
3. A properly sailed boat uses the following to steer:
   a. rudder, body weight, and sail trim
   b. rudder, jib trim and body weight
   c. rudder, boom vang, and sail trim
4. The proper body position for a helmsman is
   a. leeward side opposite the boom.
   b. windward side opposite the boom.
   c. at the transom.

II. Matching

1. Helmsman
2. Watching out for other boats
3. Crew tasks
4. Helmsman tasks

a. Main sheet and tiller
b. Driver
c. Crew and helmsman tasks
d. Boat balance and lookout

III. Exploring Sailing
(discussion or writing)

1. How is the boat balanced by the helmsman and crew?
2. Describe two different ways you can stop a sailboat.
3. Why is the crew position very important on a sailboat?

IV. Mastery Activities

1. With help from your instructor, you should be able to do the following:
   a. safety position
   b. stopping
   c. starting
   d. sailing on a reach

Using the Sails

KEY CONCEPTS

- **Points of sail**
- **Heading**
- **Main & jib coordination**

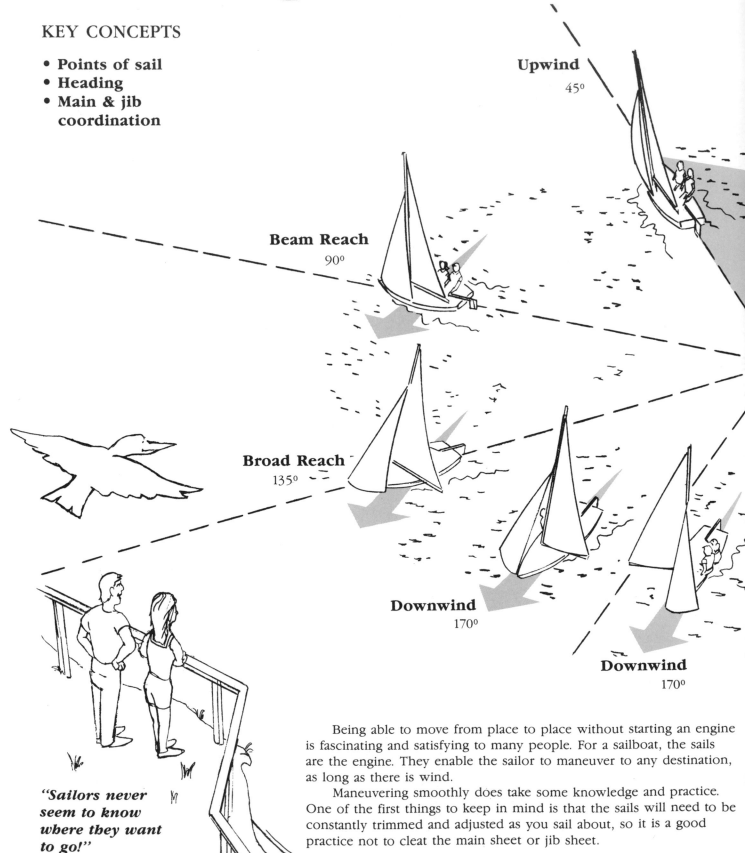

Upwind
45°

Beam Reach
90°

Broad Reach
135°

Downwind
170°

Downwind
170°

"Sailors never seem to know where they want to go!"

Being able to move from place to place without starting an engine is fascinating and satisfying to many people. For a sailboat, the sails are the engine. They enable the sailor to maneuver to any destination, as long as there is wind.

Maneuvering smoothly does take some knowledge and practice. One of the first things to keep in mind is that the sails will need to be constantly trimmed and adjusted as you sail about, so it is a good practice not to cleat the main sheet or jib sheet.

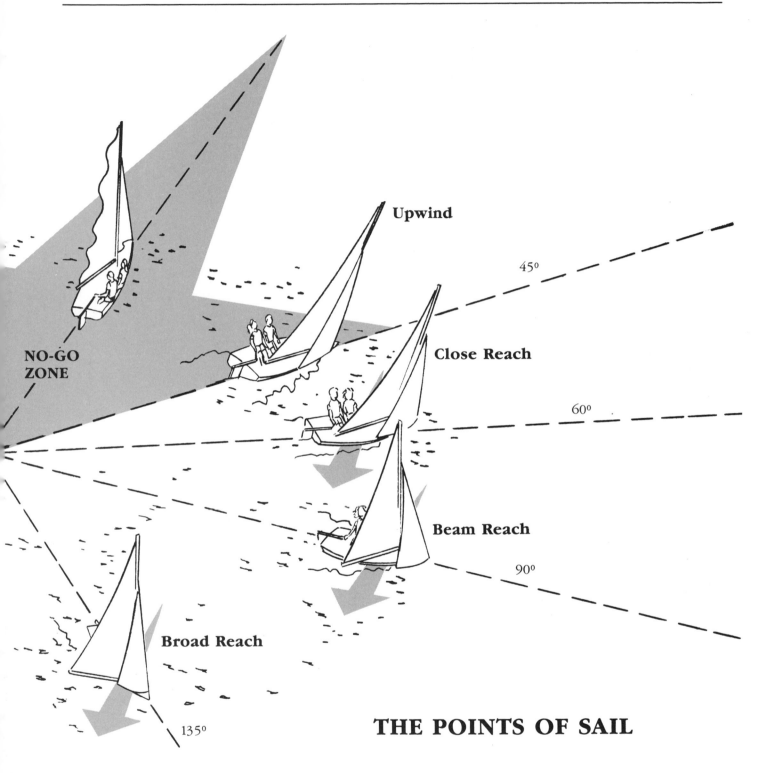

Upwind

45°

Close Reach

60°

NO-GO
ZONE

Beam Reach

90°

Broad Reach

135°

THE POINTS OF SAIL

As you hold the sheets in your hand, you will develop a feel for what the wind is doing to the sails.

Points of Sail 10 11

As the boat changes direction relative to the wind, you will be moving on different **points of sail**. Points of sail are the angles or sectors within a full 360 degree circle. There are six general points of sail: **downwind, broad reach, beam reach, close reach, upwind,** and **the no-go zone.**

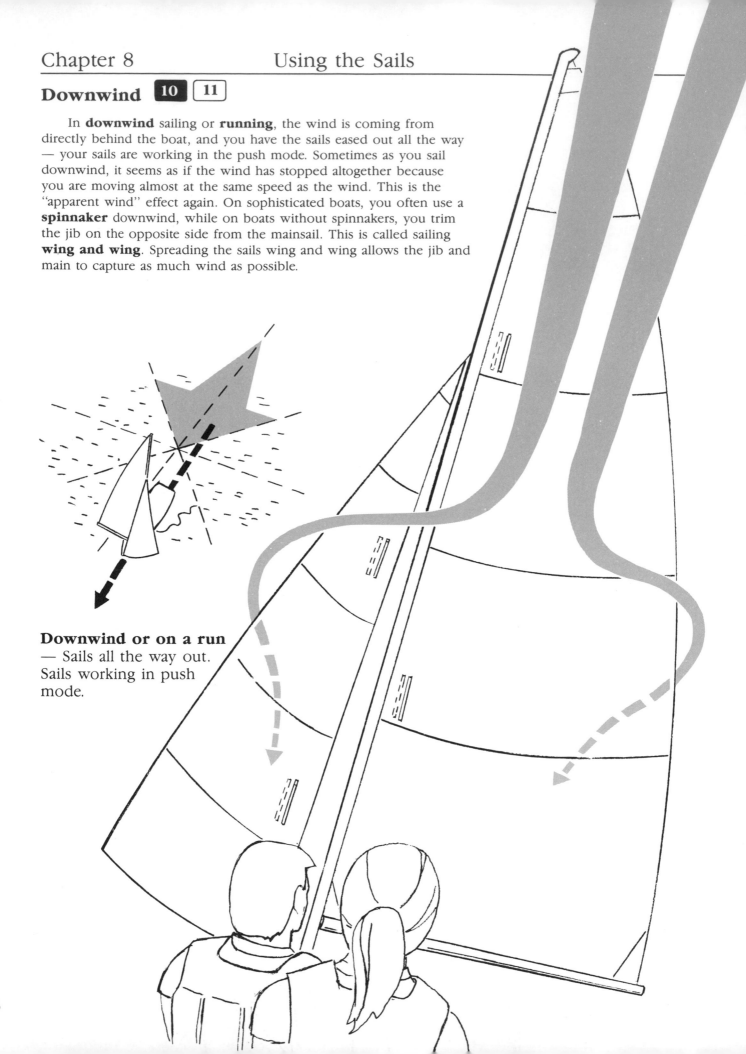

Using the Sails

Downwind 10 11

In **downwind** sailing or **running**, the wind is coming from directly behind the boat, and you have the sails eased out all the way — your sails are working in the push mode. Sometimes as you sail downwind, it seems as if the wind has stopped altogether because you are moving almost at the same speed as the wind. This is the "apparent wind" effect again. On sophisticated boats, you often use a **spinnaker** downwind, while on boats without spinnakers, you trim the jib on the opposite side from the mainsail. This is called sailing **wing and wing**. Spreading the sails wing and wing allows the jib and main to capture as much wind as possible.

Downwind or on a run — Sails all the way out. Sails working in push mode.

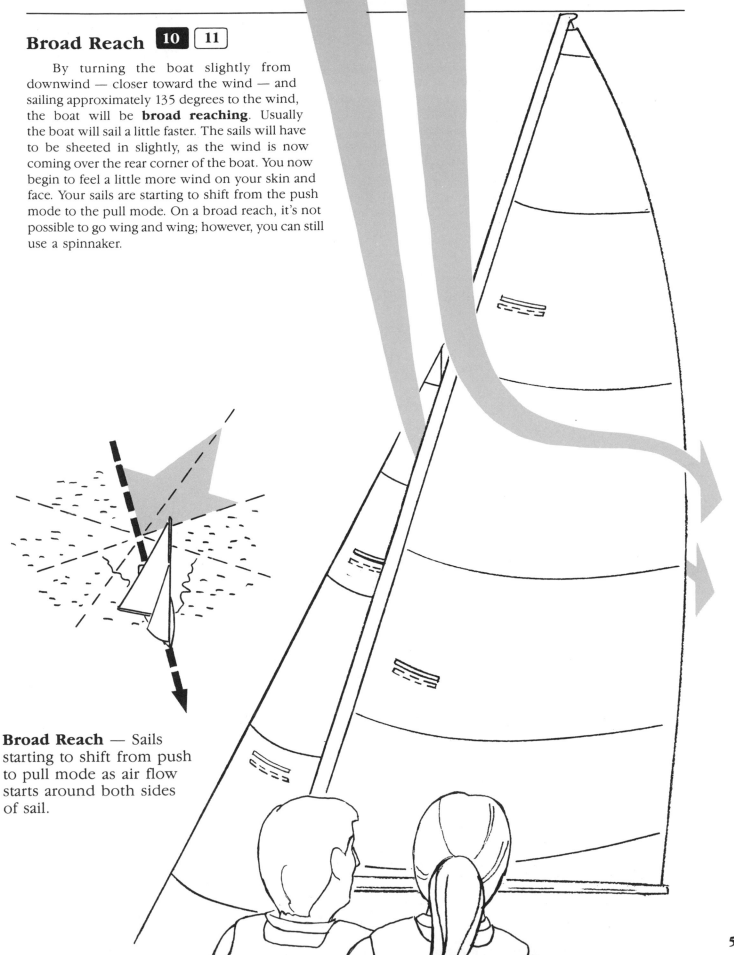

Broad Reach 10 11

By turning the boat slightly from downwind — closer toward the wind — and sailing approximately 135 degrees to the wind, the boat will be **broad reaching**. Usually the boat will sail a little faster. The sails will have to be sheeted in slightly, as the wind is now coming over the rear corner of the boat. You now begin to feel a little more wind on your skin and face. Your sails are starting to shift from the push mode to the pull mode. On a broad reach, it's not possible to go wing and wing; however, you can still use a spinnaker.

Broad Reach — Sails starting to shift from push to pull mode as air flow starts around both sides of sail.

Beam Reach 10 11

A **beam reach** is when the wind is coming directly over the side of the boat. This means that the angle to the wind is approximately 90 degrees. For most boats this is the fastest point of sail — your sails are now operating in the pull mode. Some lightweight dinghies may even rise up on top of the water and accelerate rapidly. This is called **planing**, and normally requires the breeze to be at least medium strength and the sails to be trimmed properly. Planing is one of the most exhilarating thrills in sailing.

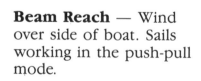

Beam Reach — Wind over side of boat. Sails working in the push-pull mode.

Close Reach 10 11

A boat on a **close reach** is starting to make progress toward the wind, with the angle to the wind approximately 60 degrees. Now that you are moving against the wind you will feel more breeze on your skin as the forward motion of the boat adds to the apparent wind. As you sail closer to the wind and pull the sails in more, the boat also will want to tip or **heel** more than when beam reaching or sailing downwind. This is normal.

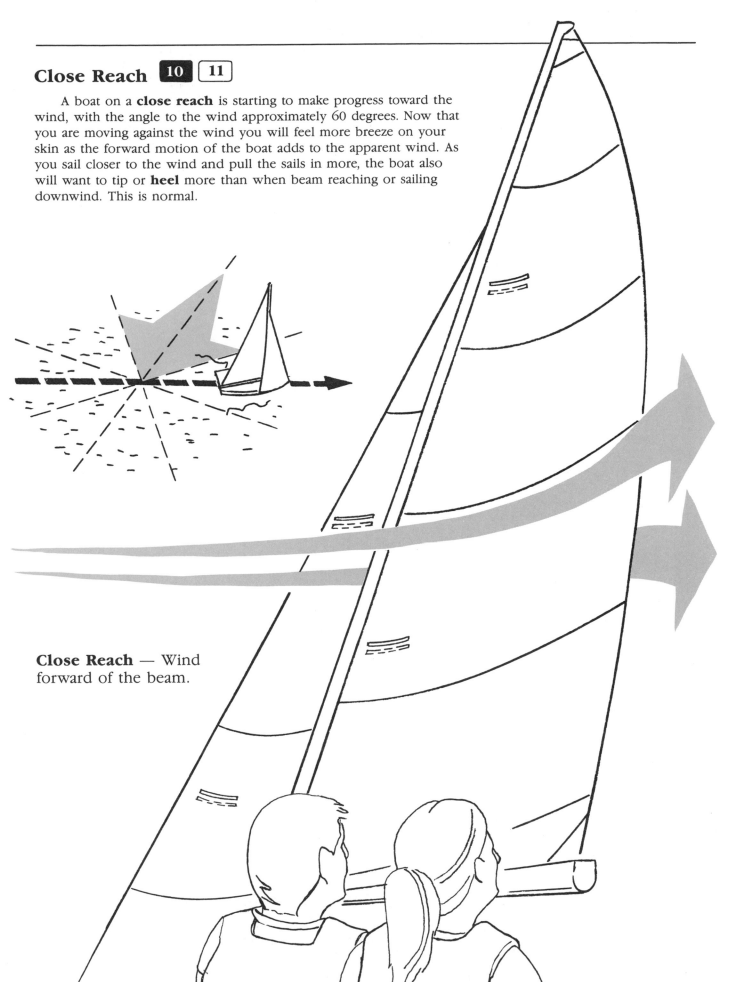

Close Reach — Wind forward of the beam.

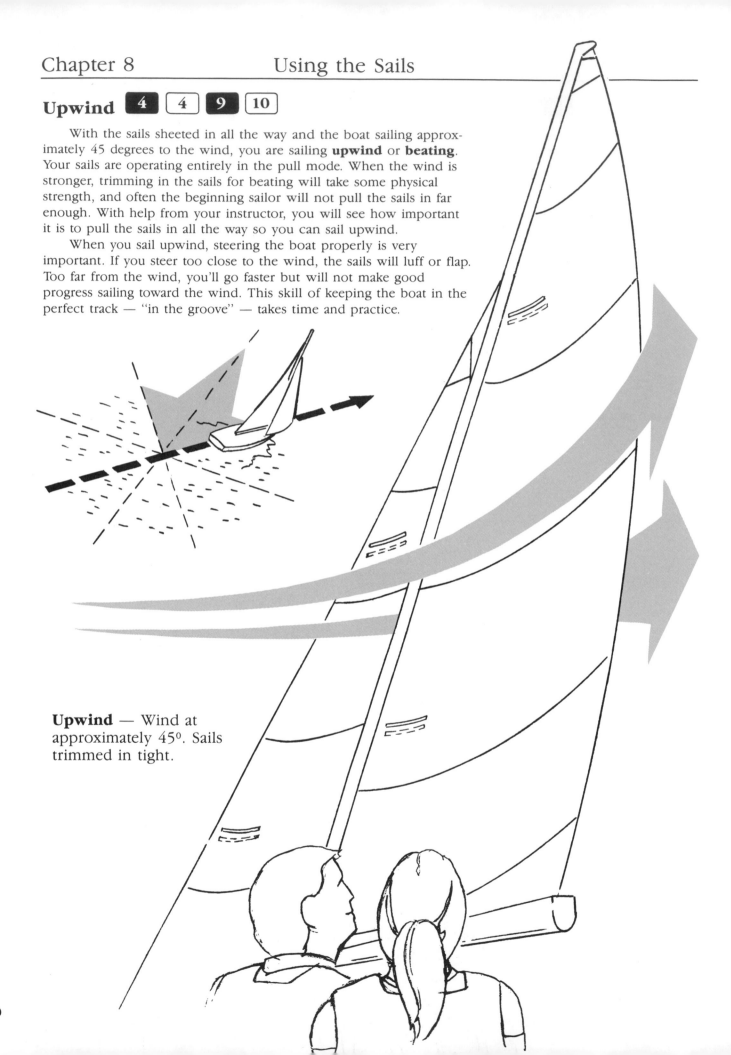

Upwind   4   4   9   10

With the sails sheeted in all the way and the boat sailing approximately 45 degrees to the wind, you are sailing **upwind** or **beating**. Your sails are operating entirely in the pull mode. When the wind is stronger, trimming in the sails for beating will take some physical strength, and often the beginning sailor will not pull the sails in far enough. With help from your instructor, you will see how important it is to pull the sails in all the way so you can sail upwind.

When you sail upwind, steering the boat properly is very important. If you steer too close to the wind, the sails will luff or flap. Too far from the wind, you'll go faster but will not make good progress sailing toward the wind. This skill of keeping the boat in the perfect track — "in the groove" — takes time and practice.

Upwind — Wind at approximately 45°. Sails trimmed in tight.

No-Go Zone 4 4

Between 45 degrees and the source of the wind is an area in which a sailboat cannot sail. The sails will flap and the boat will slow down and stop. This area is referred to as the **no-go zone**. Some highly efficient boats may sail a few degrees closer to the wind than 45 degrees; however, most dinghies will be doing well sailing that close to the wind.

Steering into the no-go zone is an excellent way to slow the boat — a maneuver often used in docking.

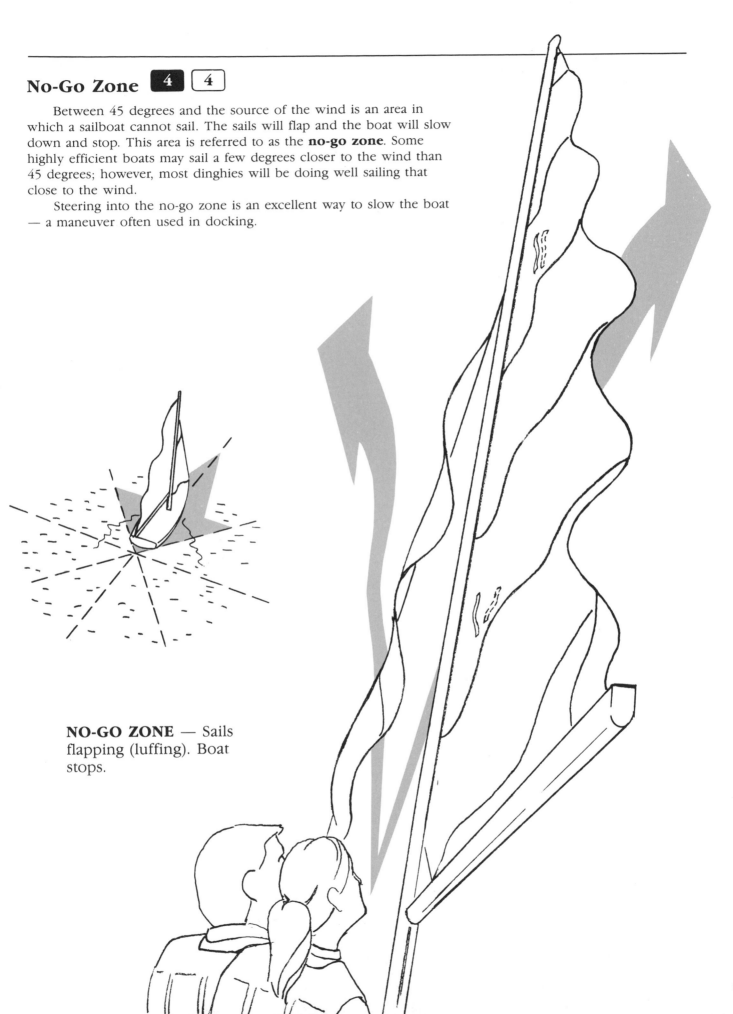

NO-GO ZONE — Sails flapping (luffing). Boat stops.

Heading

When a boat sails on a point of sail, the direction the bow points is referred to as your **heading**. Your heading determines your sail trim and helps the helmsman and crew coordinate adjustments to the main and jib. As the helmsman, you should say, "We are going to sail on a beam reach," or "We are changing course to a close reach." This helps the crew to react.

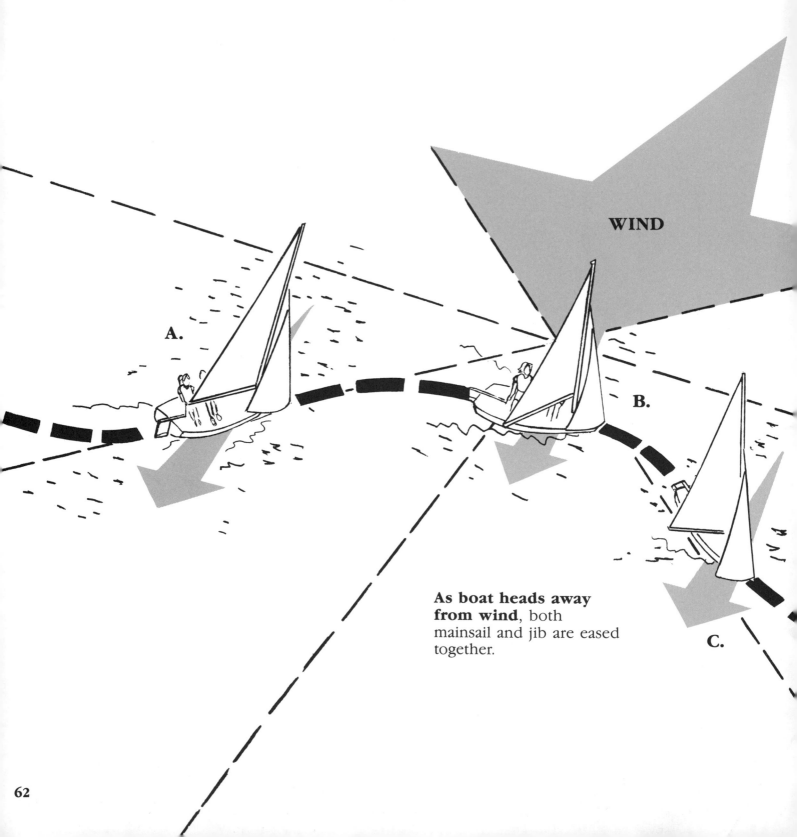

WIND

As boat heads away from wind, both mainsail and jib are eased together.

Using the Main and Jib Together ⬛12 ⬜13

Sailing on a sloop rigged boat, with a main and jib, you should try to trim the two sails to work in harmony. As you change your heading, both sails must be adjusted accordingly. If you are going from a beam reach to a broad reach, the main and jib must be eased together. If you are going to head up from a close reach to upwind sailing, the main and jib must be trimmed in together. Without the sails being trimmed in harmony, they will work against each other and not perform at their best. When the helmsman decides to change headings, it is important that he or she let the crew know whether it is time to ease or trim the jib. This makes for good communication.

As boat heads up toward wind, both mainsail and jib are trimmed back in together.

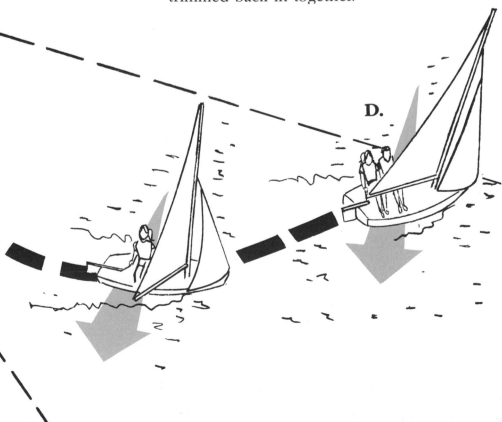

D.

Review Exercises

I. True or False
1. Sailing 90 degrees to the wind is called a beam reach.
2. When sailing upwind, your sail is in the push mode.
3. When sailing downwind, your sail is in the push mode.
4. Planing is when the boat lifts and accelerates, usually on a reach.

II. Multiple Choice
1. The no-go zone is referred to as
   a. a section of water where there is no wind.
   b. an angle to the wind between 0 and 45 degrees where the sails cannot move the boat forward.
   c. dangerous waters.

2. A broad reach is approximately how many degrees to the wind?
   a. 105 degrees
   b. 135 degrees
   c. 145 degrees

3. The direction a boat is sailing toward is commonly called the boat's
   a. path.
   b. point of sail.
   c. heading.

III. Matching
(match the words with the correct letters on page 62-63)
1. Beam reach
2. Close reach
3. Broad reach
4. Upwind

IV. Exploring Sailing
(discussion or writing)
1. What is the easiest way to stop a sailboat?
2. Why is sailing upwind the most difficult of all points of sail?

Chapter 9

Maneuvering Upwind

"I guess you can throw out the old saying about the shortest distance between two points being a straight line!"

KEY CONCEPTS

- **Sailing upwind**
- **Tacking**
- **In irons**
- **Communication**
- **Tacking sequence**
- **Tacking problems**

Learning to sail a boat upwind is one of the most rewarding parts of learning to sail. The key is coordinating both steering and sail trim. You also have to react to changes in wind strength and direction.

Sailing upwind requires proper body position, correct angle of heel, and steering at a specific angle toward the wind. In the illustration, you can see some important upwind sailing techniques. For instance the helmsman and crew sit in the center of the boat with the helmsman always steering from the windward side of the boat — opposite the boom. Ideally, the boat should have a small amount of heel to leeward. The centerboard is all the way down and sails are trimmed tight. The helmsman can use the telltales on the jib to help steer a course where the wind is a about 45-degree angle to the bow. When sailing upwind, the sails are in the pull mode.

`9` `10`

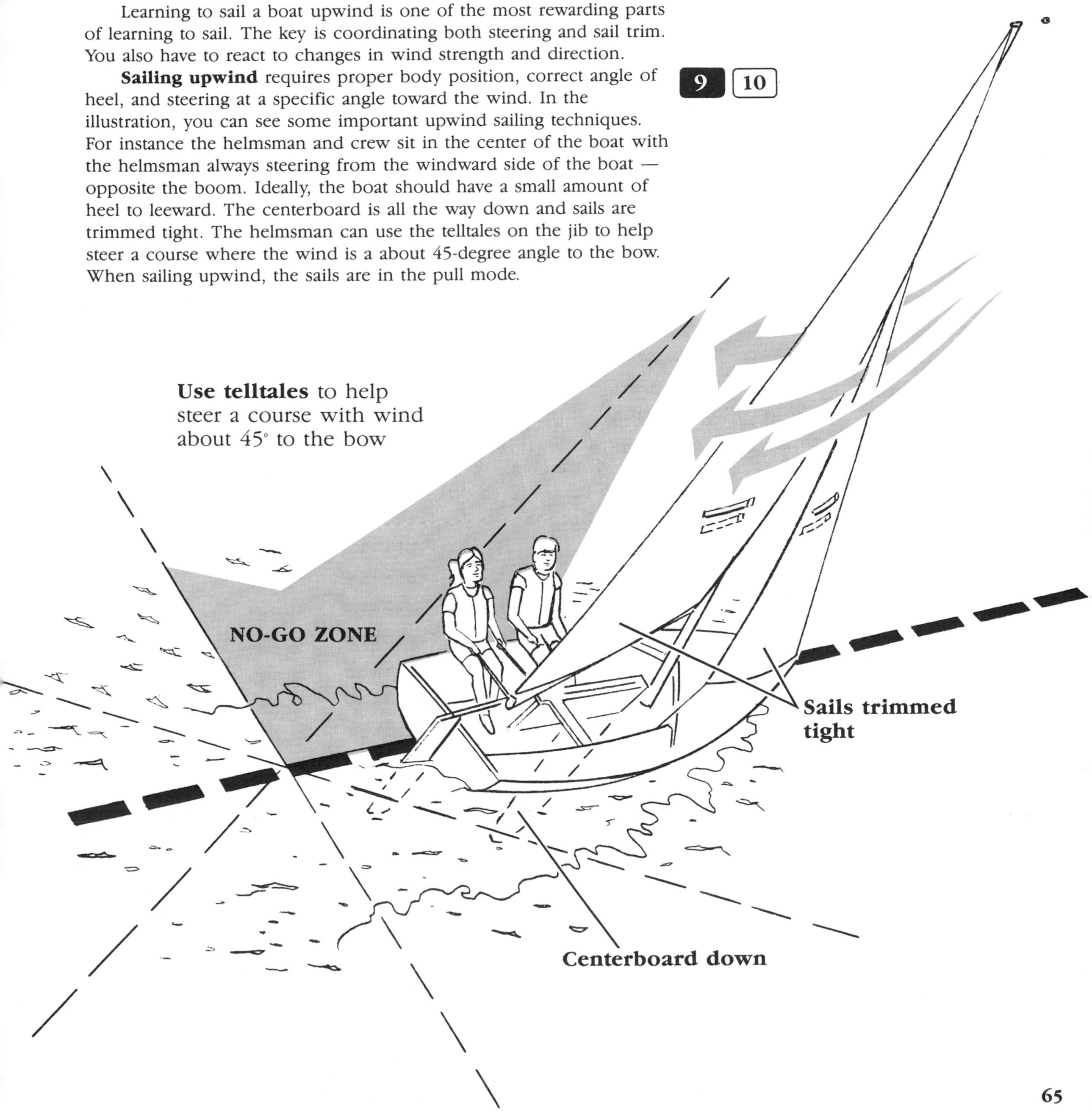

Use telltales to help steer a course with wind about 45° to the bow

NO-GO ZONE

Sails trimmed tight

Centerboard down

As we stated in the previous chapter, a sailboat cannot sail directly into the wind but can sail approximately 45 degrees to the wind. By sailing a course at 45° to the wind with the wind on one side of the boat, and then on the other, you can sail a "zig-zag" course and make progress toward the wind.

Sailors often refer to this progress against the wind as "climbing the ladder" or "beating to windward." To accomplish these zig-zag patterns will require **tacking**. Tacking is changing the side the wind hits your boat by steering the bow through the source or "eye" of the wind — the no-go zone.

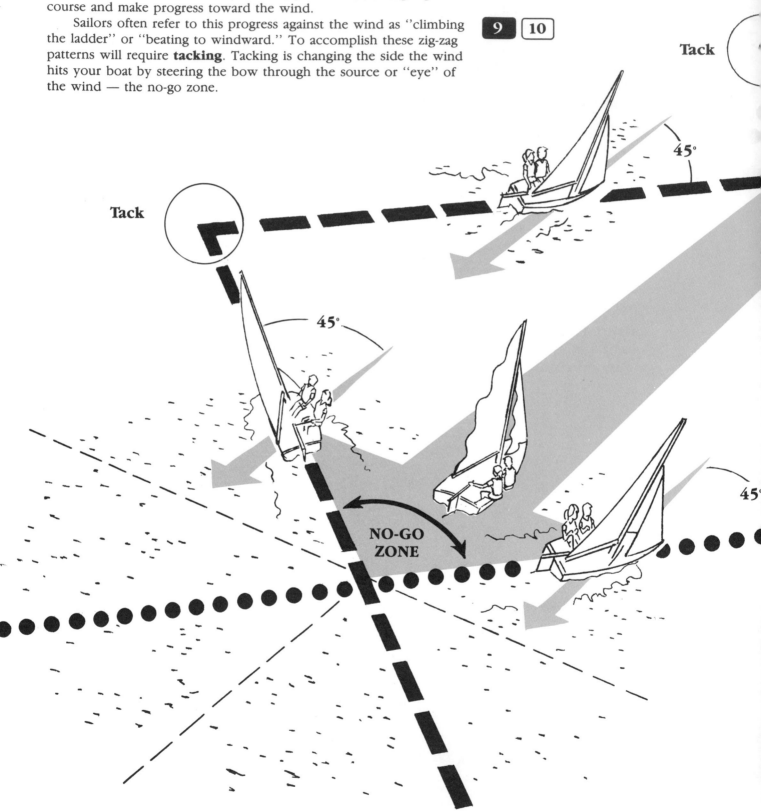

9 **10**

Tack

45°

Tack

45°

45°

NO-GO ZONE

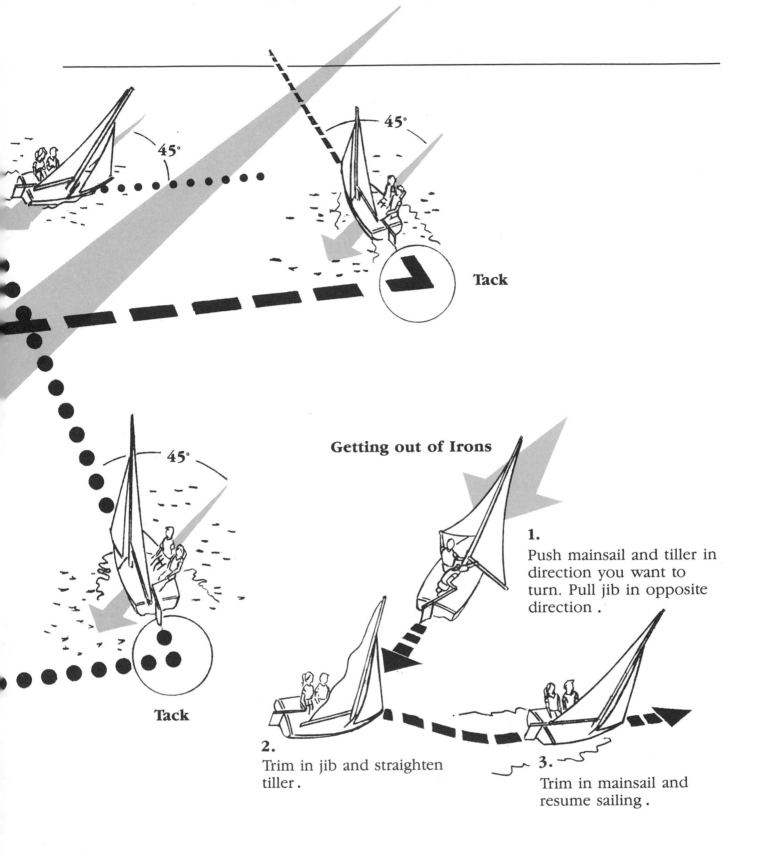

45°

45°

Tack

Getting out of Irons

1.
Push mainsail and tiller in direction you want to turn. Pull jib in opposite direction .

45°

Tack

2.
Trim in jib and straighten tiller .

3.
Trim in mainsail and resume sailing .

Before you start a tack, you must be sailing fast enough to pass through the no-go zone without stopping. If you keep in the no-go zone too long, the boat will stop and start drifting backwards. This condition is called being **in irons**. The easiest way to get out of irons is to push both the tiller and the boom in the same direction you want to turn. If the boat has a jib, the crew should pull it to the side opposite from the boom. Getting in irons happens even to the best of sailors.

Hand Exchange While Tacking 9 10

How well the helmsman switches the tiller and main sheet from one hand to the other often makes the difference between a good tack and a bad tack. Perfecting this hand exchange should be a number one priority for the helmsman. Practice it on land (use the tacking land drill described in Appendix) until you can do it smoothly and automatically.

Whether you use a tiller or tiller extension, the basic steps remain the same, even though the timing of the steps may change:

1. Push the tiller towards the sail.
2. Cross the boat, facing forward.
3. Switch hands.
4. Turn body to face mainsail.
5. Adjust the sails and heading for new tack.

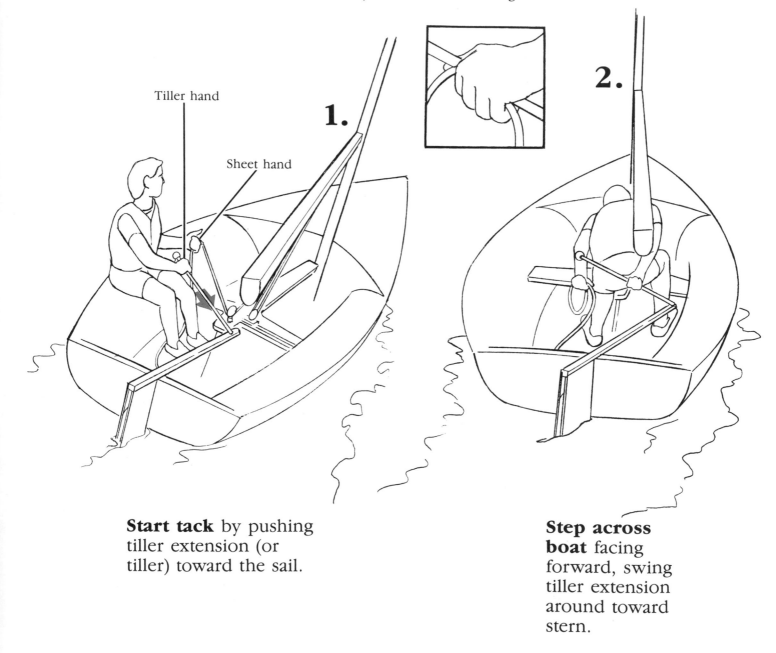

Tiller hand

Sheet hand

1.

2.

Start tack by pushing tiller extension (or tiller) toward the sail.

Step across boat facing forward, swing tiller extension around toward stern.

You switch hands by reaching your sheet hand (still holding the sheet) behind your back and grabbing the tiller or tiller extension. Your other hand lets go of the tiller or tiller extension and grabs the main sheet in front of your body.

The timing of when you switch hands will vary depending on whether a tiller or tiller extension is used. If a tiller is used, you switch hands after you have crossed the boat and are starting to turn your body — about halfway through the tack. If you use a tiller extension, the timing can vary from halfway through the tack to after the tack has been completed. Many expert dinghy sailors prefer to switch hands after the tack, because they feel it gives them better control of boat balance and trim. When switching hands after the tack, you will complete the tack still facing forward steering with your tiller hand behind your back and holding the sheet in your sheet hand. Then you reach your sheet hand behind your back to start the hand exchange.

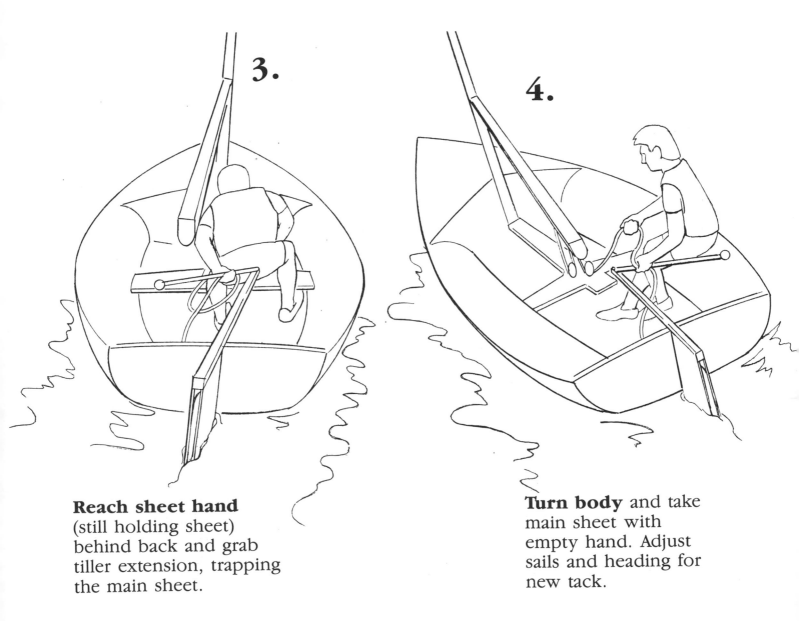

3.

Reach sheet hand (still holding sheet) behind back and grab tiller extension, trapping the main sheet.

4.

Turn body and take main sheet with empty hand. Adjust sails and heading for new tack.

Communication

To tack well requires good communication between helmsman and crew. Since the helmsman is steering and in command, he or she should give all the voice commands. If the boat is sailing upwind and the telltales are flowing smoothly, the helmsman starts the maneuver by stating "prepare to tack," or "ready about." This means the crew should get ready to uncleat the jib and to move from one side of the boat to the other.

Once the crew is ready, he or she should respond by saying "ready." When the helmsman starts to turn the boat, he or she will say "hard-a-lee," which indicates that the tiller is being pushed hard to leeward. The crew knows the tack is beginning.

It is best to practice tacking with land drills first before trying it on the water. In medium to light winds, a normal tack should take about five to seven seconds.

Crew Assistance

In tacking, the crew plays a vital role. He or she must help with boat balance and tack the jib while keeping a good lookout. Spotting land references and checking to make sure the way is clear, the crew provides important information for the helmsman. When first learning to sail, most helmsmen have their eyes inside the boat, coordinating the main sheet and tiller. The crew can act as the helmsman's second pair of eyes until the tack can be accomplished smoothly.

Tacking Problems

It is common to make mistakes when you are learning to tack. Some of the common mistakes are listed, but with help from land drill practice and your instructor, it will not take long before you master the tack.

Problems	**Solutions**
1. The boat stops turning while in the no-go zone.	**1.** Start your tack by pushing the tiller more quickly toward the sail.
2. You forget to change jib sheets and sheet the jib on the wrong side.	**2.** When you change position in the boat, drop the old jib sheet and grab the new one.
3. The boat is turned too far and the tack ends with the boat sailing on a reach rather than upwind.	**3.** Before tacking, choose a landmark to help establish your new course heading. As you finish your tack, aim your boat at this landmark. Remember to pay more attention to what's going on outside the boat rather than inside the boat.

TACKING STEPS

2.

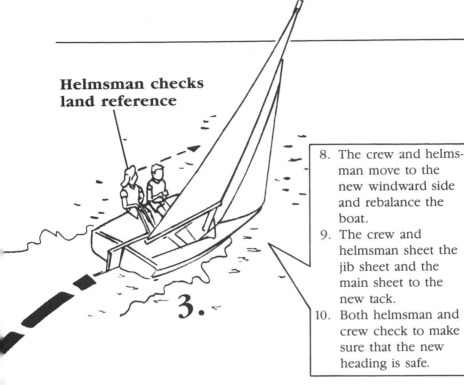

Helmsman checks land reference

8. The crew and helmsman move to the new windward side and rebalance the boat.
9. The crew and helmsman sheet the jib sheet and the main sheet to the new tack.
10. Both helmsman and crew check to make sure that the new heading is safe.

3.

5. The helmsman calls out, "tacking" or the traditional "hard a-lee" and pushes the tiller towards the sail.
6. As the boat turns into the wind, the sails will begin to luff and the crew releases the jib and moves with the helmsman towards the center of the boat.
7. The helmsman completes the hand exchange, while the crew sheets in the jib with the new jib sheet.

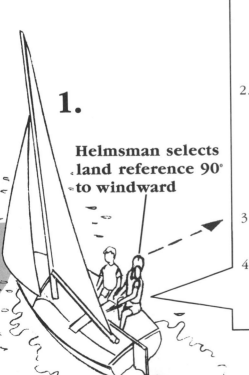

1.

Helmsman selects land reference 90° to windward

1. The helmsman and crew look around to make sure it is safe to tack and the boat has good boat speed. The sails are trimmed properly and the sail telltales are flowing smoothly.
2. The helmsman calls out to the crew, "prepare to tack" or "ready about," and selects a land reference to steer for at the completion of the tack (approximately 90 degrees to windward of the centerline of the boat).
3. The crew uncleats the jib and replies, "ready," while still holding the jib sheet.
4. If the helmsman or crew spots some obstruction or problem, he or she would reply, "no" or "not ready."

Review Exercises

I. Fill in the Blanks

1. When the helmsman begins the actual tack by turning the tiller, he or she calls out _____.
2. Sailing toward the wind source at 45° is called _____ sailing.
3. At about _____ degrees to the wind, the boat is sailing upwind.
4. To complete a successful tack, the bow of the boat always goes through the _____ zone.
5. A good tack should take approximately _____ seconds.

II. Multiple Choice

1. How does the crew best help the helmsman when first learning to tack?
   a. Talks the helmsman through the tack.
   b. Spots land references and checks to make sure the way is clear.
   c. Holds the main sheet for the helmsman while he or she changes tiller between hands.
   d. Screams and shouts.
2. Why are land references so important when first learning how to tack?
   a. They help you find your way home.
   b. They allow the crew to spot danger.
   c. They help the helmsman steer the boat in the right direction after a tack.
3. Why must the sail telltales be flowing smoothly before a successful tack?
   a. They indicate that the boat has good speed for a tack.
   b. They determine the sail trim before a tack.
   c. They tell you which way to move the tiller.

III. Exploring Sailing
(discussion or writing)

1. Could you tack with the main sheet cleated? What safety problems could this create?
2. Why would tacking be more difficult in stronger winds?

IV. Mastery Activities

1. **Shore**. Practice on land to a point of mastering the main sheet and tiller exchange before trying it on the water.
2. **Water**. Complete five tacks in a row without oversteering or getting in irons. Each tack should take no longer then ten seconds.

Maneuvering Downwind

"Did you have to put so many onions on that hamburger?"

KEY CONCEPTS

- **Sailing downwind**
- **Sailing by the lee**
- **Jibing**
- **Types of jibes**

Sailing downwind — with the wind coming directly over the stern — offers great speed and enjoyment. It is often the sailor's favorite point of sail because it's so easy.

When sailing downwind, the boat is in the push mode. The sails are sheeted out all the way to expose as much sail area as possible to the wind's pushing force. To sail downwind, simply choose a heading and steer smoothly with the sails sheeted out. Because the wind is pushing on only one side of the sail, the telltales do not work in their normal way. You will find the boat is stable and easy to sail. Because you are travelling at nearly the same speed as the wind, the feel of the wind on your face and body will be greatly reduced.

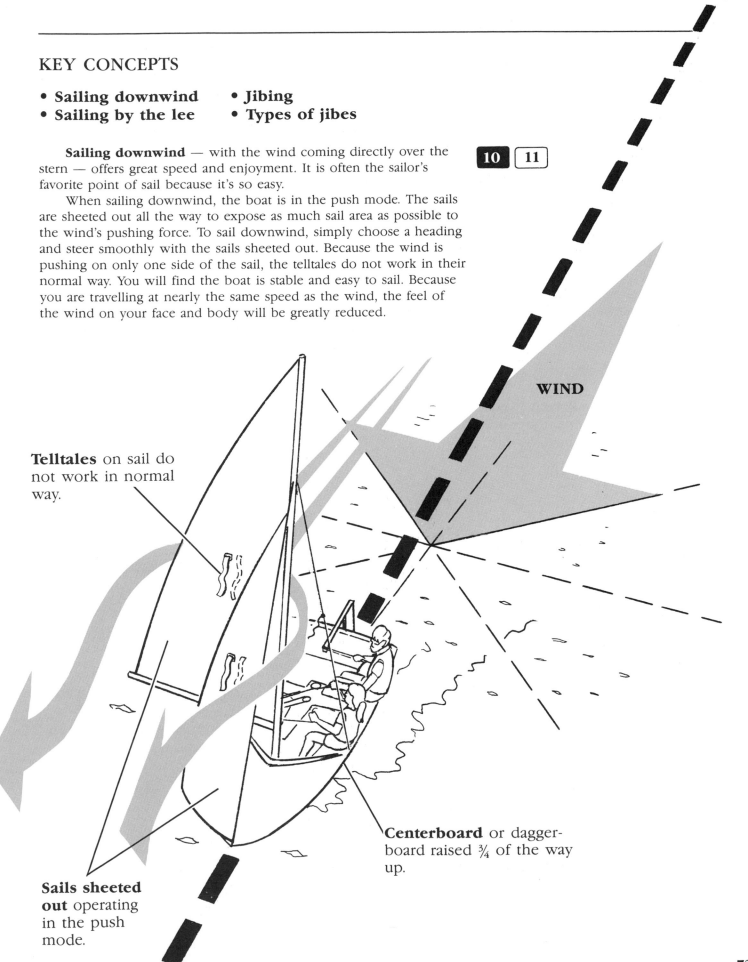

10   11

WIND

Telltales on sail do not work in normal way.

Centerboard or dagger-board raised ¾ of the way up.

Sails sheeted out operating in the push mode.

Downwind Maneuvers

Downwind, the maneuver of changing the wind from one side of the boat to another is called a **jibe.**. A jibe is the downwind version of a tack, since it involves moving the sails across the boat from one side to the other.

A jibe requires good wind sensing, especially knowing the wind direction. By knowing the exact direction of the wind, you can anticipate when to make your jibe, safely switching the sails from one side of the boat to the other. If you're not aware of the wind direction, the sails and the boom can suddenly slam across the boat when you don't expect it. This is called an accidental jibe. To prevent it, you should always be fully aware of your boat and the sails relative to the wind.

One of the best ways to avoid an accidental jibe is to avoid sailing **by the lee**. When you sail dead downwind, the wind is coming directly over the stern, down the centerline of the boat. When you sail by the lee, the wind moves toward the side of the boat that the sails are on. When this happens, the wind can catch the sail on the

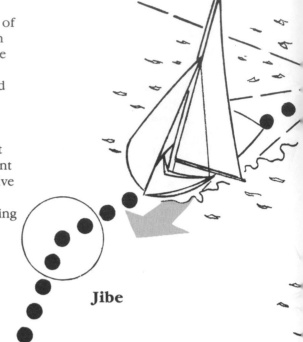

Jibe

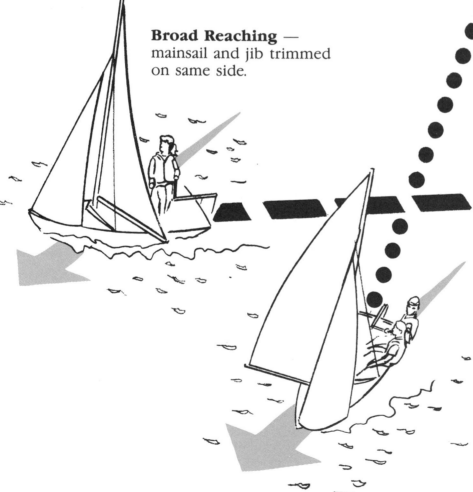

Broad Reaching — mainsail and jib trimmed on same side.

Downwind, the wind comes directly over the stern. Jib and mainsail can be trimmed "wing and wing."

wrong side and jibe the mainsail across the boat. One of the signs that you are by the lee is that the jib will lose its wind, because the mainsail captures the air that would normally fill the jib. You can also watch the telltale at the top of the mast (sometimes called a "masthead fly"), the telltales on the windward shroud, and the ripples on the water as indicators of the wind direction.

Also important downwind is the centerboard or daggerboard. It should be raised three-quarters of the way up.

Types of Jibes

There are two types of jibes. The correct and safe jibe is often referred to as an **S-jibe**. The S-jibe is controlled, with proper handling of the boat and sails by the helmsman and crew. Sometimes as the mainsail swings across the boat and fills (with wind) on the other side, the boat will heel and turn too much. In stronger winds it could end with a capsize. To overcome this problem, briefly center the tiller as the boom crosses the center of the boat and swings to the other side. As you do this, your boat's path will trace an elongated "S". In the S-jibe, the main sheet and boom are pulled across the centerline and then eased out smoothly, all under control.

The other kind of jibe — the **C-jibe** or **slam jibe** — occurs when the boat is turned and the sail comes flying across unassisted, heeling the boat, and putting strain on the rigging and gear. To avoid uncontrolled jibes will require practice moving the boom from one side of the boat to the other. Since there is a lot of coordination involved in a smooth jibe, practice on shore is helpful to reduce the chances of a slam jibe or a capsize.

Jibe

Masthead Fly

Wind coming over same side as sail.

When sailing "by the lee" the wind can catch the sail on the wrong side and cause an accidental slam jibe.

Chapter 10

Jibing Steps **10** **11**

Jibing is similar to tacking; however, the timing is a little more important in the jibe. The normal procedure involves the following steps.

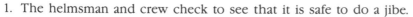

1. The helmsman and crew check to see that it is safe to do a jibe.
2. The helmsman states, "prepare to jibe."
3. The crew responds, "ready to jibe," if all is ready.
4. The helmsman determines the exact location of the wind.
5. The helmsman picks a land reference to steer towards on the new jibe.
6. The helmsman moves the tiller gradually away from the boom, slowly turning the boat. The crew lets the jib luff.
7. The helmsman slowly starts to pull in the main sheet.

8. Grabbing all of the main sheet, the helmsman brings the boom to the boat's centerline and says, "jibe ho."
9. The helmsman lets the boom cross the centerline and eases out the main sheet. As the boom crosses the centerline, the helmsman briefly centers the tiller — which makes the "S."
10. The helmsman switches the main sheet and the tiller to opposite hands and then helmsman and crew reposition themselves on the new windward side opposite the boom.
11. The helmsman adjusts the boom for the new heading.

12. The crew trims the jib sheet.
13. The helmsman and crew check to see that the new heading is correct and reorient themselves to the new wind direction.

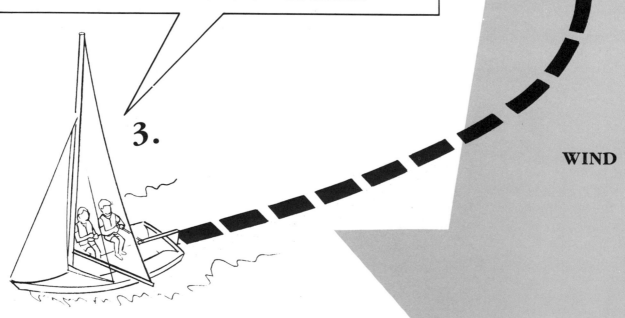

1.

2.

3.

WIND

Crew Responsibilities

In the jibe, as in the tack, the crew has an important role. In addition to handling the jib, the crew should help balance the boat, and should be the lookout for the helmsman, who is busy with the main. The crew may have to help the helmsman jibe the boom, and both the crew and the helmsman should make sure they stay low in the boat, to keep clear of the boom and keep their weight low.

You should realize that the jibe has the greatest potential for mishaps or capsizes. But if you approach jibes with this awareness, you will find that learning how to jibe will be easier.

Helmsman Responsibilities

With practice the jibe will soon be a simple maneuver. The helmsman should get used to calling out "prepare to jibe" and "jibe ho" at the proper times. This is important even after years of experience.

In light air, the jibe will become simple and routine. However, as the wind becomes stronger, the jibe is more demanding. The force of the boom and mainsail crossing the centerline can sometimes jerk the boat. It will be best to practice in stronger winds after you can jibe easily in light air. You will notice that to jibe properly in stronger air requires a keen wind sense and steering ability. And always remember, if the air is too strong for a safe jibe, you can steer around into the wind and tack the boat instead.

Hand Exchange While Jibing

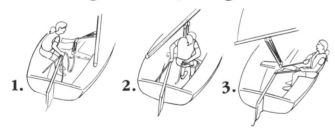

Just like tacking, it's important to know how to exchange the main sheet and tiller with your hands. **1.** Just before you grab the main sheet to throw the boom across the boat, transfer the sheet from your sheet hand to your tiller hand. Grab the main sheet between the boom and the cockpit with your sheet hand, and pull the boom across the boat. **2.** As the boom crosses the boat, step across the boat facing forward, pass your old sheet hand behind your back and grab the tiller extension or tiller. Release the tiller from your other hand. **3.** Adjust the main sheet to the new heading.

Tips for Easier Jibing

1. Practice the land drills first (see Appendix) until you perfect the hand and tiller exchanges.
2. Before the jibe, try to locate the wind direction by wind sensing or looking at the masthead fly or the telltale on the windward shroud.
3. Lower the centerboard halfway.
4. Make sure all the sheets are free and clear of any entanglements.
5. Turn the boat very slowly while jibing.
6. Keep an eye on the new course sailed.
7. Make sure the crew and helmsman talk through the maneuver.
8. Practice at first in smooth seas and light winds.

Review Exercises

I. True or False

1. A jibe is when the stern of the boat is turned through the wind and the sails cross the centerline.
2. An S-jibe is a controlled jibe.
3. "Sailing by the lee" is when the wind could unexpectedly jibe the boat.
4. The first step in jibing for the helmsman is pushing the tiller.
5. Wind sensing is very important before jibing.
6. Sailing together as a team is not necessary for jibing in a two-person boat.
7. Jibing is the opposite of tacking.
8. Turning the tiller fast will make jibing easier.
9. The crew's only responsibility in jibing is to bring the jib across the centerline.
10. The C-jibe is an unsafe jibe.

II. Exploring Sailing
(discussion or writing)

1. Describe in your own words how to do a safe S-jibe for your boat.
2. How can you best prevent an accidental jibe from happening?

III. Mastery Activities

1. Complete three consecutive S-jibes on the water.
2. Complete jibes with excellent communication between crew and helmsman.

Chapter 11

Understanding Capsize

"Fred, I don't think you're going to find that contact lens."

KEY CONCEPTS

- **Capsizing: It's part of sailing**
- **Windward and leeward capsize**
- **Capsize safety rule**
- **Scoop recovery method**
- **Walkover recovery method**
- **Turtling**
- **Mast in mud**
- **Entering and exiting**

Capsizing sometimes occurs in sailing dinghies. As you learn to sail, or become more experienced and start sailing in stronger winds, there's a chance your boat may capsize. It is nothing to be afraid of — it is a natural part of dinghy sailing. Even the most experienced sailors capsize. Your instructor will show you the best and quickest ways to recover from a capsize, and once you have mastered the recovery techniques, you may even find that it's fun to do.

Most centerboard boats are self-rescuing, which allows you to right the boat and be sailing again in a few minutes. Self-rescuing boats have built-in buoyancy which keeps the boat from sinking and makes capsize recovery easier. (Make sure the drain plugs in air tanks or flotation bags are securely fastened before you go sailing.)

There are two ways that a boat will capsize. The most common way is for the boat to roll over to leeward, away from the wind. The sails will lie on the water downwind from the boat. The other way, the boat rolls over to windward, toward the wind. This happens less frequently, but when it does, it usually happens quicker.

Causes of Capsize 5 5

There are a number of reasons why sailboats capsize:

1. A sudden gust of wind catches the sailor by surprise and overpowers the boat.
2. A poorly executed jibe unbalances the boat and makes it heel or roll too much.
3. A broken tiller or hiking strap puts the boat out of control.
4. Letting go of the tiller or main sheet makes the boat suddenly turn or change its angle of heel.
5. Quick turns in heavy air force the boat to roll over.

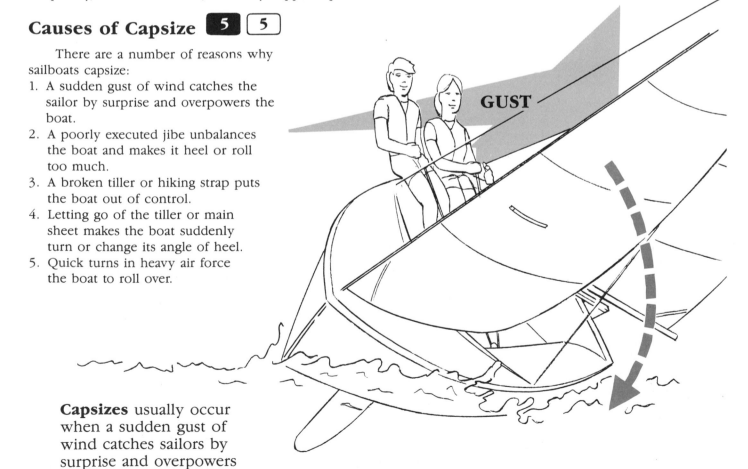

Capsizes usually occur when a sudden gust of wind catches sailors by surprise and overpowers the boat.

GUST

79

There are ways to avoid a capsize. Most important is to sail with the main sheet uncleated, or at least ready to release quickly if a sudden gust hits. It's also important to keep the boat balanced by adjusting your weight and sail trim. If a boat heels too much, you will lose control. Avoid sudden and unexpected changes in sail trim and weight position that will unbalance the boat. And remember to watch for puffs and gusts so that you are prepared to react.

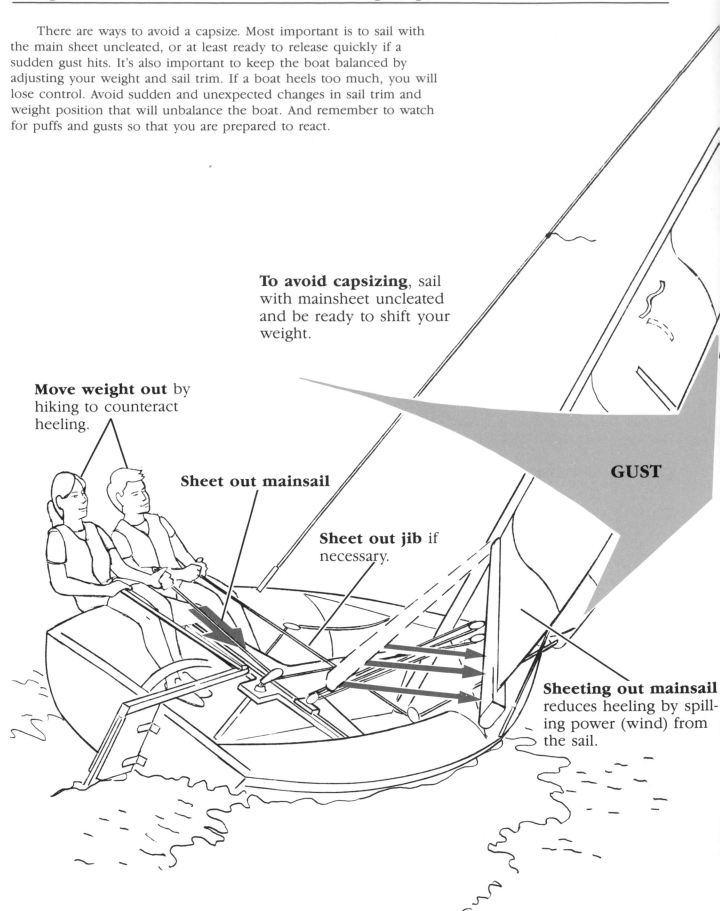

To avoid capsizing, sail with mainsheet uncleated and be ready to shift your weight.

Move weight out by hiking to counteract heeling.

Sheet out mainsail

Sheet out jib if necessary.

GUST

Sheeting out mainsail reduces heeling by spilling power (wind) from the sail.

The Capsize Safety Rule 5 5

If you do capsize, there is one important rule that you should always remember — **stay with the boat**. Even if you don't think you can turn the boat upright, don't try to swim to shore. The shore is always further than it looks. If the boat cannot be righted, climb up onto the hull. You will be more comfortable, and rescuers will be able to see you better. Stay with the boat and you will be rescued sooner.

When swimming around a capsized boat, you should avoid swimming underneath the hull or sails. It is easy to get confused or lose your orientation.

Students who wish to become expert sailors should be able to right a capsized boat. With your life jacket on and the boat acting as a floating raft, there is nothing to fear. The best place to learn and practice capsize recovery methods is in shallow water or a swimming pool. This will allow you to master the techniques before doing it in the open water.

Stay with the boat after capsizing! **Never** try to swim ashore.

Avoid swimming under hull or sails.

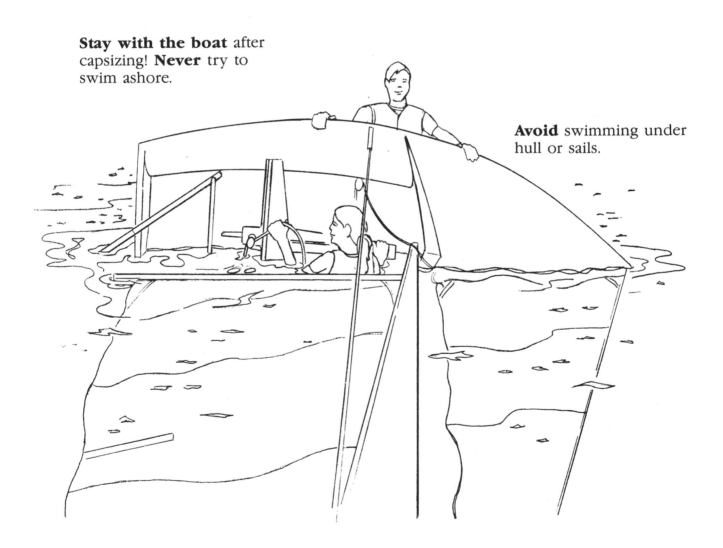

Scoop Recovery Method 5 5

If a gust of wind does surprise you and your boat capsizes, it's usually a simple matter to get it back up again. The **scoop capsize recovery** is the best method for boats that are sailed by two or more people. As the boat rights, a person is "scooped" into the boat, and this person can then balance the boat as it becomes upright and place it in the safety position. This person can also help the other person into the boat. It's important that the sailors keep in constant touch with each other during the capsize recovery. The steps for the scoop recovery method are quite easy.

1. **A** supports mast at gooseneck to prevent boat from turtling while **B** moves to centerboard, keeping in constant contact with boat.

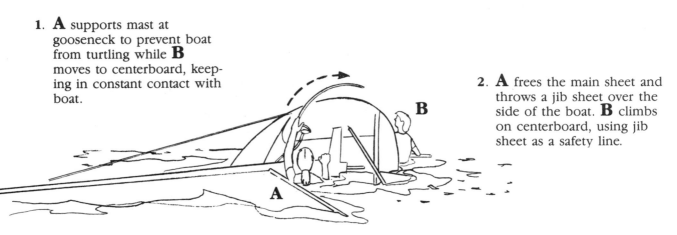

2. **A** frees the main sheet and throws a jib sheet over the side of the boat. **B** climbs on centerboard, using jib sheet as a safety line.

3. **B** leans out on centerboard while **A** holds onto stationary object in cockpit and kicks.

4. As boat swings upright, **A** is "scooped" into cockpit.

5. **A** balances the boat and places it in the safety position (wind abeam, sails luffing) and then helps **B** aboard at stern.

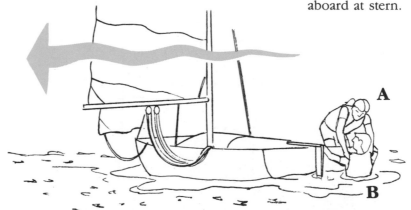

Traditional Recovery Method 5 ⎡5⎤

In the traditional method the boat is righted with no one in it. However, the boat can quickly capsize again, especially in stronger winds, because no one is in the boat to balance and control it. To minimize this problem, the boat should be positioned so that its bow is pointed into the no-go zone. This may require the crew to rotate the boat in the water, which can be slow and time consuming because the sails in the water act like a brake when rotating the boat. Once the boat is righted, the person at the bow helps to hold the boat into the wind and control it until the other person climbs in and takes control. Because of these problems, the scoop method is better and gets you up and sailing sooner.

1. **A** and **B** rotate boat so that hull is facing into wind.

2. **B** stands on centerboard until boat swings upright.

3. Meanwhile, **A** holds boat in position.

4. **B** climbs into boat at stern, gains control and places boat in safety position.

5. **A** swims around to stern and is helped aboard by **B**.

Walkover Recovery Method 5 5

Many sailboats can be righted as the capsize occurs, using the **walkover method**; however, this procedure takes lots of practice. When the boat is overpowered, it often drags its boom in the water, which slows the capsize. With practice, the sailor can climb over the high side of the boat onto the centerboard before the boat goes all the way over. This part of the maneuver is the most difficult, and if the helmsman hesitates for a few moments the boat will tend to turn upside down.

Once over the top, the sailor should place both feet on the centerboard and grip the edge of the boat or **gunwale**. As you lean backwards, the boat will start to come up and you scramble back into the cockpit.

All of this should be done quickly, in one fluid motion. But it takes practice. In good weather and warm water, it's often fun to capsize the boat on purpose and right it without getting wet, using this method.

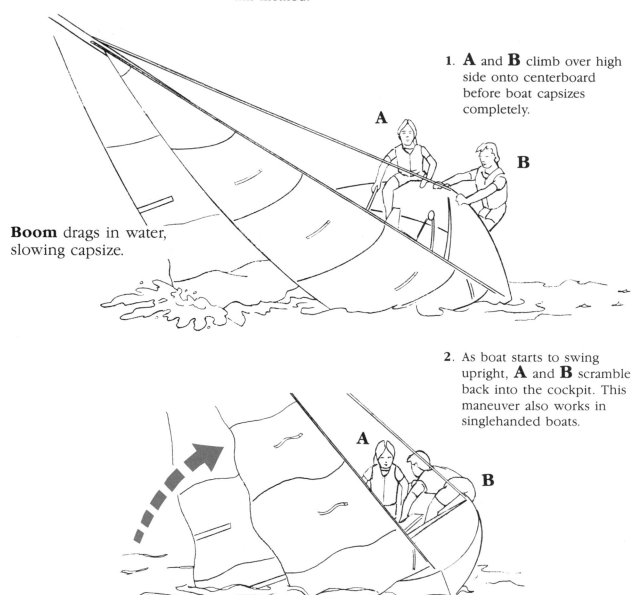

1. **A** and **B** climb over high side onto centerboard before boat capsizes completely.

Boom drags in water, slowing capsize.

2. As boat starts to swing upright, **A** and **B** scramble back into the cockpit. This maneuver also works in singlehanded boats.

Capsize Problems

When your boat capsizes, it is possible that it will continue to turn over until it is upside down, with the mast pointing straight down. This type of capsize is called "turning turtle," or **turtling**.

A turtled capsize can be prevented by placing flotation in the top of the sail or in the mast. Righting a turtled boat is usually difficult, since an upside-down hull is very stable and the submerged sails will resist your efforts. Another problem is that the centerboard or dagger-board may slip back into its housing, and is no longer in the "down" position.

Your first step is to rotate the turtled boat into a horizontal capsize position with the hull lying on its side and the sails to leeward. To get the extra leverage to do this, you may have to pull a sheet across the hull to the windward side, stand on the windward rail, and lean back. The boat should slowly rotate to the normal capsize position. Then you can follow the usual procedure for righting the boat.

If you can't right the turtled boat by yourself, you will need help from your instructor or fellow sailors. However, you should learn how to right a turtled boat without assistance. Each boat will respond slightly differently, depending on the size, shape and weight distribution.

Return boat to normal capsize position by leading sheet around to windward side and leaning back.

When boat turtles, centerboard will often slide back into trunk. Put centerboard in down position after boat has been turned onto its side.

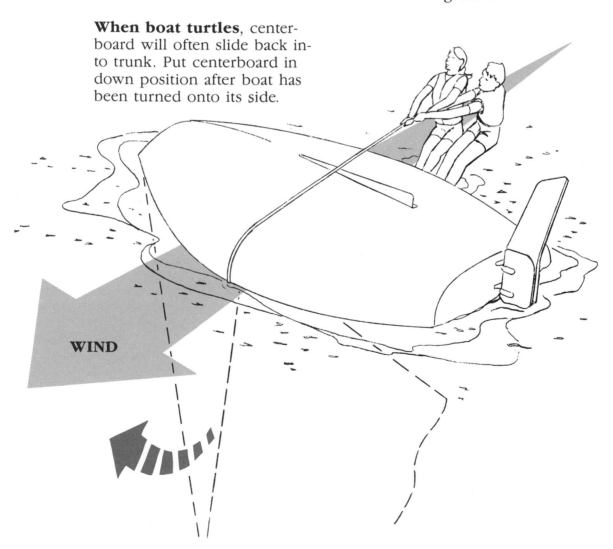

WIND

Some older types of centerboard boats that do not have modern self-rescuing characteristics are sometimes used to teach sailing. Trying to do a self-rescue recovery of these boats is difficult, if not impossible. Outside assistance, such as a powerboat, is often needed to help get the water out of the boat or tow it to shore. The problem with this kind of boat is that it floats very low in the water once you have turned it upright. And with so much water in the boat, it will be impossible to sail fast enough to drain the water out through the automatic bailers. At times when you try bailing the water with a bucket, the water outside the boat will often flow in as quickly as you bail the water out. Also because the boat is nearly awash, it tends to tip over unless you take extra care to balance it. A person, outside the boat, may have to steady the boat by holding the gunwale, while another person bails rapidly with a bucket. If you need outside assistance, remember to **stay with the boat** until help arrives.

Mast in the Mud

If a boat turtles in shallow water, the mast will hit the bottom and can stick in the mud or sand. You will need to act quickly to prevent the mast from becoming bent or detached from the boat. The helmsman and crew should get off the boat quickly, so their weight won't make the mast sink deeper into the mud. To free the mast, try swimming to the bow of the boat and turning the boat into the wind. Be careful about climbing on the boat, since your weight could end up driving the mast further into the mud. If the mast won't free up, you will need outside assistance.

Entering and Exiting the Boat

During a capsize, there are preferred ways of leaving and re-entering the boat. As the boat goes over, you should fall into the water feet first, not head first. Don't dive into the water. With practice, you will find it quite easy to drop into the water between the boom and the deck.

In a scoop recovery, one person is scooped into the boat and is then in a position to assist the second person. If both people are in the water when the boat rights, the stronger should enter the boat over the windward side of the transom, and put the boat in the safety position. Once in the safety position, the other person should be helped into the boat, also over the windward side of the transom. The person in the boat should face the person in the water, grab the person underneath the shoulders of the life jacket, and hoist. It may take a three-count to get the person into the boat. Once the person gets his or her chest over the transom, a leg should be swung into the boat. You should practice this procedure.

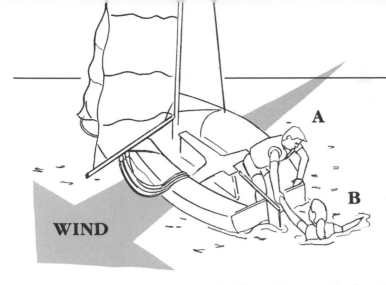

WIND

1. After **A** has put the boat into the safety position, **B** approaches windward side of stern.

2. **A** grabs crew **B** by the shoulder straps of **B's** life jacket and starts a "three-count."

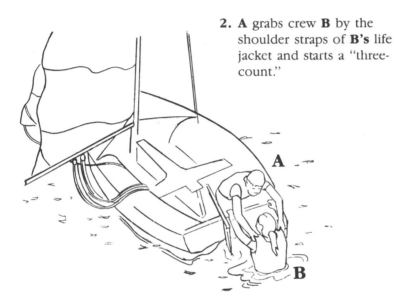

3. On the count of "three," **A** pulls **B** until his or her chest is over the transom. **B** swings a leg into the boat and climbs aboard.

Review Exercises

I. Matching

1. Turtling
2. Scoop recovery
3. Walkover recovery
4. Capsize safety rule

a. Never swim away from any capsized boat.
b. A capsized boat with the mast pointing toward the bottom.
c. Capsize recovery for experienced sailors.
d. Capsize recovery where a person is scooped into the boat during re-righting.

II. Fill in the Blanks

1. Capsize is a _____ part of dinghy sailing even for the most experienced sailor.
2. By turning the boat into the _____, you can free a mast stuck in the mud.
3. When both people are in the water, the _____ person should enter the re-righted boat first.
4. _____ in the mast or the top of the sail can greatly reduce the chance of turtling.

III. Exploring Sailing
(discussion or writing)

1. List the major causes of capsize.
2. Describe how a person helps another person enter the boat after a capsize.
3. List the rules for capsize safety.

IV. Mastery Activities

1. Perform a successful scoop recovery.
2. Complete a successful walkover on a singlehanded boat.
3. Re-enter the boat without assistance after a capsize.
4. Complete one traditional recovery.

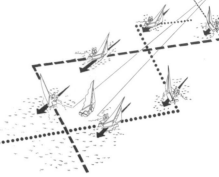

Review of Fundamental Sailing Skills

These are the fundamental sailing skills that you should be able to do at this point in your course. Review these skills when you go sailing and check off the ones you can successfully complete. Then have your instructor review your skills.

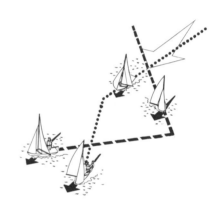

Sailing Upwind

Student self-evaluation ☐
Instructor evaluation ☐

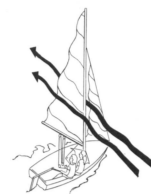

Determine Wind Direction and Speed

Student self-evaluation ☐
Instructor evaluation ☐

Slowing a Boat

Student self-evaluation ☐
Instructor evaluation ☐

Sailing Downwind

Student self-evaluation ☐
Instructor evaluation ☐

Rig a Boat

Student self-evaluation ☐
Instructor evaluation ☐

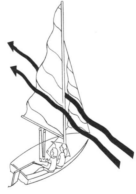

Safety Position

Student self-evaluation ☐
Instructor evaluation ☐

Capsize Recovery

Student self-evaluation ☐
Instructor evaluation ☐

Starting and Stopping

Student self-evaluation ☐
Instructor evaluation ☐

Turning a Boat

Student self-evaluation ☐
Instructor evaluation ☐

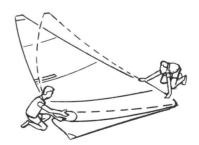

De-Rig a Boat

Student self-evaluation ☐
Instructor evaluation ☐

The following questions cover some situations that you will encounter when sailing a boat. If you can answer these and have learned the skills listed on the previous page, you can now sail and are ready to go on to Part 2 (Chapters 12-20). If you have any problems with these fundamental sailing skills, now is a good time to work with your instructor to get them right.

Review Question #1

For each of the sails, how would you adjust the sheet to improve the speed of the boat?

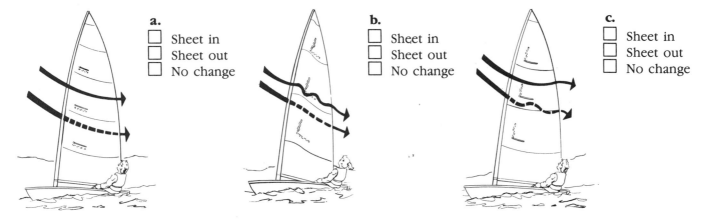

a.
☐ Sheet in
☐ Sheet out
☐ No change

b.
☐ Sheet in
☐ Sheet out
☐ No change

c.
☐ Sheet in
☐ Sheet out
☐ No change

Review Question #2

For each of the sails, how would you move the tiller to improve the speed of the boat?

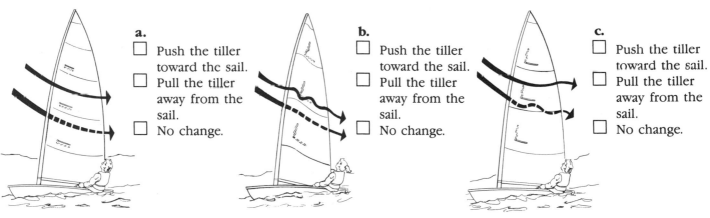

a.
☐ Push the tiller toward the sail.
☐ Pull the tiller away from the sail.
☐ No change.

b.
☐ Push the tiller toward the sail.
☐ Pull the tiller away from the sail.
☐ No change.

c.
☐ Push the tiller toward the sail.
☐ Pull the tiller away from the sail.
☐ No change.

Review Question #3

a. To turn the boat left, you would

☐ move the tiller to the left.
☐ move the tiller to the right.

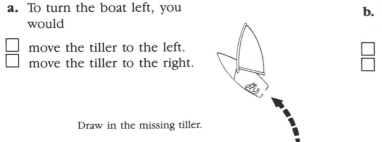

Draw in the missing tiller.

b. To turn the boat right, you would

☐ move the tiller to the left.
☐ move the tiller to the right.

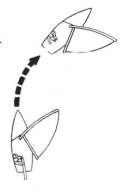

Draw in the missing tiller.

Review Question #4

a. To stop this boat, you would

☐ sheet in.
☐ sheet out.

b. To stop this boat, you would

☐ turn away from the wind.
☐ turn toward the wind.

Review Question #5

To turn this boat into the no-go zone, you would

☐ pull the tiller away from the sail.
☐ push the tiller toward the sail.

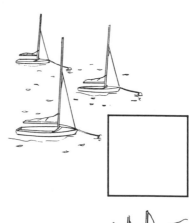

Review Question #6

Draw the correct sail position for the safety position and mark the wind direction arrow in the box.

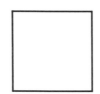

Review Question #7

For each example, draw the wind direction arrow in the box.

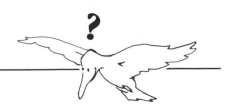

Review Question #8

For each point of sail, draw the correct sail position and draw the wind direction arrow (in the box).

 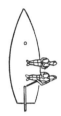 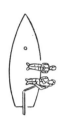  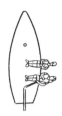

Upwind   **Reach**   **Downwind**

Review Question #9

Match the number with the correct letter/s.
What is the boat doing at:

1 _____   A. Heading off
2 _____   B. Heading up
3 _____   C. Jibing
4 _____   D. Safety Position
5 _____   E. Tacking
6 _____   F. Turning away from wind
              G. Turning into no-go zone
              H. Turning toward the wind

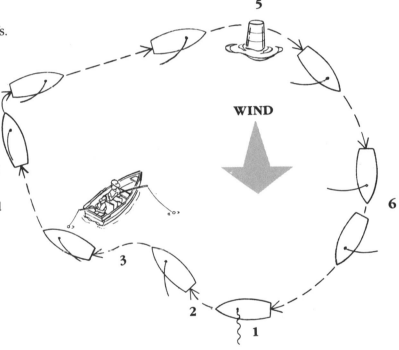

Review Question #10

Your boat has capsized. You and your crew plan to right the boat using the scoop capsize recovery method.

a. Do you have to rotate the boat so the bow is pointed into the wind? ☐ Yes ☐ No

b. What are the positions that you and your crew should take when re-righting a boat?

☐ Both people put their weight on the centerboard.

☐ One person holds the bow and the other gets on the centerboard.

☐ One person holds the rudder and the other gets on the centerboard.

☐ One person holds onto the inside of the cockpit and kicks, and the other puts his or her weight on the centerboard.

c. Should the main sheet be pulled in all the way and cleated? ☐ Yes ☐ No

Chapter 12

Man-Overboard Recovery

"It's good to be back!"

KEY CONCEPTS

- **Man-overboard recovery methods**
- **Prevention**

During a lifetime of sailing, you may have to rescue someone who falls off a boat — a "man-overboard" or MOB. In sailing dinghies, a person may be holding onto something that breaks, such as a hiking strap, tiller extension or jib sheet. Or the person may slip or get hit by the boom.

Falling overboard is serious. It is part of the sailor's code that, if you hear the words **"man-overboard,"** you should assist in any way possible in making the recovery.

Learning the man-overboard recovery procedure is easier than it first appears. The part that takes practice is putting the boat in position for the final approach to the person in the water, after you have made your tack.

The key is to never let the boat luff directly into the wind, but instead to approach the man-overboard on a close reach. You then sheet out the sails to stop the boat next to the MOB. You should make contact with the person from the windward side of the boat, then put the boat in the safety position while you help the person move to the transom and get in the boat. If the MOB can't reach the boat, hold out a paddle or boat hook for the person to grab. Use the same method as shown on page 87 (Chapter 11, Understanding Capsize) to bring the person into the boat. During man-overboard recovery, it is important that the people in the boat constantly keep watching and talking with the person in the water.

For practice, a five-gallon plastic jug filled with water is an excellent "dummy." The weight of the water will give you an idea of what it takes to pull a wet sailor into a boat.

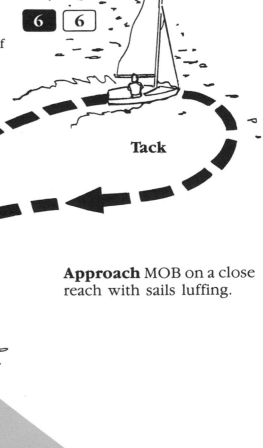

Approach MOB on a close reach with sails luffing.

Tack

WIND

Alternative Recovery Methods   6   6

Because of the wide variety of boats, you should be aware of other methods for recovering someone. These alternative methods will provide back-up systems for the basic method.

The first is jibing after the person has fallen in the water. It should only be used when the winds are light. In stronger winds, the jibe could result in a capsize if the boat is short-handed or the person in the boat is inexperienced.

A second alternative is to "quick stop" the boat by tacking immediately after the person has gone over, leaving the jib cleated. With the jib cleated, the boat turns and drifts toward the man overboard. As you drift downwind, the main is sheeted out fully and luffing. This method keeps the boat closer to the MOB, which allows for better communication and visibility. This method will work in light winds, but leaving the jib cleated in strong winds could cause a capsize.

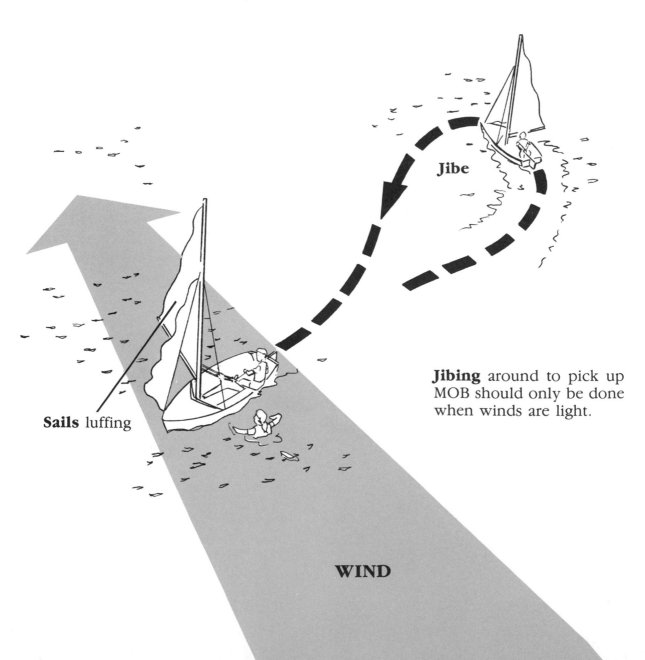

Jibe

Jibing around to pick up MOB should only be done when winds are light.

Sails luffing

WIND

Prevention

Most man-overboard occurrences are the result of misjudgement and could be prevented with a better understanding of the boat and its forces. It is important to make sure the boat and its equipment are in good condition. For instance, check the boat thoroughly before sailing, especially the hiking straps, tiller extension, and sheets. Wear nonskid shoes and hold onto the boat as you move about. Finally, listen to those marine forecasts and check the sky for threatening weather, to avoid the heavy winds that can cause accidents.

Many sailors are surprised when man-overboard accidents happen right at the dock or the mooring. Sometimes, reaching for a mooring line can cause you to lose your balance and fall into the water. Transferring sails from the boat to the shore can also cause a slip, as a boat may move or the sail bag block your view. Never be afraid to ask for help as you step from one boat to another or onto the shore. Think before you step!

Review Exercises

I. True or False

1. The greatest cause of man-overboard is human error.
2. Man-overboard can happen at a mooring.
3. Worn hiking straps are a common cause of man-overboard.

II. Multiple Choice

1. The final approach to pick up a man-overboard should be
   a. upwind.
   b. on a close reach.
   c. downwind.

2. The best place to approach a man-overboard is at
   a. the bow.
   b. the transom.
   c. the windward side of the boat.

3. The best way to keep in contact with a man-overboard is
   a. throwing a line.
   b. talking and constant watching.
   c. swimming after the man-overboard.

III. Exploring Sailing
(discussion or writing)

1. List three associated skills for man-overboard.
2. Draw the preferred man-overboard route.

IV. Mastery Activities

1. Successfully complete a man-overboard recovery on the first attempt.
2. Sucessfully complete one alternative man-overboard procedure on the first attempt.

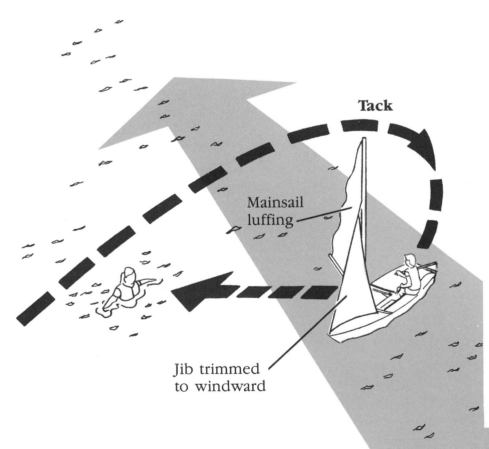

Tack

Mainsail luffing

Jib trimmed to windward

With "quick-stop" method, boat drifts down to man overboard.

WIND

95

Chapter 13

Leaving and Returning

"You always knew they'd make it, didn't you, Jim?"

KEY CONCEPTS

- **Glide zone**
- **Mooring**
- **Docking**

Leaving and returning to a dock or mooring are a challenging part of sailing. Timing and working with the wind are the main ingredients in executing these maneuvers successfully.

The Glide Zone

The **glide zone** is the distance a boat will coast when it is turned into the no-go zone, or if the sails are let out to flap, until the boat stops. Each boat has a different glide zone, depending on its weight and size. The strength of the wind also affects the glide zone. Higher wind velocities will slow down the boat more quickly, because the wind and waves act to push the boat backward. In lighter and medium winds, the boat will glide a longer distance. The length of the glide zone can vary from one boat length to several, depending on the boat and conditions. Getting a feel for how much your boat will coast or glide is very important when you dock, moor, and anchor.

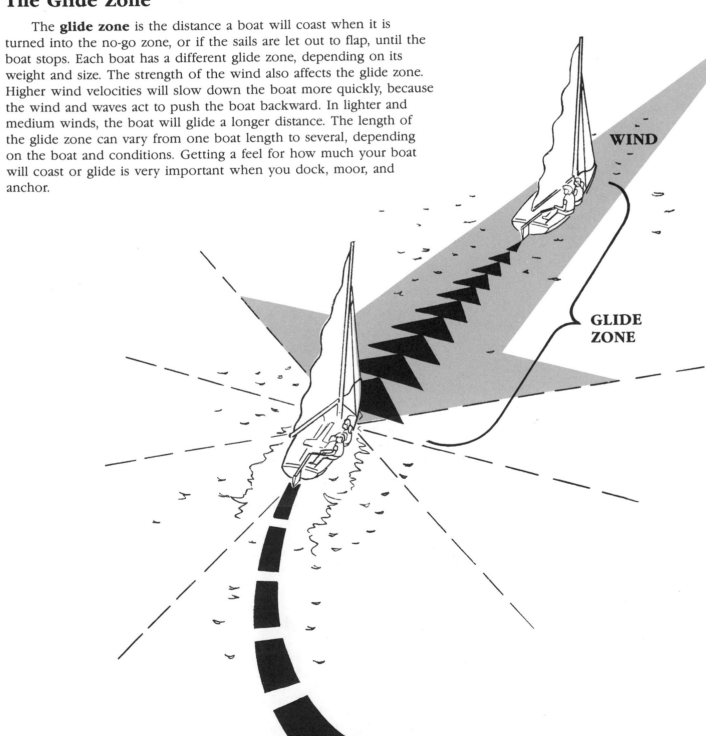

WIND

GLIDE
ZONE

Mooring 13 14

Returning to a mooring requires taking into account the boat's speed and point of sail as well as the glide zone. Wind direction doesn't seriously affect the procedures for leaving and returning to a mooring (unlike docking). When tied to a mooring, boats usually swing so they are pointing into the wind.

The best way to approach a mooring is to sail on a beam reach downwind of the mooring as though you were going to pass it. When directly downwind, turn the boat into the no-go zone and use the glide zone to coast to a stop at the mooring. It is generally best to under-shoot the mooring for safety reasons. Even experienced sailors sometimes make more then one pass before they glide up to the mooring correctly.

If you have trouble reaching a mooring this way, you can sail the boat upwind from the mooring, turn into the no-go zone, lower the sails, and drift or paddle downwind to the mooring.

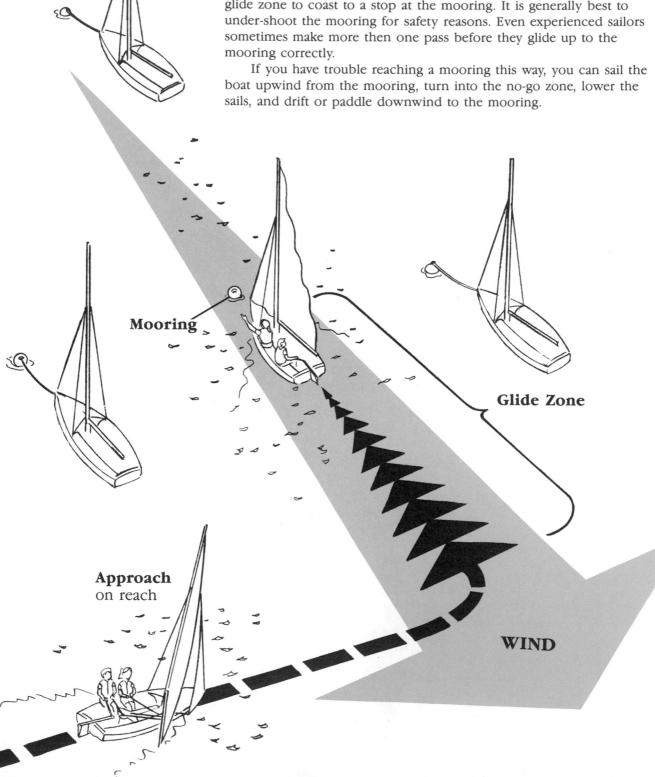

Mooring

Glide Zone

Approach
on reach

WIND

Docking — Leeward Side 13 14

Leaving the dock from the leeward side — with the wind blowing away from the dock — is easy, since the wind is pushing the boat away from the dock. First, lower the centerboard and raise the sails with the boat pointing into the wind (no-go zone). Then push or turn the bow of the boat away from the dock, ease the sails, and steer the boat away, on a reach.

When you first start to sail, the easiest way to return to a dock or mooring is to approach the dock slowly on a reach with the sails trimmed so they are partially luffing. As you get close to dock, sheet out the sails until they are completely flapping. The boat will slowly come to a stop. You have stopped the boat by putting it in the safety position. You can use this "safety position" method when returning to the leeward and windward sides of a dock. Its disadvantage is that it needs a lot of dock space. If there are other boats tied to the dock or returning to it, this method might not work.

As your sailing skills improve, you should start to use a better way of returning to a dock, by turning the boat into the no-go zone. You will approach the dock sailing on a reach or sailing upwind. As you sail up to the dock, turn the boat into the no-go zone and glide until the boat stops. After the boat is tied to the dock, lower the sails. It's always best to approach the dock slowly and to under-shoot the dock. If you do under-shoot — that is, miscalculate the boat's glide zone — paddling is a perfectly acceptable way to get back to the dock.

You should always plan an escape route in case you are unable to dock because of a wind shift, another boat, approaching too fast, or some other reason.

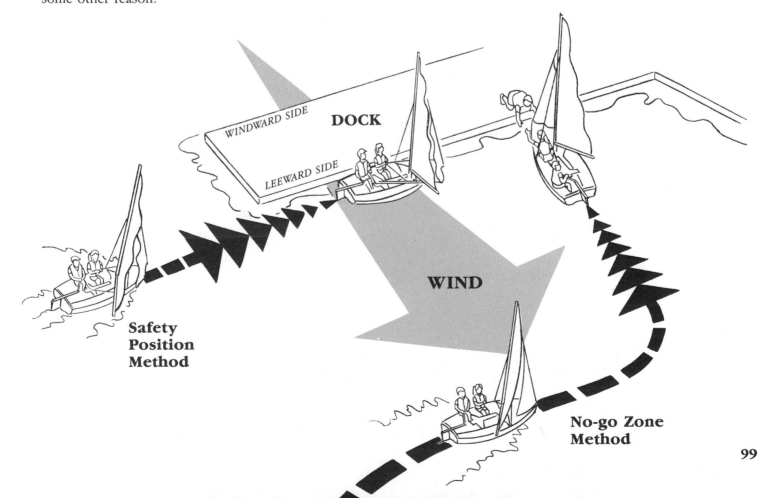

WINDWARD SIDE **DOCK**

LEEWARD SIDE

Safety Position Method

WIND

No-go Zone Method

Docking — Windward Side **13** **14**

Leaving the dock when the wind is blowing the boat onto the dock requires careful timing. As you raise your sails, the boat should be pointed into the wind. The difficult part is that you will have to begin sailing upwind as soon as you start to leave, but the wind will tend to push you back onto the dock.

As you start sailing away, trim your sails tightly for sailing upwind. Sail until it is time to tack, then repeat the zig-zag pattern of sailing upwind until you're well clear. As you push off from the dock, it's important to give the boat a firm shove to gather some forward speed so the centerboard will work and keep the boat from going sideways. When sailing a boat with a mainsail and jib, you must use both sails to get maximum initial speed.

Sailing a boat off the windward side of a dock isn't easy. If possible you should move the boat around to the leeward side and leave from there.

Returning to the windward side of the dock, you should sail to a point several boat lengths directly upwind of the dock. Turn into the wind, drop the sails, and turn back toward the dock, letting the wind blow you to the dock. If you have a jib, you can leave it up after the main is down and let it carry you closer to the dock. As you get near, lower the jib or let it flap, and drift down to the dock. Be sure you lower your sails well to windward.

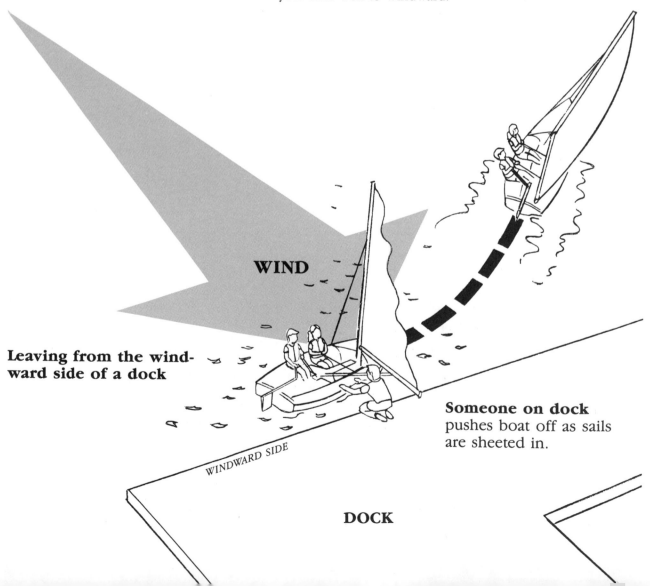

WIND

Leaving from the windward side of a dock

WINDWARD SIDE

Someone on dock pushes boat off as sails are sheeted in.

DOCK

When coming back to a dock, it is not unusual to find the wind direction is different than when you left, and you may have to make your landing on a different side. For this reason, you should always think ahead and have a firm plan of how to leave and return to the dock safely from all directions. Remember your "escape route," in case you don't make it the first time, and visualize your glide zone. Always remember that it's better to approach too slowly than too fast. Good judgement and planning are what it is all about.

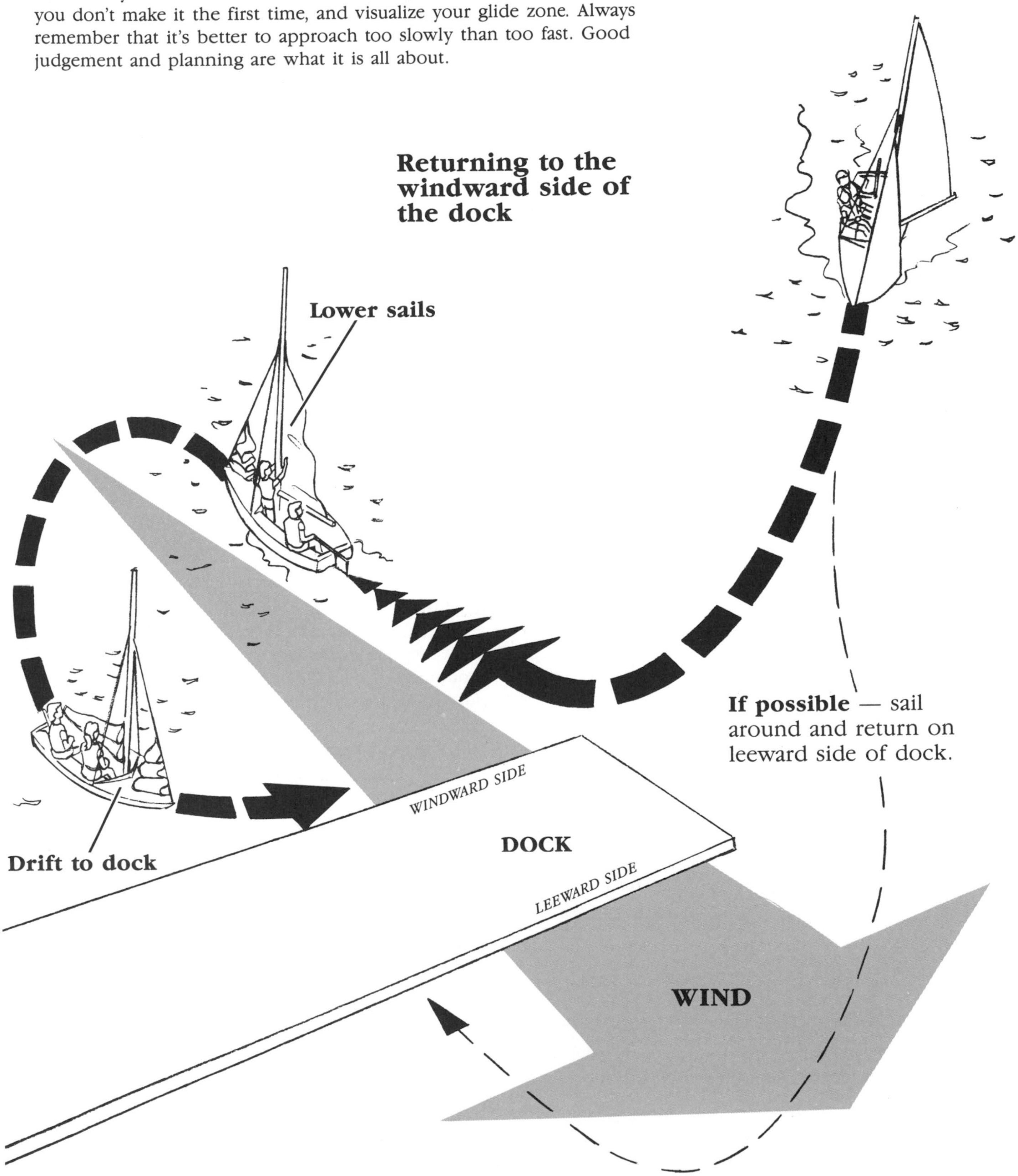

Returning to the windward side of the dock

Lower sails

If possible — sail around and return on leeward side of dock.

Drift to dock

WINDWARD SIDE

DOCK

LEEWARD SIDE

WIND

Typical Docking Problems and Solutions

Problem #1: Boat doesn't maneuver well — slides sideways when leaving.

Solution #1: Make sure the centerboard and rudder are all the way down.

Problem #2: I forgot to check the wind direction at the dock.

Solution #2: Have your crew check the wind direction too, and ask him or her to remind you. Or, prepare a check list of items to do before leaving the dock and include "wind direction" on it. Put the list between two pieces of transparent contact paper to prevent it from getting wet and attach it to the boat where you can see it.

Problem #3: The boat does not want to sail away from the dock on the windward side.

Solution #3: Ask someone on the dock to give the boat a big push while you trim the sails quickly. You may also have to paddle a little to get going.

Problem #4: I always under-shoot the dock.

Solution #4: Don't worry. Time and practice will correct this. This problem is usually caused by turning the boat into the no-go zone too soon — before you have reached the bottom of the glide zone. In the beginning, it can be tricky estimating where the glide zone starts. Practice by turning the boat into the no-go zone and see how far the boat will glide before it stops. Try using a reference mark to judge the length of the glide zone. Estimate the length of the glide zone in number of boat lengths. For instance, if you turn into the no-go zone seven boat lengths away from the dock and the boat stops two boat lengths short of the dock, the glide zone is only five boat lengths long, and you should turn into the no-go zone five boat lengths away from the dock.

If you find it difficult to estimate boat lengths, try using a land-mark. As you approach the dock, sail on a beam reach downwind of the dock at what you think will put you at the bottom of the glide zone. Sight down the centerline of the boat to a landmark. Turn into the no-go zone. If you under-shoot on your first approach, on your second approach position your boat on a landmark that is further upwind.

Problem #5: If I am sailing too fast and will over-shoot, how do I slow down quickly?

Solution #5: First of all, make sure that you have turned your boat into the no-go zone and the sails are completely flapping. If you are still going too fast, you have not estimated enough distance for the glide zone. You can quickly slow the boat by "backing" the sails (see next page).

You can quickly slow the boat by "braking" with your mainsail. This maneuver is called **"backing"** the mainsail. You do this by pushing the mainsail out until the wind fills the **back** side of the sail. When this happens, you are putting your boat into the push mode (remember the push-pull principle), but the wind will be trying to push the boat backwards. The boat will stop quickly, and if you continue to "back" the mainsail, the boat will start to sail backwards. For this maneuver to work successfully, you must push the mainsail out all the way — the boom should be in the same position as it is when sailing downwind. Practice this maneuver in open water — clear of obstacles. It could help you out of an awkward situation.

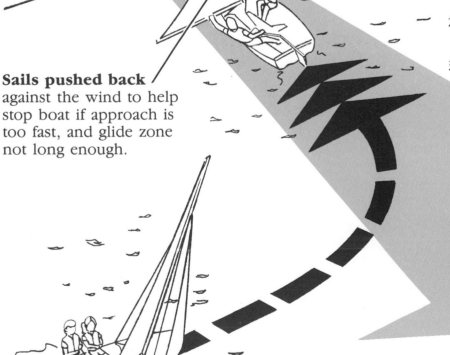

DOCK

Sails pushed back against the wind to help stop boat if approach is too fast, and glide zone not long enough.

WIND

I. Matching

1. A permanent anchor with a float
2. The distance a boat moves when in the no-go zone
3. The best way to return to a dock
4. The most difficult dock maneuver
5. The best way to leave a dock

a. Slowly
b. Mooring
c. Glide zone
d. Leaving a dock's leeward side
e. Leaving a dock's windward side

II. Exploring Sailing
(discussion or writing)

1. Why is the glide zone so critical for docking and mooring?
2. How can some of the techniques you learned to get out of irons be applied to leaving the leeward side of a dock?
3. How would you leave and return to a beach?

III. Mastery Activities

1. Leave and return to a mooring in different wind conditions.
2. Leave and return to the leeward side of a dock in different wind conditions.
3. Return to a windward side of a dock.

Chapter 14

Sailing Well: Improving Your Skills

"I think Jimmy and Carol are finally getting the bang of it."

KEY CONCEPTS

- **Sailing a course**
- **"In the groove"**
- **Feathering**
- **Weather helm**
- **Centerboard adjustment**
- **Sail trim**
- **Balance**
- **Water reading**
- **Safety habits**

As you spend more time sailing, you will soon begin to master the many different skills. You will want to work on keeping the boat sailing at the proper angle of heel, fore-and-aft balance, sail trim, and centerboard position. Sailing well involves developing a "feel" for whether your boat is moving at its best. Sailing well also involves a keen awareness of currents, wind, weather, and safety.

Sailing a Course

One of the things that all good sailors should master is the ability to **sail a course**. Sailing a course simply means sailing from point A to point B, no matter what the wind direction or conditions. There are usually many different ways of doing it.

The direction of the wind will determine the point of sail. If you must sail on a reach or run to get there, the direct route is usually the best. Just aim your boat at the destination and sail. Every time the wind direction shifts slightly, you should change the trim of the sails to keep them working at their best.

If your destination is to windward, into the no-go zone, you will have to sail upwind to get there, tacking once or several times.

When you are more experienced, you will automatically tack or jibe to a new course without having to think about it.

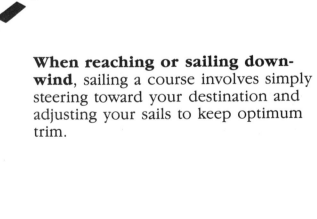

When reaching or sailing downwind, sailing a course involves simply steering toward your destination and adjusting your sails to keep optimum trim.

WIND

Steering Well Upwind

As you steer upwind you should know how to respond to changes in wind speed and direction. You react to these changes by steering the boat toward and away from the wind and keeping the telltales flowing back smoothly.

When sailing upwind or close-hauled, you will find that there is a **"groove,"** or lane, to steer in, similar to a traffic lane on a road. The sides of the groove (the white lines on the road) can be seen by the telltales on the sail. If you start to cross the **windward** side of the groove, the telltales on the windward side of the sails will flutter or stall while the telltales on the leeward side will continue flowing back smoothly. If you start to cross the **leeward** side of the groove, the telltales on the leeward side of the sail will droop and stall, while the windward telltales will continue flowing smoothly.

When you are "**in the groove**," both windward and leeward telltales will flow smoothly. The groove is not very wide — just turn the bow of the boat a few degrees, and you will find the sides.

Because the wind is constantly changing, you will have to make small adjustments with the tiller to stay "in the groove." You should get in the habit of steering the boat by touching the windward side of the groove periodically and steering back into the groove. This technique will keep you sailing as close to the wind as possible and still maintain boat speed. Experienced helmsmen may do this as often as every five or ten seconds. This sounds difficult at first, but after a little practice you will find yourself doing it without even thinking about it.

SAILING UPWIND "In the Groove"

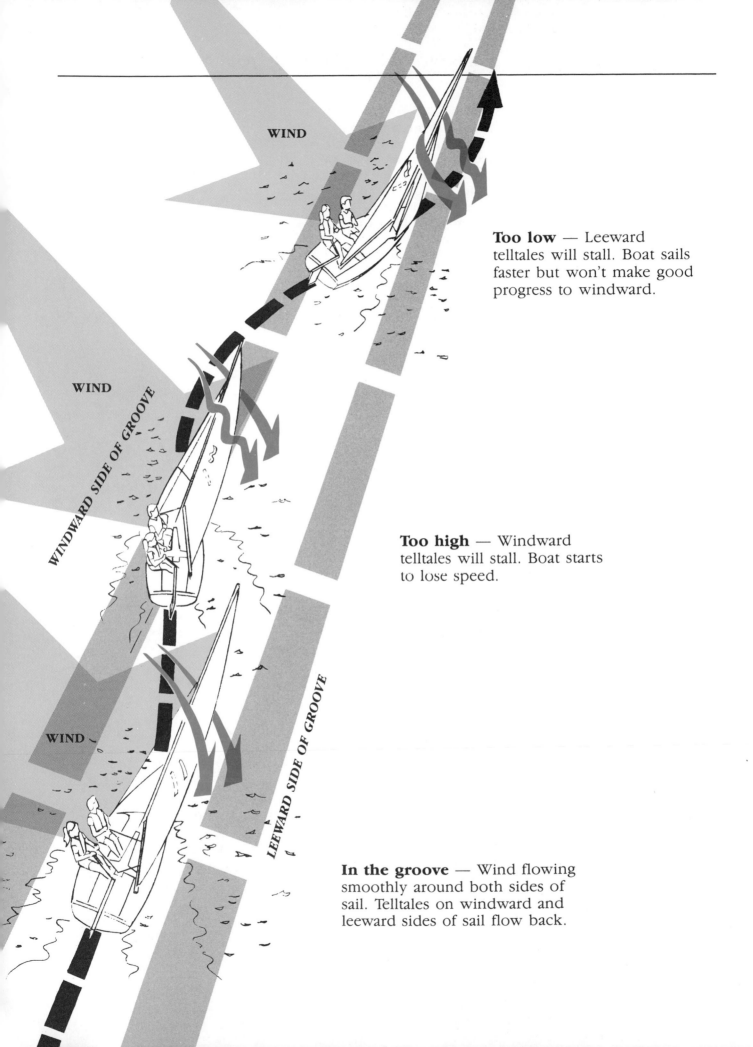

WIND

Too low — Leeward telltales will stall. Boat sails faster but won't make good progress to windward.

WIND

WINDWARD SIDE OF GROOVE

Too high — Windward telltales will stall. Boat starts to lose speed.

LEEWARD SIDE OF GROOVE

WIND

In the groove — Wind flowing smoothly around both sides of sail. Telltales on windward and leeward sides of sail flow back.

Feathering

As the wind increases or a puff hits, the boat can be over-powered. When a sailboat is overpowered, it will heel too much, go slower, and may even capsize. To overcome this situation, you can move your weight, change sail trim, or change the shape of the sails. Experienced helmsmen also use a steering technique called **feathering**, to help de-power the boat and keep it stable. Feathering is steering to keep the boat at the windward side of the groove, or just past the groove, for long periods of time.

The sails, particularly the jib, will luff slightly, with the windward telltale fluttering and stalling, and at times even the leeward telltale may also flutter. It takes skill and practice to feather the boat and keep it moving forward and level. When feathering, you should steer with the tiller extension, and both you and your crew should be **hiking**, or leaning out beyond the windward side of the boat.

WIND

Feathering, or pinching, helps de-power the sails and keeps the boat from heeling too much.

As the wind increases, the helmsman will usually have to apply added pressure to the tiller by pulling on it to counteract the boat's tendency to turn toward the wind. This is called **weather helm**. When sailing upwind, a small amount of weather helm often helps to steer the boat close to the wind. But too much weather helm on any point of sail is a sign that the boat is heeling too much or being over-powered. The crew and helmsman can reduce weather helm by hiking out, sheeting out the mainsail a little, or feathering the boat. The amount of pressure on the helm will vary, depending on the wind and wave conditions.

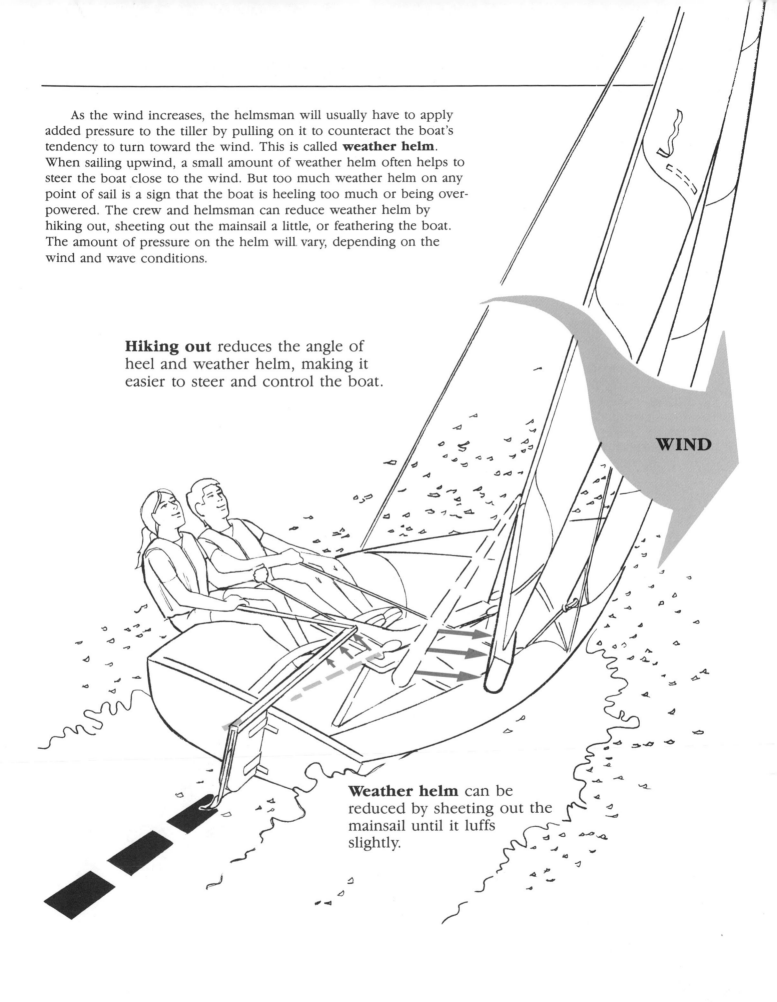

Hiking out reduces the angle of heel and weather helm, making it easier to steer and control the boat.

WIND

Weather helm can be reduced by sheeting out the mainsail until it luffs slightly.

Centerboard Position

The centerboard or daggerboard has different positions for different points of sail. Upwind and on a close reach, the centerboard is kept all the way down. On a beam reach, the board is raised to about halfway up, and as you turn to a broad reach or downwind, it is raised to three-quarters up.

When maneuvering upwind, you need all the centerboard to keep the boat from being pushed sideways, but when sailing downwind, the sideways force is reduced and you do not need as much centerboard. Raising the centerboard for downwind sailing also reduces the amount of surface friction, which in turn produces small increases in boat speed.

Sail Trim 12 13

As you become sensitive to sail trim, you will find that sheeting in or out a few inches can make a world of difference in how the boat performs. You will also learn to coordinate the sheeting of the mainsail and jib. The helmsman and crew should sheet in (**trim**) and sheet out (**ease**) the sails in unison. You should learn to sheet in the sails when turning toward the wind and to sheet out when turning away from the wind.

Outhaul

Boom Vang

Traveller

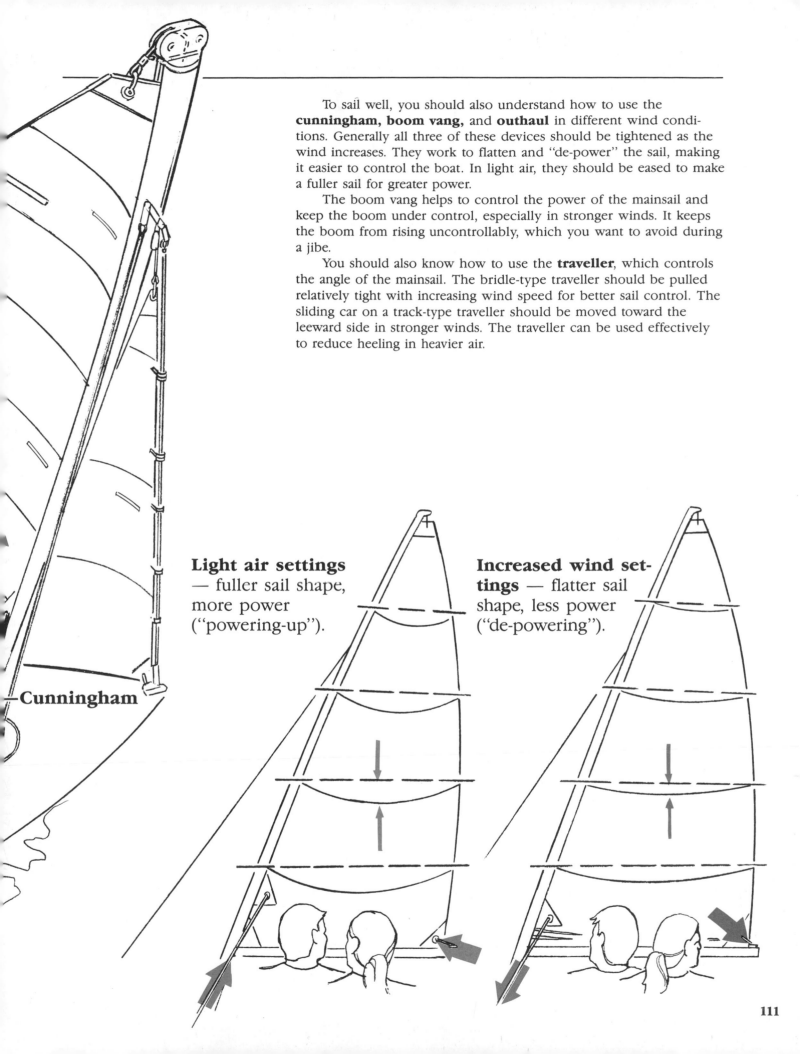

To sail well, you should also understand how to use the **cunningham, boom vang,** and **outhaul** in different wind conditions. Generally all three of these devices should be tightened as the wind increases. They work to flatten and "de-power" the sail, making it easier to control the boat. In light air, they should be eased to make a fuller sail for greater power.

The boom vang helps to control the power of the mainsail and keep the boom under control, especially in stronger winds. It keeps the boom from rising uncontrollably, which you want to avoid during a jibe.

You should also know how to use the **traveller**, which controls the angle of the mainsail. The bridle-type traveller should be pulled relatively tight with increasing wind speed for better sail control. The sliding car on a track-type traveller should be moved toward the leeward side in stronger winds. The traveller can be used effectively to reduce heeling in heavier air.

—Cunningham

Light air settings — fuller sail shape, more power ("powering-up").

Increased wind settings — flatter sail shape, less power ("de-powering").

Boat Balance 12 13

The angle of heel, or side-to-side balance, is different for different points of sail. Upwind, heeling the boat slightly to leeward is good. Downwind, particularly in light and medium air, you may want the boat to be heeled slightly to windward to help neutralize the rudder (the weather helm) and allow the sails to become most efficient.

When the boat moves from one point of sail to another, you should move your weight smoothly to achieve the correct balance or angle of heel. As the wind increases, you will have to move your weight further to the high (windward) side to maintain the proper angle of heel.

Chapter 7, "Your First Sail," discussed how to turn the boat by moving your weight from side to side. As you become more accomplished, you should use this concept when turning the boat. When you move the tiller to turn the boat toward the wind, move your weight a little to leeward at the same time, by leaning into the boat. This will help to turn the boat using less tiller movement. When you turn the boat away from the wind, move your weight a little to windward by leaning out.

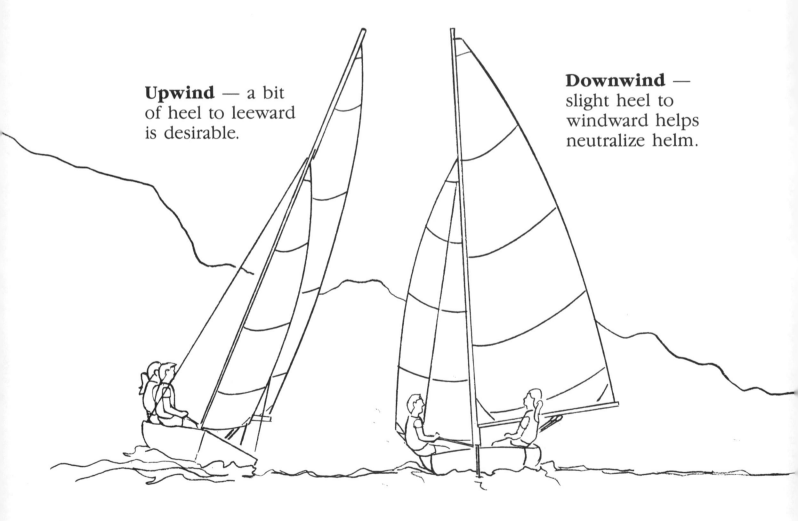

Upwind — a bit of heel to leeward is desirable.

Downwind — slight heel to windward helps neutralize helm.

Water Reading

By looking at the ripples that the wind makes on the water, you should be able to detect puffs and lulls and determine the wind direction within a few degrees. Puffs on the water will look darker, while lulls will look lighter and smoother. Being able to read puffs and lulls will let you react before they affect you. When you approach a puff, you should begin easing the mainsail seconds before the puff hits, to help keep the boat balanced. This will allow you to control the boat rather than letting the boat control you.

Safety For Master Sailors

As you begin to sail well, you will automatically check all the different items on the boat that deal with safety. Every time you go sailing, you should:

1. Check the weather forecast.
2. Bring the right kind of clothes and remember that it is better to overdress than underdress.
3. Always wear your life jacket, making sure it fits comfortably and is suitable for your body and weight.
4. Be sure you understand how to right a capsized boat.
5. Make sure that you have safety equipment such as a paddle, bailer, spare line, and anchor.
6. Make sure that the boat is drained properly and that the air tanks are empty and dry and the plugs are secured.
7. If the water is cold, sail with a wet suit or dry suit, under a PFD.
8. Establish an upper wind speed for your skill. When the wind blows harder than that, consider it unsafe to go sailing.
9. Always make sure that somebody on shore or at the sailing club knows what time you expect to be back from your sail.
10. Always bring something to drink and some sunblock for those hot sunny days.

As a master sailor, you will understand all the safety principles around the waterfront and on the water. **Sailing safe is being a master sailor!**

Review Exercises

I. Matching

1. Water reading
2. Feathering
3. Traveller
4. Sailing well
5. Boom vang

a. Tighten in heavy air
b. Observing the wind on the water
c. Purposely steering so that the forward edge of the sail luffs
d. Sailing safely
e. Controls the angle of the mainsail

II. True or False

1. Sailing well and mastering various techniques takes time and practice.
2. The centerboard or dagger-board should be three-quarters up when sailing downwind.
3. In most states, safety equipment is not necessary for sailing.
4. The boom vang is normally used to sheet in the sails.

III. Exploring Sailing
(discussion or writing)

1. Why do you feather upwind in heavier winds?
2. Why is it important to establish a maximum wind speed for your sailing ability?

IV. Mastery Activities

1. Sail a rectangular course successfully, using all points of sail, tacking, jibing, and using proper sail trim.
2. See the appendix for additional water drills.

Chapter 15

Right-of-Way

"Bill's still not too sure of his right-of-way rules."

KEY CONCEPTS

- **Avoiding collisions**
- **Right-of-way**
- **Five basic rules**

A natural question at this point in your sailing is, what is the best way to avoid danger and collisions? Keeping track of wind changes and paying attention to your surroundings will always help prevent problems.

The sailing community has "rules of the road" for sailboats and powerboats to avoid collisions. Racing sailors use a more complex set of rules, and additional rules are used for navigation and cruising. However, as you learn to sail you can safely operate your boat by understanding just a few basic **right-of-way** rules.

Avoiding Collisions 12 13

Unless the danger is straight ahead, one of the best ways to avoid a collision is simply to turn the tiller toward the danger. When you turn the tiller **toward** the danger, you will be turning the boat **away** from the danger. This is a good rule to remember whenever you forget what to do. You can also avoid a collision by slowing or stopping the boat. Whichever method you use, it's a good idea to do it early so the other boat knows what your intentions are. With only a little practice you will soon be able to avoid other boats safely without having to think about it.

Remember to look around before you tack or jibe and check for other boats to leeward. Don't forget to check those blind spots behind the sails frequently.

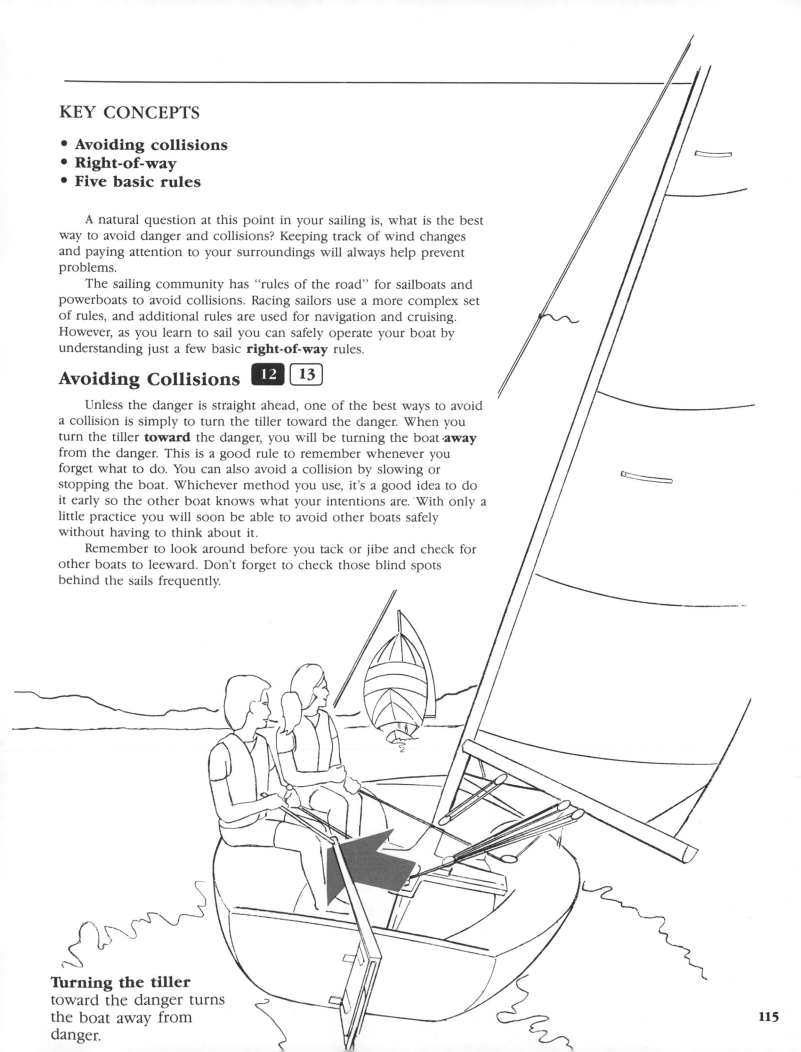

Turning the tiller toward the danger turns the boat away from danger.

Right-of-Way [12] [13]

Whenever two boats meet, one boat will have right-of-way. The boat with right-of-way is supposed to maintain heading and speed so the other boat can safely avoid it. However, the right-of-way boat should always be prepared to avoid a collision, in case something prevents the other boat from staying clear. When sailboats are involved you need to know what **tack** they are sailing on, as well as the basic right-of-way rules, to determine which boat has right-of-way.

Basic Rule 1 [12] [13]

[10] [11]

When two sailboats on *different* tacks meet, **the boat on starboard tack has right-of-way over the boat on port tack.** When a sailboat is on *starboard tack*, the starboard (right or green) side of the boat is the side nearest to the wind, which will be the "high" side when sailing upwind. When a sailboat is on *port tack*, the port (left or red) side is the side nearest to the wind, or the "high" side when sailing upwind. When you are on starboard tack, you have right-of-way over any sailboat on port tack. You should politely say to a sailor on port tack, *"Starboard"* or *"I have right-of-way."* This will remind them that you are the right-of-way boat and they must stay clear of you.

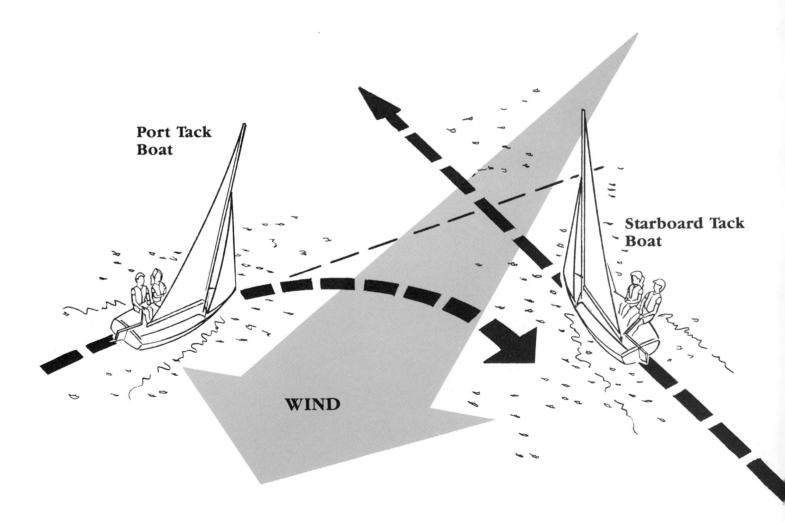

Port Tack Boat

Starboard Tack Boat

WIND

Basic Rule 2 `12` `13`

When two sailboats on the *same* tack meet, **the leeward boat has right-of-way over the windward boat.** For example, when two boats are both sailing on starboard tack but on different points of sail so they are on a collision course, the boat closer to the wind source must keep clear. The boat further from the wind has right-of-way. To remind the windward boat, the leeward boat should say, *"I'm leeward boat — please stay clear."*

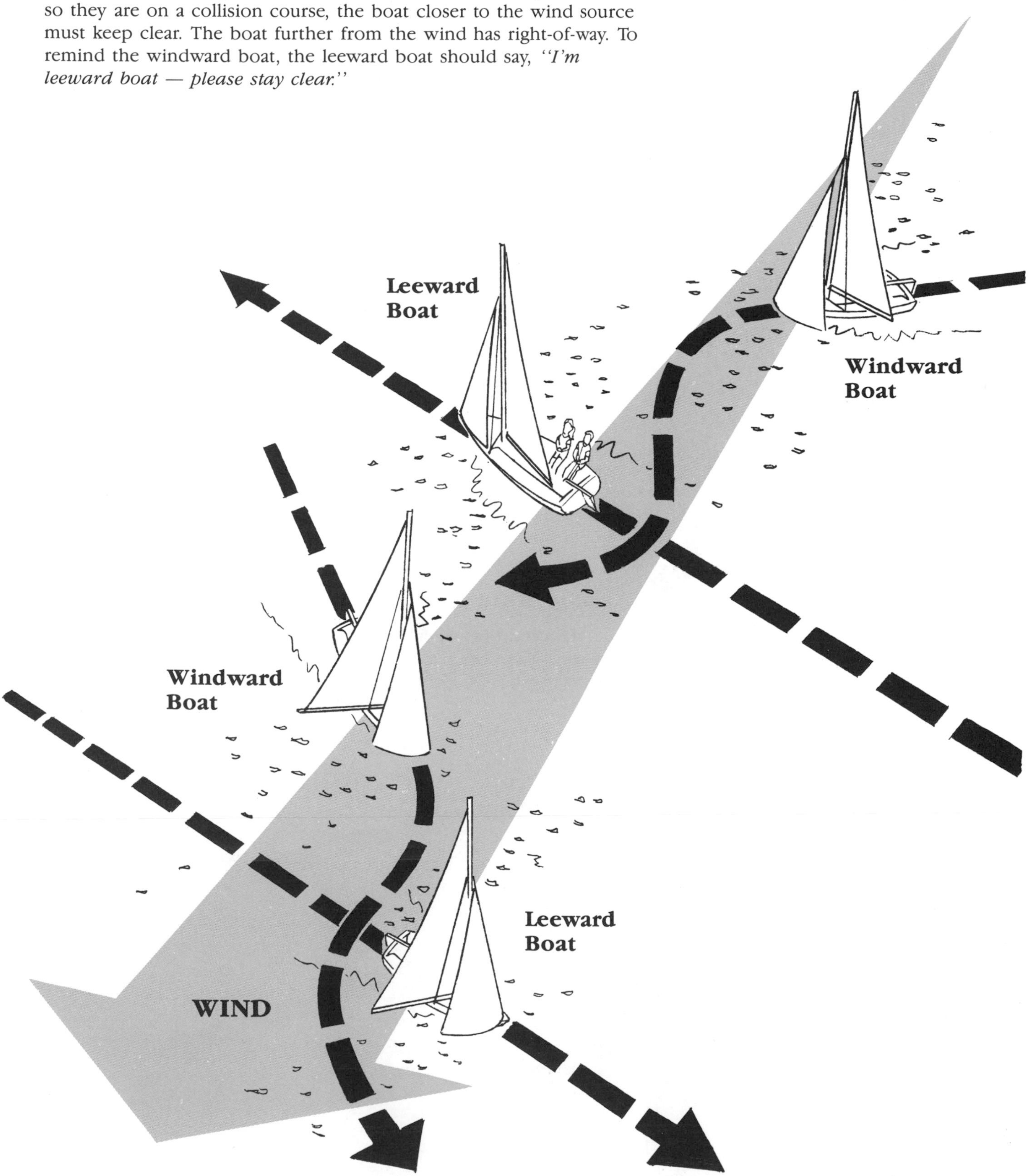

Leeward Boat

Windward Boat

Windward Boat

Leeward Boat

WIND

Basic Rule 3 **12** **13**

A boat sailing on a tack has right-of-way over any boat that is tacking or jibing. If you are going to tack or jibe you must be certain that the water around you is clear of other boats during your maneuver.

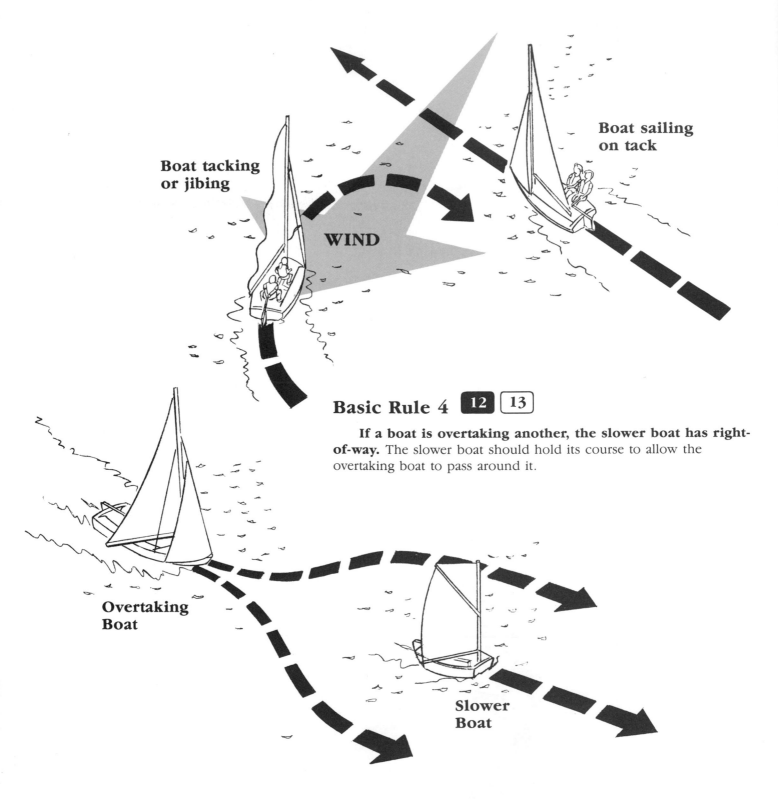

Boat tacking or jibing

WIND

Boat sailing on tack

Basic Rule 4 **12** **13**

If a boat is overtaking another, the slower boat has right-of-way. The slower boat should hold its course to allow the overtaking boat to pass around it.

Overtaking Boat

Slower Boat

Basic Rule 5 12 13

Sailboats generally have right-of-way over powerboats.
Powerboats that are the same size as your sailboat will have more maneuverability and can avoid you. However, bigger power vessels can not stop and start quickly, and it may take them a long time to turn. They may also have to operate in deeper water or channels. So when you are in danger of colliding with a bigger powerboat it will usually be best for you to simply stay clear. This is also true for ships, tugs, and barges.

Remember, when on the water keep up your environmental awareness and make sure that you are staying clear of other boats and obstacles. Always be on the lookout for other boats — especially to leeward of you, which are difficult to see behind the sails. And finally, if in doubt, stay clear.

Review Exercises

I. True or False

1. A boat on port tack has right-of-way over a boat on starboard tack.
2. A boat tacking must keep clear of a boat on a tack.
3. A leeward boat on the same tack has right-of-way over windward boats.
4. When danger approaches, turn the tiller toward the danger.
5. The crew does not need to look out for other boats.

II. Exploring Sailing
(discussion or writing)

1. How do you best avoid a collision?
2. What is the crew role in avoiding collisions?
3. Describe the five basic right-of-way rules.

III. Mastery Activities

1. Sail successfully in a crowded area, avoiding dangers and collisions.

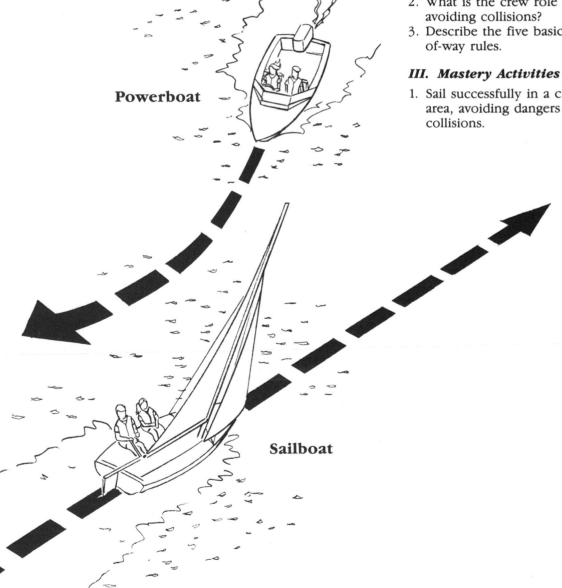

Powerboat

Sailboat

Chapter 16

More Seamanship Maneuvers

"I disagree. Holding this tiller is VERY tiring!"

KEY CONCEPTS

- **Paddling and sculling**
- **Anchoring**
- **Towing**
- **Coming alongside**

Seamanship skills allow you to use a boat in tight places, or when there is too little or too much wind. Rowing, paddling, sculling, anchoring, and towing are some of the seamanship maneuvers, and knowing how to come alongside an anchored boat is a useful skill.

Rowing, Paddling and Sculling

When maneuvering around a dock or other restricted areas, you may have to use muscle power. There are three ways a sailboat can be propelled without using the sails: paddling, rowing or sculling. Paddling and rowing can be done for a long time, while sculling is used for short distances.

Paddling works best with at least two people in the boat. One person steers with the rudder while the other paddles from the side of the boat. If the centerboard is all the way down, the boat will track nicely through the water, and the paddler needs only to paddle from one side.

If two people paddle, from the port and starboard sides of the boat, they are, in effect, rowing, and this is obviously faster than paddling. A few dinghies are even equipped with oarlocks for oars.

For short distances, it is often easiest to scull the boat. In sculling, you move the tiller and rudder repeatedly back and forth, using it as a paddle at the stern.

If you have lowered the sails, they should be **furled** or **stowed**, so they won't blow in the water or get in your way.

When paddling, keep the boat level. Person paddling should use long, even strokes.

Sculling is best for short distances.

Anchoring

There may be times when you have to anchor your boat. If the wind has died and the current is carrying you in the wrong direction, you will want to anchor until the current changes or the wind increases. Or perhaps you want to stop sailing to have a picnic, or because a squall is approaching. The safety equipment on your boat should always include an anchor and plenty of anchor line.

The ratio of the anchor line length to the water depth is called **scope**. Normally for every foot of water depth, you should have seven feet of line, or a scope of 7 to 1 to ensure that the anchor will hold properly against wind, current and waves. For ten feet of water, you would use 70 feet of anchor line. It is important to know the water depth where you sail so you can have enough anchor line onboard.

A good way to set an anchor is the following:

1. Get the anchor ready, making sure the line is not tangled on anything and is coiled. Tie the end of the line to the boat so it can't fall overboard by accident.
2. Turn the boat into the wind (the no-go zone).
3. Once the boat stops, lower the anchor and let the boat drift away from the anchor by easing the anchor line. When lowering the anchor, don't throw it; drop it slowly into the water.
4. When you have let out ample scope, give the line a sharp tug to make the sure the anchor has caught in the bottom.
5. Adjust the line and secure it to the bow of the boat.
6. Lower the sails and furl them. (If it is calm and you are waiting for the wind to return, you can leave the sails up.)

Bruce Anchor

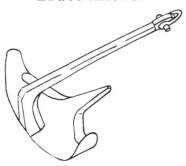

Lightweight, or Danforth anchor

Plow or CQR Anchor

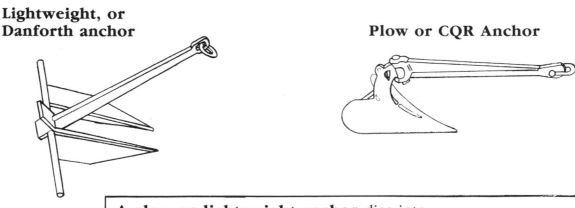

A plow or lightweight anchor digs into the sea bottom when pulled at a low angle to the bottom, and releases when pulled up vertically.

Raising the Anchor

When pulling up the anchor, take in the line until the boat is over the anchor. Then pull it directly upward, breaking the anchor free from the bottom. Coil the line as you bring the anchor up, and, if it is dirty, swish it back and forth in the water to clean it. When the anchor is back in the boat, stow it so it won't get in your way or get lost if you capsize.

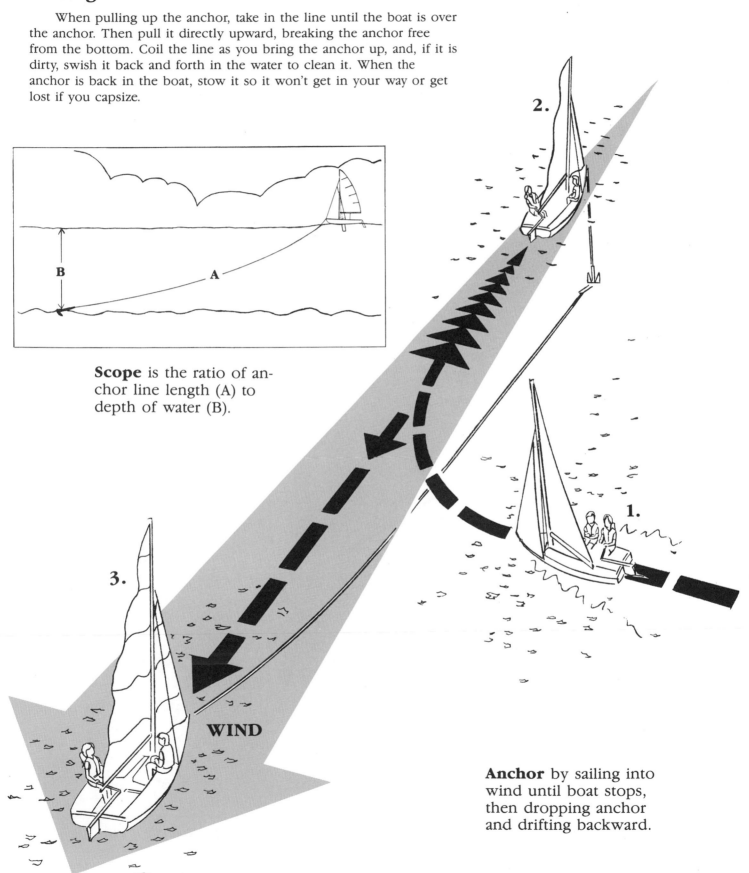

Scope is the ratio of anchor line length (A) to depth of water (B).

WIND

Anchor by sailing into wind until boat stops, then dropping anchor and drifting backward.

Towing

If you get becalmed or your boat has a breakdown, you may want to get a tow back to the dock. You should understand the best way to pick up or throw a towline. For "picking up," the towlines will be either thrown to you or slowly dragged through the water past your boat.

Many sailing dinghies have a line, called a **painter**, permanently attached to the bow of the boat. If you use the painter for towing, the tow boat will usually pass alongside and take it. If the tow boat plans to tow a group of sailboats, it may drag a long line behind it for you to tie your painter to. A polypropylene line is often used because it floats on top of the water and is easy to see. To pick up this towline, position the boat parallel to the towline and pick it up as the line comes by. Take your painter and tie it to the towline using a rolling hitch (see Chapter 18 for knots).

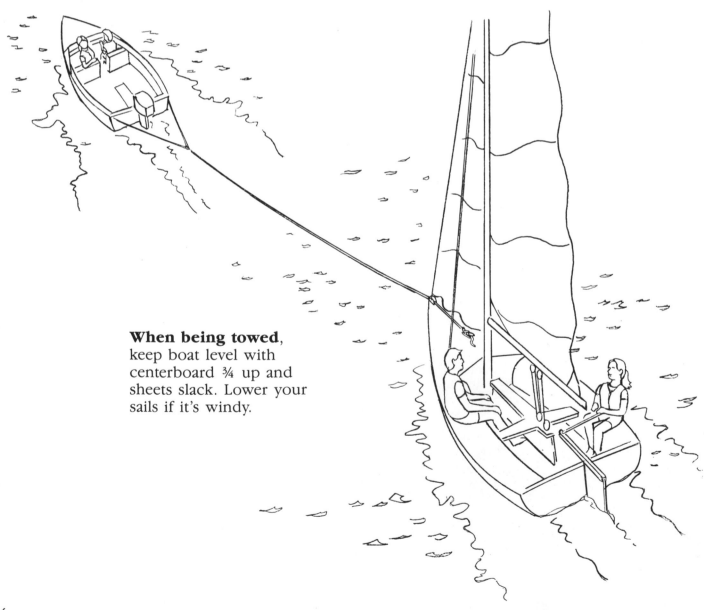

When being towed, keep boat level with centerboard ¾ up and sheets slack. Lower your sails if it's windy.

Coming Alongside Another Boat

Sometimes, it may be necessary to come alongside another boat to change crew or pick up equipment. This can be done without lowering your sails. If a boat is anchored in little or no current, its bow will be pointing into the wind. There are two ways to come alongside such a boat using the **glide zone**. Approach the anchored boat on a reach, turn the boat into the wind (the no-go zone), and slowly coast or glide to a stop alongside the boat. Be careful that your fingers don't get between the boats.

In the second method, you approach the anchored boat, sailing slowly on a beam reach ("safety position") with the sails luffing. Stop at the back end (transom) of the boat by sheeting out the sails until they flap.

It is important when you come alongside that you do it slowly. It is better to under-shoot your location and have to try it again, rather than come in too quickly and crash. Never come alongside a boat by sailing a broad reach or downwind. You cannot stop the boat from these positions. Remember, *the best way to stop a boat is either to luff the sails or to turn the boat into the wind.* You can practice coming alongside by sailing up to a mooring or buoy instead of an anchored boat.

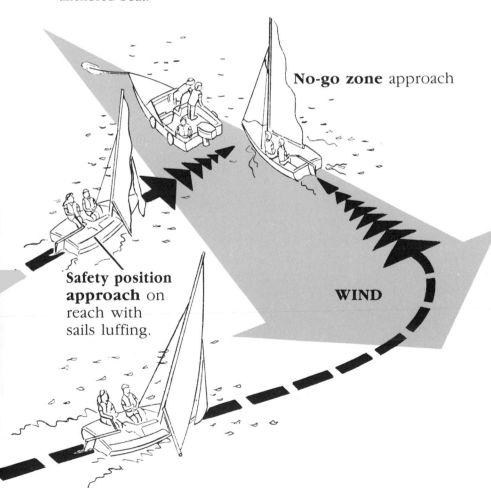

No-go zone approach

Safety position approach on reach with sails luffing.

WIND

Review Exercises

I. *Multiple Choice*

1. The best way to stop a boat is
   a. turn into the no-go zone.
   b. paddle to stop the boat.
   c. scull backwards.
2. The recommended scope for anchor line is
   a. 7 to 1.
   b. 1 to 70.
   c. 1 to 1.
3. When coming alongside another boat, it is best to
   a. over-shoot the glide zone.
   b. under-shoot the glide zone.
   c. drag your feet.
4. Sails that are properly secured are
   a. furled/stowed.
   b. stored.
   c. moored.
5. What is usually used in coming alongside a boat or dock?
   a. Downwind approach
   b. Tow boat
   c. No-go zone

II. *Matching*

1. Paddling
2. Glide zone
3. Scope
4. Painter

a. The distance it takes to slow the boat by water and skin friction
b. Propelling the boat with one paddle
c. Ratio of length of anchor line to depth of water
d. Permanently attached to the boat

III. *Exploring Sailing*
(discussion or writing)

1. List the steps for anchoring.
2. Describe how you come alongside a boat.

IV. *Mastery Activities*

1. Return to a dock and mooring safely on five different days with different wind directions.
2. Set and raise an anchor properly.
3. Pick up a tow from a powerboat in medium air on the first attempt.

Chapter 17

Weather and Currents

"Why us?"

KEY CONCEPTS

- **Barometer**
- **Anemometer**
- **High pressure**
- **Low pressure**
- **Jet stream**

- **Wind movement**
- **Offshore wind**
- **Onshore wind**
- **Tides and currents**

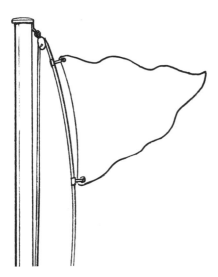

As a sailor you will become aware that the weather is constantly changing. No two days are ever exactly the same. Even if the wind is blowing from the same direction as yesterday, the waves and wind speed may have changed.

A safe sailor must learn to identify the signs of good sailing weather and the warning signs of poor weather.

Information **11** 12

You can obtain weather information from a number of sources. Besides the U.S. Coast Guard and the National Weather Service, other good sources of information include newspapers, with their detailed weather maps, and radio, television, and cable stations with their weather reports and forecasts. The best sources for wind speed and poor weather are marine forecasts and aviation reports — often available by telephone. The U.S. Coast Guard also uses an advisory system that displays different flags to indicate wind speed and warnings.

Small craft warning signal. A single red triangular flag is flown on shore to indicate winds up to 38 m.p.h. and conditions unsafe for small boats.

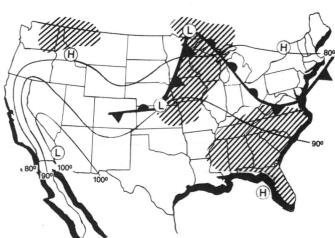

Weather maps for two consecutive days show high pressure (**H**) and low pressure (**L**) systems moving across the country from west to east. Weather maps are found in many newspapers.

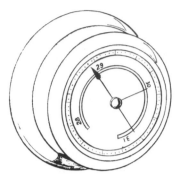

A barometer
measures atmospheric
pressure.

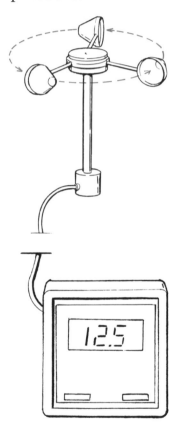

An anemometer
measures wind speed.

Measuring Weather

One of the best devices for predicting weather is the **barometer**, which indicates pressure changes of different air masses. Generally, when the barometer is rising, it indicates fair weather and good sailing conditions. When the barometer starts to fall, poor weather may be on its way. Television weather reports usually give the barometric pressure and indicate whether it is rising or falling.

The **anemometer** is used to detect wind speed. Many sailing sites have an anemometer that shows how strong the wind is blowing at the waterfront. It is a good idea to check the anemometer, especially when the wind is blowing from the shore and is difficult to judge.

Moving Weather

In North America, weather systems normally move from west to east. These systems are referred to as low and high pressure systems and may originate in Canada, the Pacific Ocean, the Gulf of Mexico, or even the Atlantic Ocean.

The **high pressure system**, identified by a large "H" on the weather map, usually denotes drier, cooler air, and you can generally expect good sailing conditions. The cool air tends to sink to the earth's surface and cause an increase in pressure.

The **low pressure system** is identified by an "L" on the weather map and usually denotes relatively warm air that has a tendency to rise, creating lower pressure and a fall in the barometer. Low pressure systems may have strong winds, rain, and storms.

High-pressure systems are generally associated with cumulus or high, stratus-type clouds, while the low-pressure system is generally associated with low-level clouds. As a sailor, it is important to understand that clouds can move faster than the surface wind, which means the approaching weather system may first appear at higher altitudes. Fast moving clouds may bring higher wind speeds, and slow moving clouds lower winds.

The **jet stream** is a snake-like river of air that circles the earth about 35,000 feet above the earth's surface. It controls the location and movement of the high and low pressure systems.

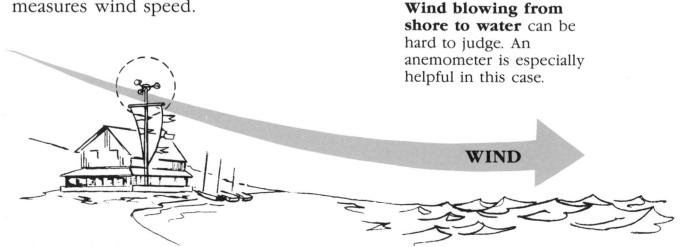

**Wind blowing from
shore to water** can be
hard to judge. An
anemometer is especially
helpful in this case.

WIND

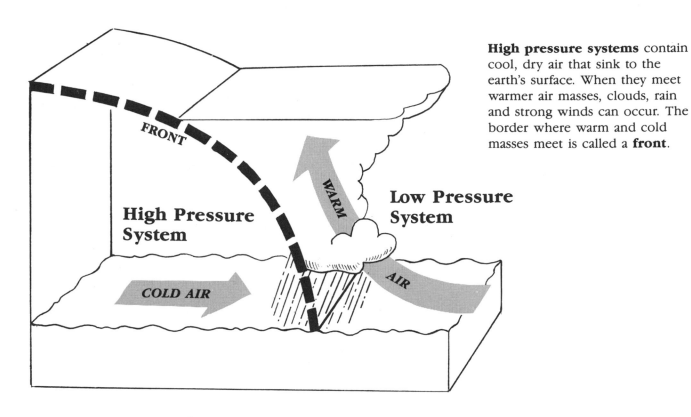

High pressure systems contain cool, dry air that sink to the earth's surface. When they meet warmer air masses, clouds, rain and strong winds can occur. The border where warm and cold masses meet is called a **front**.

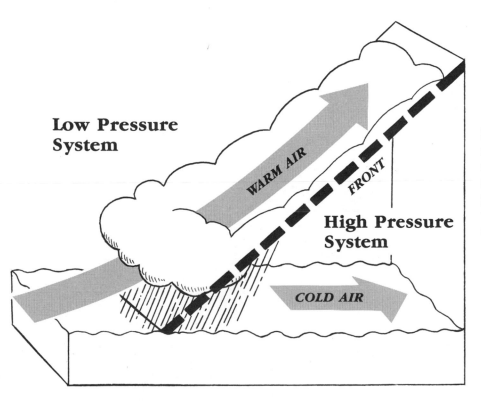

Low pressure systems contain relatively warm air that has a tendency to rise. They generally move more slowly than high pressure systems and the rain and wind created when they meet cold air masses is less violent.

Wind Movement

Wind is created by pressure differences with air generally flowing from high pressure to low pressure areas. It will be altered greatly by the local topography. As you sail on a body of water surrounded by large buildings or hills, the wind speed and direction will change often. This is a unique aspect of sailing which is fun to discover and learn. Your environmental awareness will help you react to these changes.

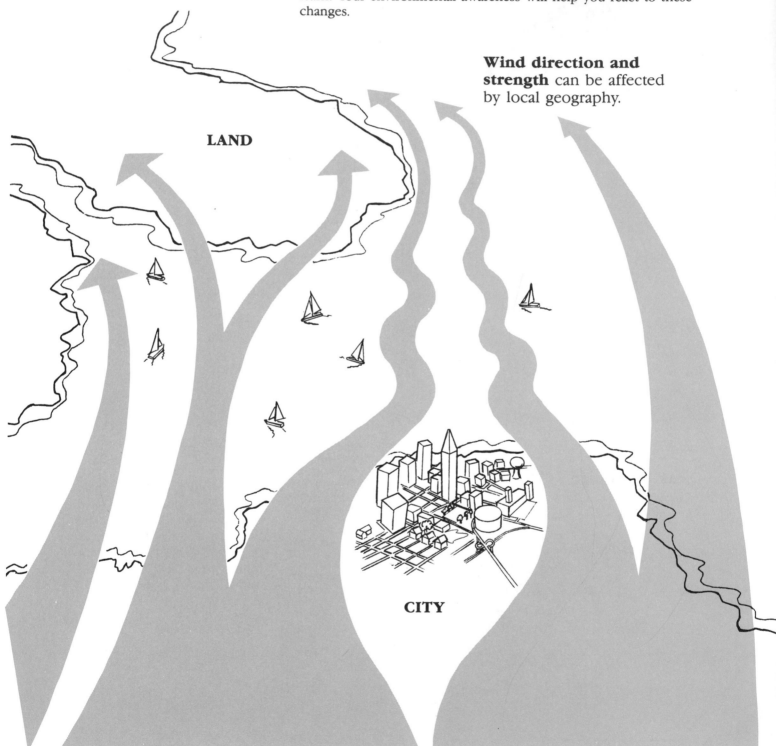

Wind direction and strength can be affected by local geography.

LAND

CITY

Water and Wind 11 12

Some winds are referred to as either offshore or onshore. **Offshore winds** blow from the land onto a large body of water and are generally affected by the local topography. Often when you stand on shore, the wind seems relatively calm. But as you move out onto the water you may find the wind to be much stronger.

OFFSHORE WIND

ONSHORE WIND

131

Onshore winds or sea breezes occur when the air blows from the water onto the shore. Sometimes onshore winds can be quite strong. They are a result of the air being pulled in by the hotter air rising over the land, particularly during the afternoon. The light to medium sea breeze is ideal for a novice sailor to sail in.

Warm air rising

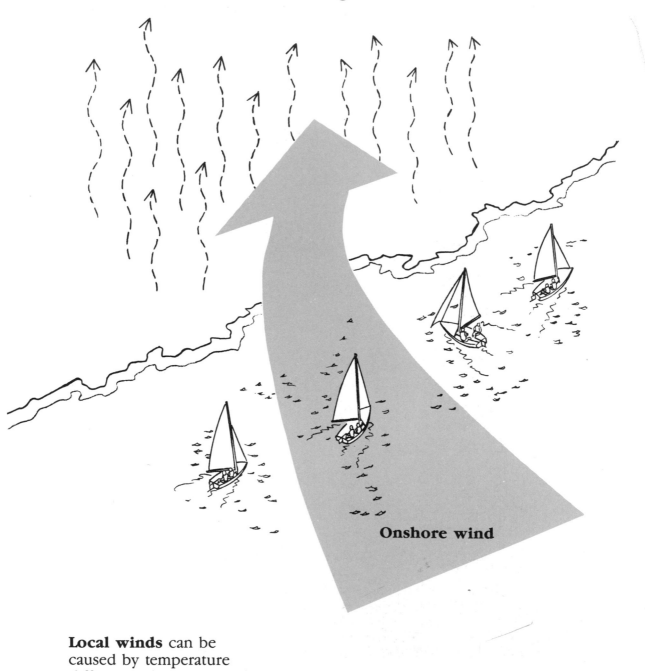

Onshore wind

Local winds can be caused by temperature differences between land and water.

Signs in the Sky

A good sailor will be constantly monitoring conditions, especially for any signs of threatening weather. Collecting weather information from television or radio is the first step to determining whether it's safe to sail. You should also know some of the early detection signs for bad weather. They are:

1. Increase in cloud cover and darkening skies.
2. Sudden decrease or increase in wind velocity.
3. Change in wind direction.
4. Lightning nearby or in the distance.
5. Thunder in the distance.
6. Gusty wind conditions.

A change in the weather can happen quickly. If there is any sign of bad weather you should head for shore. Be prepared and always watch for signs in the sky.

At the first sign of threatening weather, it is smart to head for shore.

Tides and Currents   **11**   12

Understanding tides and currents is important. Your safety and many sailing maneuvers such as docking, mooring and sailing a course are affected by them. A **current** is the **horizontal** flow of water caused by tide or differences in elevation. **Tides** are the **vertical** movement of water caused by the gravitational pull of the earth and moon. Tides occur daily at regular intervals. The difference between the height of water at low and high tide varies in different locations. Most fresh water lakes do not have tides.

Currents and tides are both affected by water depth. Deep water will increase the speed of the current or tide, and shallow water will reduce it. You can determine the direction and speed of current by using certain indicators. A floating object, such as a stick being carried along by the moving water, or water swirling past a fixed buoy or dock are good current indicators. The vertical movement of tides can be seen as the water rises or falls on a piling or beach.

Current flowing around stationary objects will create a swirl or "wake" that can help you determine its direction.

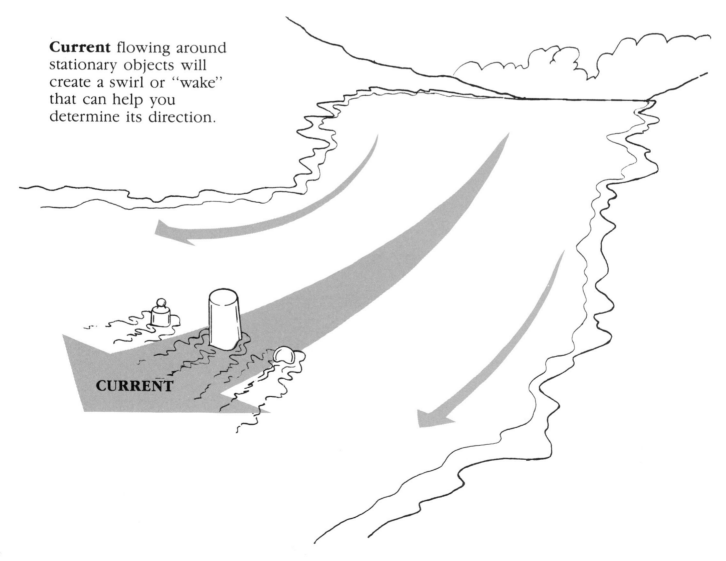

CURRENT

Currents and Tides: Questions and Answers:

Q: *How do you detect the direction current is flowing?*

A: By looking at a stationary object such as a buoy, mooring, or lobster pot. Current flowing past these objects will often create a swirl or "wake" that moves in the direction of the current.

Q: *If I can't sail against the current, what should I do?*

A: The best solution is to anchor the boat and wait for the wind to increase or wait for a tow.

Q: *How do I find out if the tide is rising or falling?*

A: Marine forecasts usually have tide reports. Tide tables can also be bought at local marine stores. Water swirling past a stationary object will show the direction of the water movement.

Q: *The boat keeps going sideways or downstream from the point where I'm steering.*

A: Steering upstream and overcorrecting will help you sail to your destination.

Q: *Do I have to compensate for current when returning to a dock or mooring?*

A: Yes. The first step is to determine what direction and speed the current is moving. Then you correct for the current during your approach. This may take some practice.

Steering up-current can correct for the effect of current on your boat's heading.

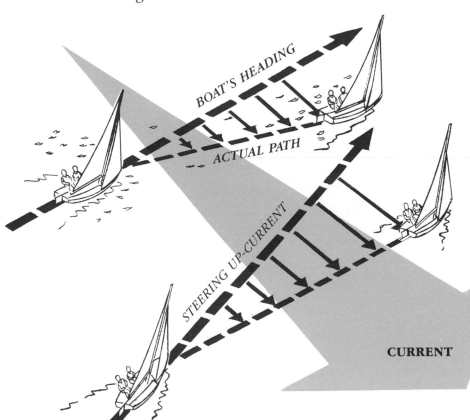

BOAT'S HEADING

ACTUAL PATH

STEERING UP-CURRENT

CURRENT

Review Exercises

I. Multiple Choice

1. How does a sailor identify a current or tide when sailing?
   a. Read a marine chart.
   b. Watch water move around a fixed object or marker.
   c. Watch the wind direction and speed.

2. How does barometric pressure allow you to predict weather?
   a. It indicates type of pressure system.
   b. It acts as a gauge to predict wind speed.
   c. Falling barometric pressure always means bright sunshine.

3. A seabreeze is
   a. an offshore wind.
   b. a wind created by the earth's rotation.
   c. an onshore wind from a large body of water.

II. Matching

1. High pressure
2. Offshore
3. Barometer
4. Current
5. Tide
6. Anemometer

a. Wind-speed measuring device
b. Water motion generated by elevation
c. Wind from the land to the water
d. Fair weather with a high barometer
e. Vertical movement of water created by gravitational forces at regular intervals
f. Device used to measure atmospheric pressure

III. Exploring Sailing
(discussion or writing)

1. Why does weather move from the west to the east in North America?
2. What is the general prevailing wind for your area?
3. What are the signs of poor weather?

Chapter 18

Knowing Those Knots and Lines

"My advice is to start over."

KEY CONCEPTS 3 [3]

- **Types of line**
- **Bowline**
- **Figure 8**
- **Cleat hitch**
- **Clove hitch**
- **Two half hitches**
- **Rolling hitch**
- **Coiling and stowing a line**

Learning about different lines and knots is a rewarding experience, and can be especially fun to do at home when the weather is bad. Tying knots correctly is **very** important and could even save a sailor's life some day.

All ropes used on a sailboat are called **lines**. Different lines are made of different materials for different uses. Nylon, for example, stretches and is used for anchors and dock lines. Dacron has very low stretch and is used for halyards and sheets. Polypropylene floats and is used for mooring pick-up lines. The lines that you will probably use most — the jib sheets and the main sheet — will be dacron.

There are a large number of knots used in sailing, but you only need to know a few to get started. In the illustrations you can see six knots that are used every day around sailboats.

1. The Figure-8 knot is a stopper knot used at the end of a tail or line.
2. The clove hitch and two half hitches are used for tying to a post, ring or eye.
3. A rolling hitch is for tying to a towline.
4. The bowline is for tying a non-slip loop for a variety of purposes. The bowline is the most widely used knot around the sailing community.
5. The cleat hitch is used for fastening a line to a cleat.

Figure 8

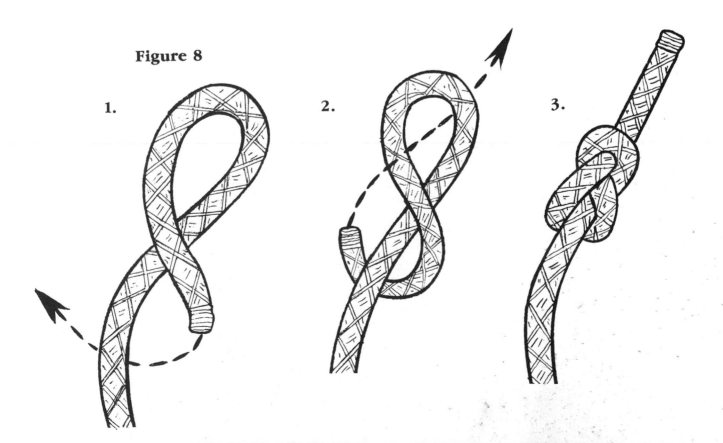

1.   2.   3.

Clove Hitch

1.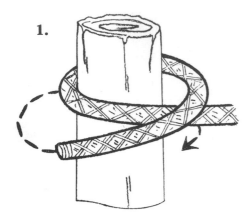

2.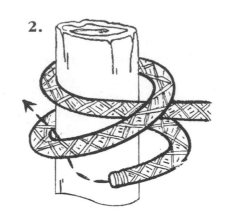

3.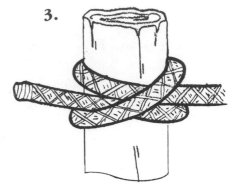

Two Half Hitches

1.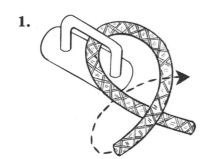

2.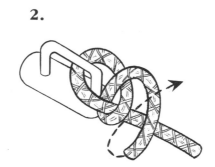

3.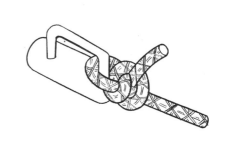

Rolling Hitch

1.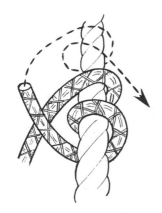

2.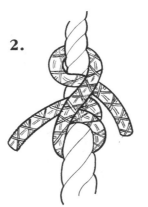

3.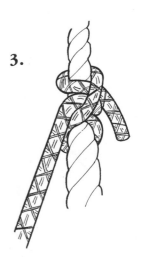

Bowline　　　　　　　**Cleat Hitch**

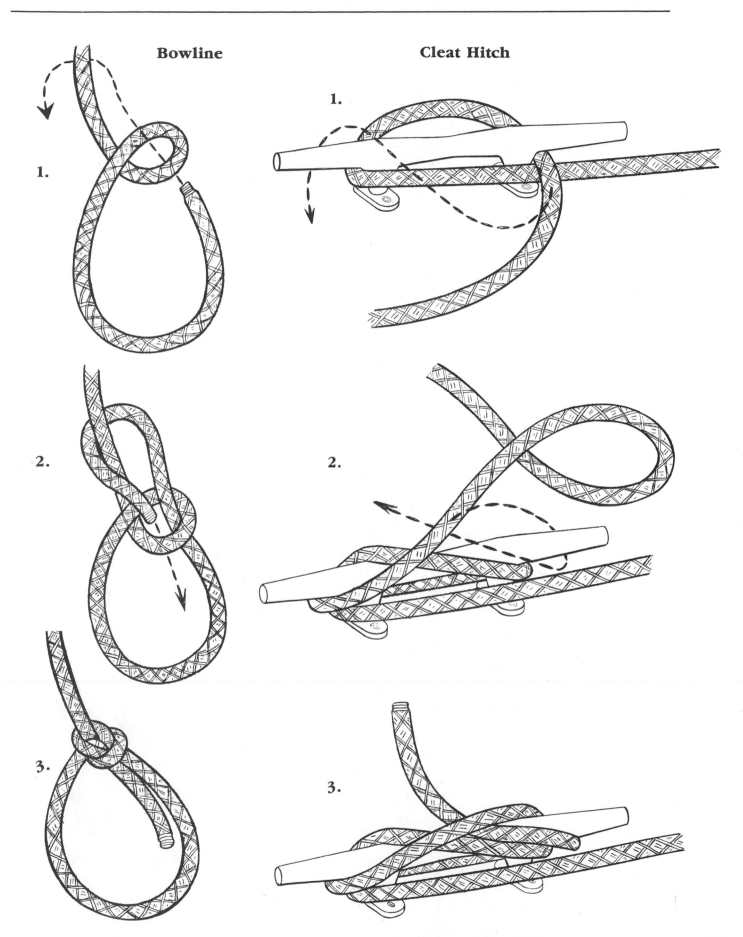

1.

2.

3.

1.

2.

3.

Throwing a line is sometimes necessary when docking or towing a boat. The line should always be coiled first, before throwing. Though it looks easy, you should practice throwing a line to make sure you can do it quickly and accurately. **Stowing a line** is best done by coiling the line and then tying it so that it is ready to use.

Knowing how to use the knots and how to coil and throw a line will make life around the sailboat much easier.

Coiling a line is easy with practice. With some lines it helps to twist the line as you coil to compensate for natural twist in the line.

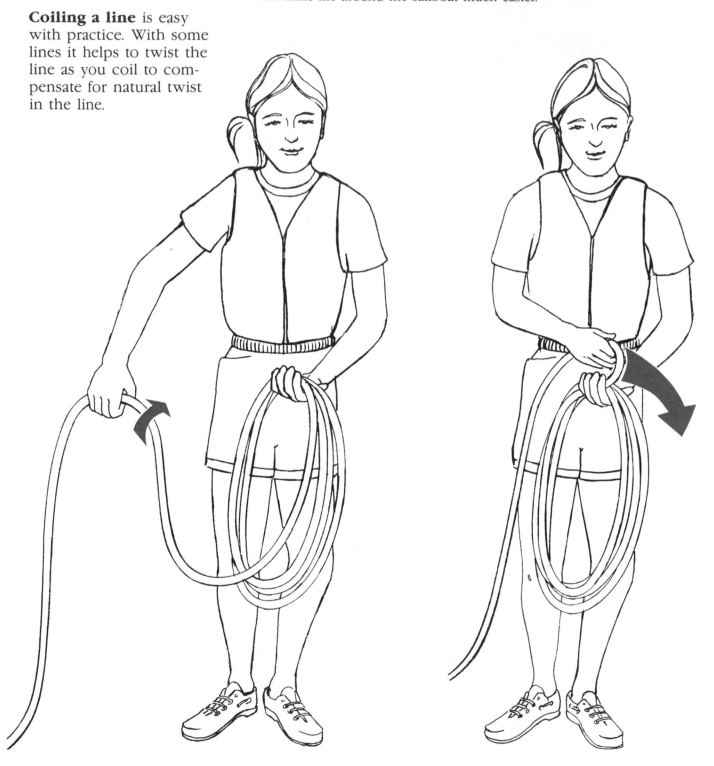

Throw a line by separating the coil into two groups...

...then throw the smallest coil and let the rest of the line uncoil from the other hand.

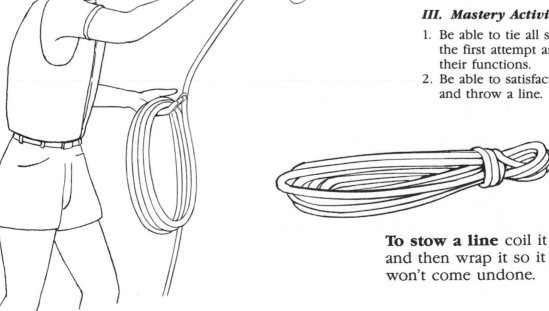

To stow a line coil it and then wrap it so it won't come undone.

I. Matching
(match the words to the correct pictures)

1. Bowline
2. Cleat hitch
3. Rolling hitch
4. Figure 8
5. Two half hitches
6. Clove hitch

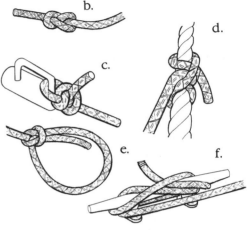

a.

b.

c.

d.

e.

f.

II. Exploring Sailing
(discussion or writing)

1. Describe the different uses of nylon, dacron, and polypropylene line.
2. Describe the steps in tying a bowline.
3. Why are sheets usually made from dacron?

III. Mastery Activities

1. Be able to tie all six knots on the first attempt and know their functions.
2. Be able to satisfactorily coil and throw a line.

Chapter 19

Decision Making in Sailing

"Is that all you can say: Yikes?"

KEY CONCEPTS

- **Judgement**
- **Anticipation**
- **Options in Decision Making**

When you are learning to sail, much time and concentration is given to how to control the boat. Now that you have the control skills, it is time to think about the decisions that you will make when you sail. In the world of sailing you are faced with thousands of decisions each time you plan to go sailing — everything from what clothes to wear to how to safely return to the harbor. Decisions are made on many different levels.

As with driving a bicycle or an automobile, good decisions revolve around safety and judgement. Judgement is based on **knowledge, experience**, and **confidence**, and will vary from person to person. The knowledge you gained through this book and your instructor is the most important ingredient toward making good decisions.

Spending more time around boats will help you greatly. And finally, the confidence you gain through practice and time on the water is invaluable.

The success and enjoyment that you have on the water depends on avoiding unpleasant surprises. To minimize these surprises that no one wants and at the same time improve your D.M.S. (Decision Making in Sailing), you should:

- Plan ahead
- Be prepared
- Anticipate the situation — think ahead of the boat
- Maximize your options — keep your options open
- Always have an escape route or bail-out plan
- Think defensively

One of the fun and challenging things about sailing is that you can usually respond to most situations in several different ways — there is no one right way. You can react to a situation by using the fundamental sailing skills such as starting, slowing, stopping, tacking, jibing, turning away from the wind, and turning toward the wind. For example, if you are approaching a right-of-way boat which is sailing upwind, you can avoid it by:

- Slowing down
- Stopping
- Turning away from the wind
- Tacking

It's your choice — your decision as to which option you are going to take based on the circumstances surrounding you.

We can all learn from challenges. Following are some challenging D.M.S. situations that demonstrate the point. Study them and you'll see what makes sailing well a satisfying challenge that lasts a lifetime.

Shown at right is a simplified chart of a sailing area that poses many typical planning challenges to recreational sailors. Included are areas with shallow water, a narrow channel with commercial water traffic, protected and open sailing areas.

Study the chart and notes below and then proceed to the following charts to test your decision making ability in situations combining different directions and strengths of wind and current.

Notes:

A. Channel opening to outer bay is narrow. Tidal current in and out can be strong. In light winds, this could pose a problem sailing against the current. Check tide tables for times of high and low tide.

B. This area is very shallow at low tide, but at high tide water is deeper, offering an alternative to using channel.

C. Channel is used for commerical water traffic and larger recreational powerboats. If sailing near channel, remember larger powerboats, tugboats and barges have to stay in channel, which is narrow. Don't expect them to give way.

D. Winds blowing from city front onto the bay can be shifty and erratic. Winds will usually be steadiest in middle of inner bay.

E. Be careful of rocks on this side of Nash Island and Gull Island.

F. Passage between Nash Island and Gull Island is very tight, making it difficult to sail through while tacking upwind. Only use this route when reaching or sailing downwind.

G. Area between the mainland and Nash Island is well protected when winds are blowing from North or South.

H. Passage under bridge is tall enough for sailboats, but very tight. Use this route only when reaching or sailing downwind.

I. Scott's Cove is well protected from all northerly winds.

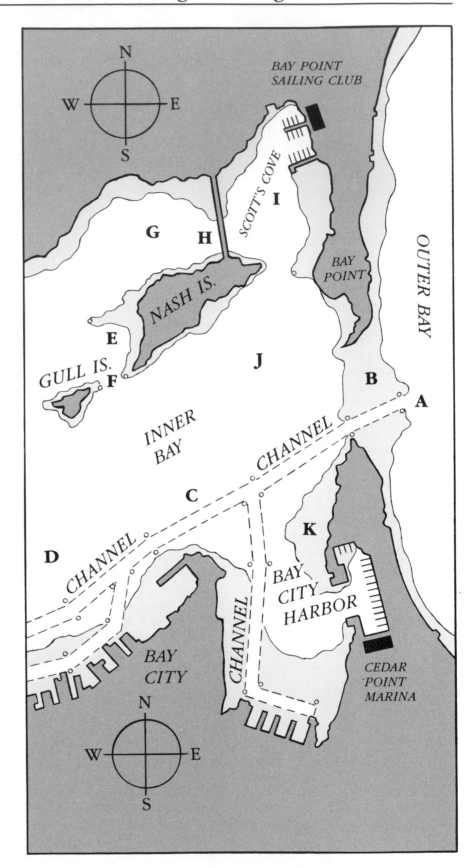

J. Open area in bay will have rougher waves in windy conditions.

K. Bay City Harbor is well protected from all but Northerly winds.

1. Plan a sail from Bay Point Sailing Club **(X)** out around Gull Island and back. The wind is from the South and the current is flowing into the Inner Bay.

2. Plan a sail from Cedar Point Marina **(Y)** around Nash Island and back. The wind is from the South and the current is flowing into the Inner Bay.

3. Plan a sail from Bay Point Sailing Club **(X)** to the Outer Bay and back. The wind is from the West and the tide is almost high.

4. Plan a sail from Cedar Point Marina **(Y)** to the Outer Bay and back. The wind is from the East and the tide is almost high.

Draw your proposed routes (try different colors for various routes) for each situation on the accompanying chart. Add comments or questions in the space below (such as points of sail, compensation for current, other boat traffic, etc.)

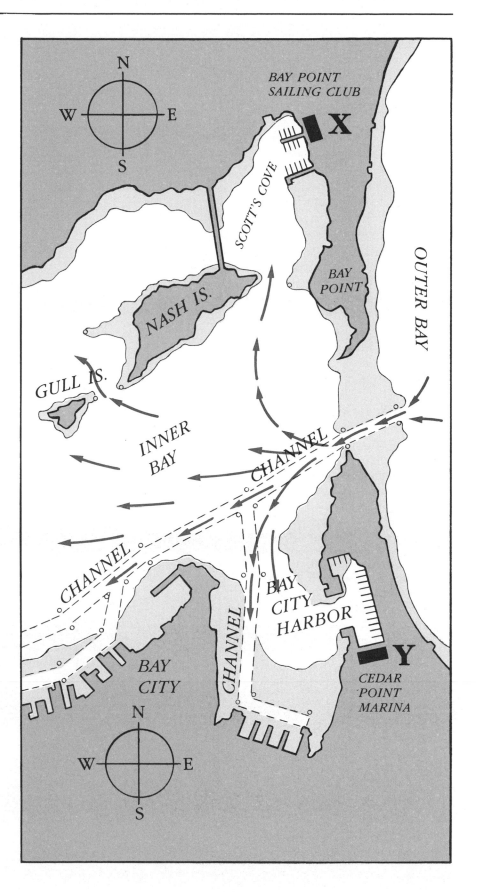

1. Plan a sail from Bay Point Sailing Club (**X**) out around Gull Island and back. The wind is from the North and the current is flowing out of the Inner Bay.

2. Plan a sail from Cedar Point Marina (**Y**) out around Nash Island and back. The wind is from the North and the current is flowing out of the Inner Bay.

3. Plan a sail from Cedar Point Marina (**Y**) to the Outer Bay and back. The wind is from the West and the current will change from going out of Inner Bay to coming in while you are in the Outer Bay.

Draw your proposed routes (try different colors for various routes) for each situation on the accompanying chart. Add comments or questions in the space below (such as points of sail, compensation for current, other boat traffic, etc.)

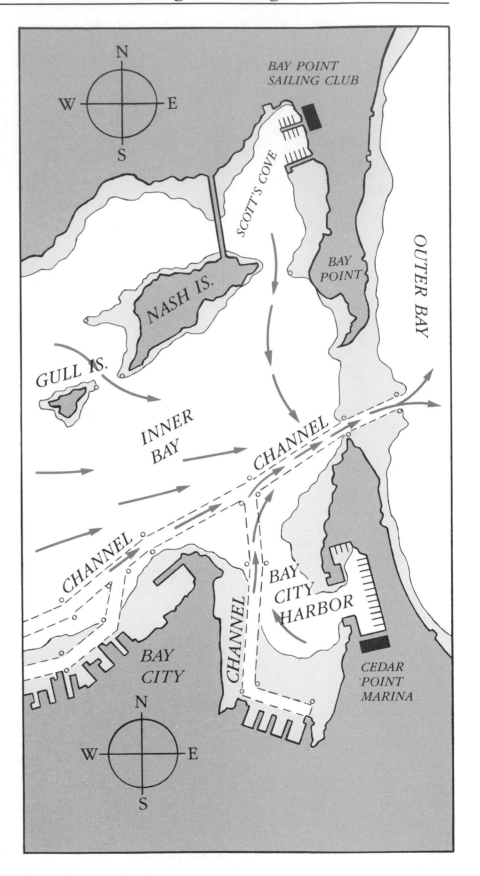

1. You are sailing in area **J** and a squall **S** is approaching with strong winds from the South. What do you do?

2. You are sailing in area **J** and a squall **N** is approaching with strong winds from the North. What do you do?

Draw your proposed routes (try different colors for various routes) for each situation on the accompanying chart. Add comments or questions in the space below (such as points of sail, compensation for current, other boat traffic, etc.)

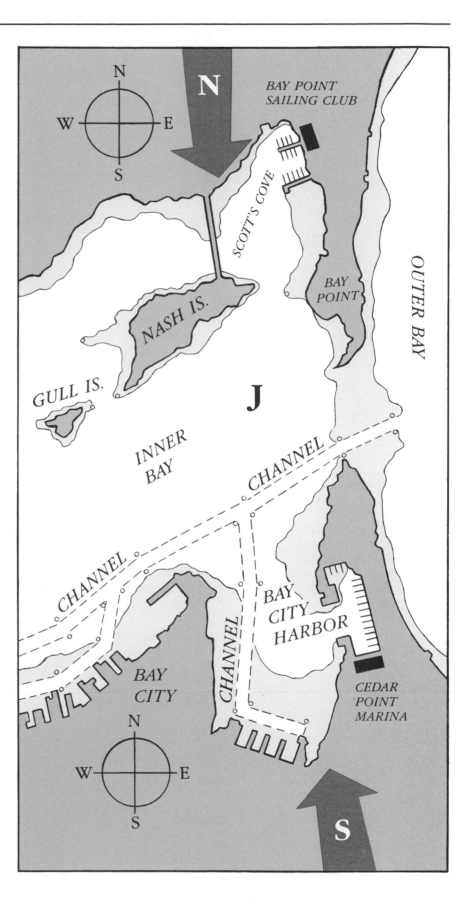

Chapter 20

New Horizons

Few sports offer as much freedom of choice as sailing. There are literally hundreds of different types of boats and sailboat classes that you can sail. Each has its own special characteristics and feel (see Appendix for a list of boats that are popular with beginning sailors). There are also many ways in which you can become involved with the sport — through organizations such as sailing clubs, sailing associations or community sailing programs, or on your own — sailing off the beach or out of a marina. Even if you don't own a boat, there are hundreds of thousands of sailboats out there that need crew.

One of the best parts of sailing is travelling with your boat to different sailing locales. Many small dinghies are easily transportable on a roof rack or small trailer, and many one-design racing classes hold national and regional events in different places each year where hundreds of sailors meet to race and socialize.

Sailboat racing is a wonderful way to develop skills quickly and make lots of friends. It's one of the few sports where beginners and champions can get out on the same course and compete together for the same prize. In most racing classes, the premium is on "smarts," not athletic ability. More than in most sports, male, female, young and old compete on an equal footing.

What makes sailing so special? Wind and water, the challenge of harnessing nature's forces in a clean and natural way, the camaraderie of other sailors. . .all contribute to sailing's enduring appeal. As you finish your introduction to sailing another thing should become evident as well. A sailor **never** stops learning. This is ultimately what makes sailing so satisfying — a sport that can last a lifetime.

The following Appendix is designed as a key to new sailing horizons. In addition to presenting more detailed information on sails, rigs, on-shore and on-water drills and sailing terminology, it lists valuable information and study sources (both books and videos) and organizations whose job it is to help you enjoy sailing more.

Sail safe, and **have fun!**

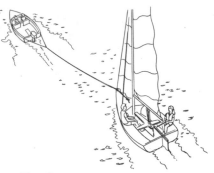

Review of Additional Sailing Skills

These are the additional sailing skills that you should be able to do by the end of your course. Review these skills when you go sailing and check off the ones you can successfully complete. Then have your instructor review your skills.

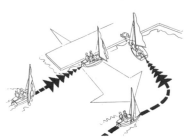

Leaving & Returning to Dock or Mooring

    Student self-evaluation ☐
    Instructor evaluation ☐

Use of Additional Sail Controls

    Student self-evaluation ☐
    Instructor evaluation ☐

Towing

    Student self-evaluation ☐
    Instructor evaluation ☐

Man-Overboard Recovery Methods

    Student self-evaluation ☐
    Instructor evaluation ☐

Five Basic Right-of-Way Rules

    Student self-evaluation ☐
    Instructor evaluation ☐

Coming Alongside Another Boat

    Student self-evaluation ☐
    Instructor evaluation ☐

Sailing a Course

    Student self-evaluation ☐
    Instructor evaluation ☐

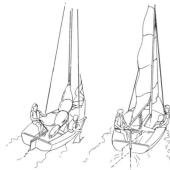

Paddling and Sculling

    Student self-evaluation ☐
    Instructor evaluation ☐

Determining Current Direction and Speed

    Student self-evaluation ☐
    Instructor evaluation ☐

Centerboard Positions

    Student self-evaluation ☐
    Instructor evaluation ☐

Anchoring

    Student self-evaluation ☐
    Instructor evaluation ☐

Basic Knots

    Student self-evaluation ☐
    Instructor evaluation ☐

Review Question #1

A puff is approaching your boat.

a. A puff means
- ☒ more wind speed.
- ☐ less wind speed.

b. What will the puff do to your boat as you sail into it?
- ☒ The boat will heel more.
- ☐ The boat will heel less.

c. What should you do as you sail into it?
- ☐ Sheet out the sail a little.
- ☒ Sheet in the sail a little.

d. Or you should
- ☒ turn the boat toward the wind a little.
- ☐ turn the boat away from the wind a little.

Review Question #2

Your crew falls overboard. The wind speed is about 10 to 12 miles per hour.

a. What is the best recovery course for you to take?
- ☒ Course 1
- ☐ Course 2
- ☐ Course 3

b. What would you be doing at points:

A _Sailing into wind + a broad to beng reach windward of man over board_

B _Starting a tack_

C _tacking_

D _falling off + turning up_

E _starting to jibe_

F _Turning windward_

Review Question #3

If your sail looks like this, what would you do with

a. the cunningham or downhaul?
- ☒ Tighten it
- ☐ Loosen it

b. the outhaul?
- ☒ Tighten it
- ☐ Loosen it

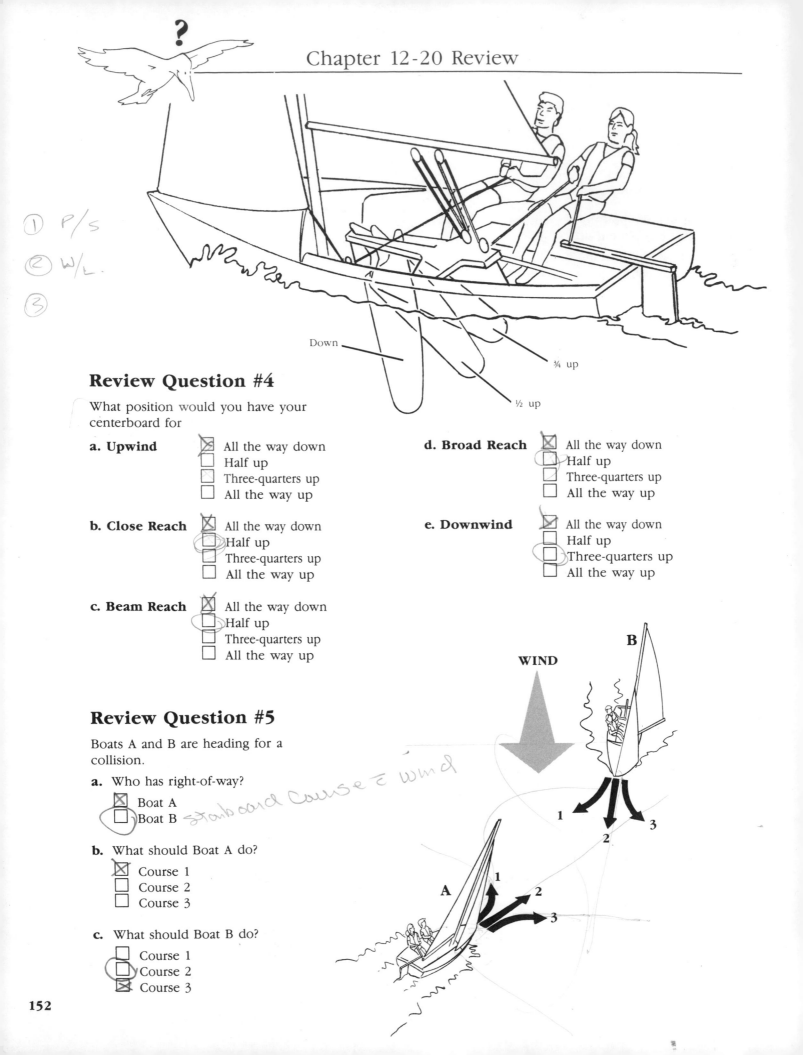

① P/S
② W/L.
③

Down

¾ up

½ up

Review Question #4

What position would you have your centerboard for

a. Upwind
- ☒ All the way down
- ☐ Half up
- ☐ Three-quarters up
- ☐ All the way up

b. Close Reach
- ☒ All the way down
- ☐ Half up
- ☐ Three-quarters up
- ☐ All the way up

c. Beam Reach
- ☒ All the way down
- ☐ Half up
- ☐ Three-quarters up
- ☐ All the way up

d. Broad Reach
- ☒ All the way down
- ☐ Half up
- ☐ Three-quarters up
- ☐ All the way up

e. Downwind
- ☒ All the way down
- ☐ Half up
- ☐ Three-quarters up
- ☐ All the way up

Review Question #5

Boats A and B are heading for a collision.

a. Who has right-of-way?
- ☒ Boat A
- ☐ Boat B   starboard course = wind

b. What should Boat A do?
- ☒ Course 1
- ☐ Course 2
- ☐ Course 3

c. What should Boat B do?
- ☐ Course 1
- ☐ Course 2
- ☒ Course 3

WIND

B

A   1   2   3

1   2   3

Review Question #6

You need a tow back to the dock. A tow boat is approaching towing a sailboat.

a. What approach course should you take to the tow boat?

☒ Course 1
☐ Course 2

b. When should you lower your sail?

☐ Before you have picked up the tow.
☒ After you have picked up the tow.

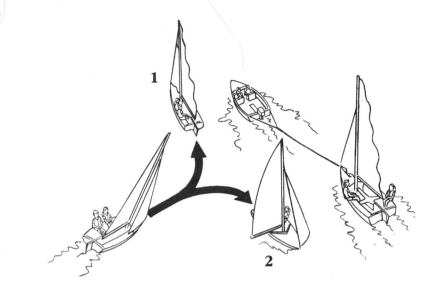

Review Question #7

What direction is the current running?

a. Draw the current arrow in the box.

b. What course would you have to sail to compensate for the action of the current?

☐ Course 1
☐ Course 2
☒ Course 3

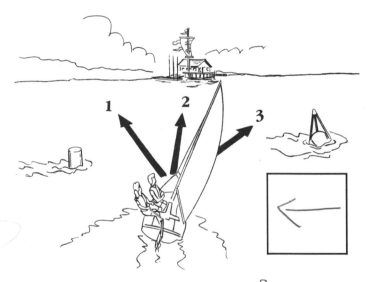

Review Question #8

What knot would you use for (more than one knot can be used for some):

1 a/e
2 a
3 e a
4 c
5 b
6 e a

Select the knot from:

a Bowline
b Two half hitches
c Figure 8
d Cleat hitch
e Clove hitch

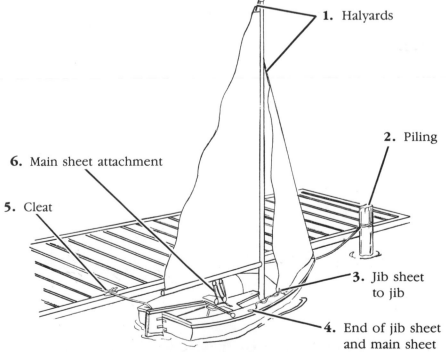

1. Halyards

2. Piling

3. Jib sheet to jib

4. End of jib sheet and main sheet

5. Cleat

6. Main sheet attachment

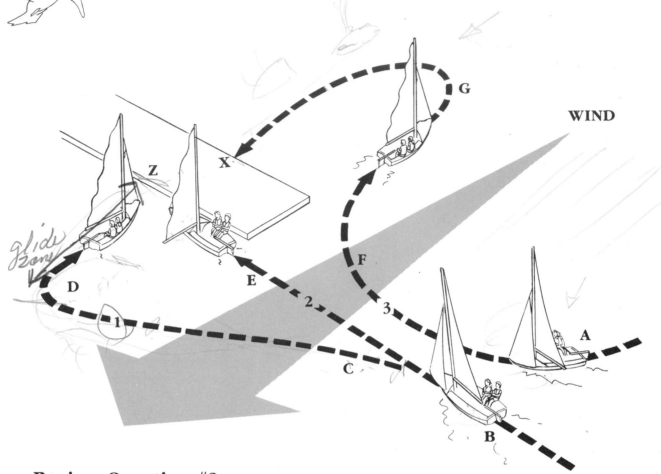

Review Question #9

Boats A and B are approaching the dock.

a. Which boat has right-of-way?

☒ Boat A

☐ Boat B

b. Which boat must stay clear?

☐ Boat A

☒ Boat B

c. Which is the best return point on the dock?

☐ Point X

☒ Point Z

d. Draw in the Glide Zone for Approach 1

e. If you take Approach 1, what would you be doing at:

C _fall off / luff sails as approaching_

D _luff sails / turn windward shut out_

f. If you take Approach 2, what would you be doing at:

E _shut mainsail out / drop speed, head in 30°_

g. If you take Approach 3, what would you be doing at:

F _turn up_

G _Jibe / shut out / sails down (bare pole) when down wind._

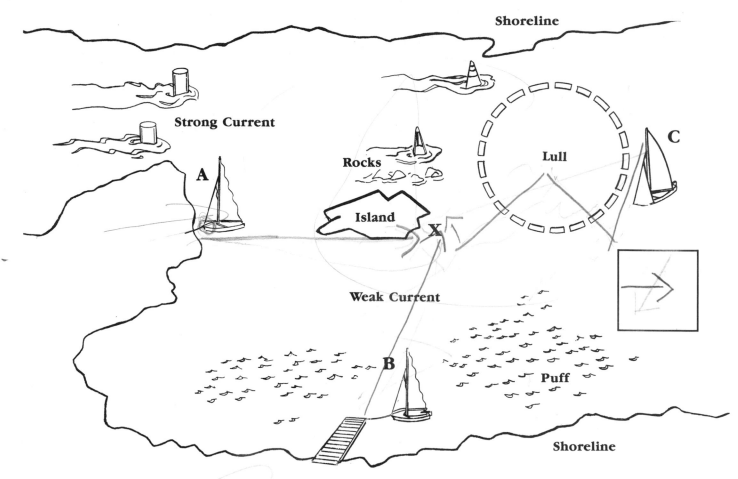

Shoreline

Strong Current

Rocks

Lull

A

C

Island

X

Weak Current

Puff

B

Shoreline

Review Question #10

Boats A, B, and C are planning to meet at destination X for a picnic.

a. Determine the wind direction and draw the arrow in the box.

b. For each boat, draw the route that would get you to destination X as quickly as possible.

c. What point of sail will each boat be sailing to reach destination **X**:

A _downwind_
B _Broad reach_
C _upwind_

d. Will boat A:

☐ Tack
☒ Jibe
☐ Sail a straight course

e. Will boat B:

☐ Tack
☐ Jibe
☒ Sail a straight course

f. Will boat C:

☒ Tack
☐ Jibe
☐ Sail a straight course

g. The sails on boat A will be:

☐ Sheeted in all the way
☐ Sheeted in halfway
☒ Sheeted out all the way

h. The sails on boat B will be:

☐ Sheeted in all the way
☒ Sheeted in halfway
☐ Sheeted out all the way

i. The sails on boat C will be:

☒ Sheeted in all the way
☐ Sheeted in halfway
☐ Sheeted out all the way

Certificate Record (Part 1) — Minimum Water Skills

The following skills are to be tested on the boat and water for mastery. It is recommended that the chronological order of skills be followed as listed. To attain mastery level, the student should be able to perform the skills safely and generally mistake free — judged on a basis that is appropriate for a learn-to-sail student. Criteria used for evaluation should include steering technique, sail trim, body position, boat-handling skill, communication and student confidence.

Student performance may be influenced by wind speed and direction, water conditions and air temperature. Recommended wind range for testing skills is three to ten knots. Regional differences in typical conditions may require that this recommended wind range be modified.

Instructor Record

Introduced   Date   Mastered   Date

☐ _____   ☐ _____   1. **Rig a Boat:** Centerboard, rudder, sails, battens, halyards, sheets, etc.

☐ _____   ☐ _____   2. **Basic Knots:** Bowline, Figure 8, Cleat Hitch, Two Half Hitches (Recommended that this test be done while rigging boat and tying boat to dock).

☐ _____   ☐ _____   3. **Leaving Dock or Mooring:** Determining wind direction and speed, determining current direction and speed, entering boat, raising sails, leaving dock, sail trim, maneuverability, departure plan, tacks and jibes, boathandling.

☐ _____   ☐ _____   4. **Starting and Stopping:** Sail trim, body position, response time (include two methods for stopping).

☐ _____   ☐ _____   5. **Safety Position:** Point of sail, sail trim, response time, holding position.

☐ _____   ☐ _____   6. **Tacking:** Steering, course heading, sail trim, body movements, helmsman/crew communication.

☐ _____   ☐ _____   7. **Jibing:** Steering, course heading, sail trim, body movements, helmsman/crew communication.

☐ _____   ☐ _____   8. **Sailing a Rectangular Course:** Steering, boat speed, sail trim, tacks and jibes, body position, body movement, course headings, helmsman/crew communication.

☐ _____   ☐ _____   9. **Man-Overboard (MOB):** Communication, recovery plan, sequence of maneuvers, boathandling, course sailed, pickup approach, bringing MOB aboard.

☐ _____   ☐ _____   10. **Maneuvering in Confined Area:** Communication, boat-handling, avoiding obstacles, right-of-way, sail trim, course sailed.

☐ _____   ☐ _____   11. **Capsize Recovery:** Recovery method (scoop method for two people), sequence of maneuvers, exiting and entering boat, communication, maintain contact with boat, PFD properly worn.

☐ _____   ☐ _____   12. **Returning to Dock or Mooring:** Approach plan, maneuverability, boathandling, sail trim, tacks and jibes, use of glide zone, tying to dock or mooring, lowering sails.

☐ _____   ☐ _____   13. **De-Rig Boat:** De-rig sails, fold sails, de-rig and stow equipment, secure and tie down boat.

Certificate Record (Part 2) — Minimum Knowledge Skills

In addition to mastering the minimum water skills, a student is expected to be familiar with the following knowledge areas: right-of-way, safety, sail parts, boat parts, points of sail, hypothermia, heat emergencies, weather, currents and tides. To successfully complete the requirements for a basic sailing certificate, you must answer 80% of the questions correctly on the knowledge test that your instructor will give you.

To prepare for your test, complete the following sample. If you score 80% (32 of 40) or more and review any questions you answered incorrectly, you should be ready for the knowledge test.

I. MULTIPLE CHOICE
(choose the best answer)

1. Places on the surface of the water that show changes in wind speed are called
   - ☐ a. lulls and lines.
   - ☐ b. puffs and true wind.
   - ☐ c. lulls and puffs.
   - ☐ d. lines and pulleys.

2. The scoop capsize recovery is the safest capsize procedure because
   - ☐ a. it keeps as little water out of the boat as possible.
   - ☐ b. it positions the boat better into the wind source.
   - ☐ c. it prevents turtling.
   - ☐ d. it allows a person to be in the boat after re-right who can control the boat and help the other person.

3. A sailor can determine current moving in the water by
   - ☐ a. water reading for puffs and lulls.
   - ☐ b. gravitational moon charts.
   - ☐ c. small eddies and ripples around fixed objects in the water.
   - ☐ d. advice from a local fisherman.

4. Warming a victim's body temperature gradually helps to relieve
   - ☐ a. heat stroke.
   - ☐ b. hypothermia.
   - ☐ c. heat cramps.
   - ☐ d. strains.

5. The mast of the sailboat can be dangerous because of
   - ☐ a. the many shrouds attached to it.
   - ☐ b. sharp edges in the mast track.
   - ☐ c. weight and length.
   - ☐ d. overhead electrical wires.

6. Besides safety in the water, the PFD aids the sailor by
   - ☐ a. its color, warmth and comfort.
   - ☐ b. its color, and protection against the boom.
   - ☐ c. its warmth, and fashionable design.
   - ☐ d. its warmth, and feature of one size fits all.

II. TRUE OR FALSE

7. High pressure systems usually have better sailing conditions than low pressure systems.

8. Port tack has right-of-way over any small powerboat.

9. The device which best prevents the boom from lifting up is called the boom head.

10. To help prevent heat exhaustion a sailor should drink plenty of fluids and wear light colored clothing.

11. Once you have passed this course it is no longer recommended that you wear a PFD.

12. A catamaran is a multihull and a Laser is a monohull.

13. There are 300 degrees in a compass.

14. Turning the bow through the wind, changing the boat from starboard tack to port tack, is called a jibe.

III. MATCHING

15. Moving the rudder repeatedly back and forth to propel the boat.

16. A boat sailing approximately 135 degrees to the wind.

17. The device which detects small changes in atmospheric pressure.

18. In a crowded waterway it is best to use _____.

19. The line used to pull a sail up.

20. An easy way to stop a boat is to turn into the _____.

- ☐ a. barometer
- ☐ b. halyard
- ☐ c. no-go zone
- ☐ d. sculling
- ☐ e. broad reach
- ☐ f. environmental awareness

IV. DEFINITIONS
(in your own words briefly define the following words)

21. Water reading

22. Upwind sailing

23. Hard-a-lee

24. Glide zone

**Certificate Record
(Part 2)** *continued*

V. BOAT IDENTIFICATION
(name the label points)

Sail

25. A _____
26. B _____
27. C _____
28. D _____

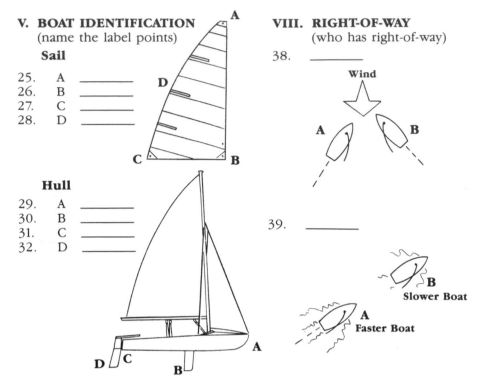

Hull

29. A _____
30. B _____
31. C _____
32. D _____

VI. POINTS OF SAIL

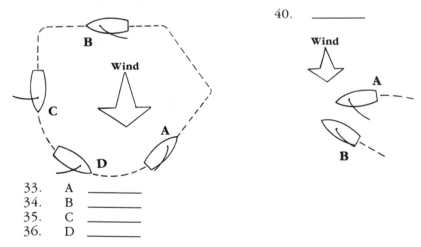

33. A _____
34. B _____
35. C _____
36. D _____

VII. DECISION MAKING IN SAILING

You have to return to the dock as quickly as possible and avoid any
hazards.
(Choose the best route for your return.)

37. _____

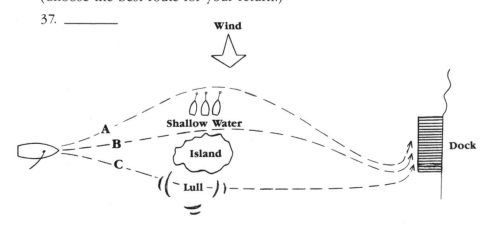

VIII. RIGHT-OF-WAY
(who has right-of-way)

38. _____

39. _____

40. _____

Course Evaluation

Dear Student:

The United States Yacht Racing Union and the American Red Cross need your evaluation and comments to help make these courses the best possible for you and future students. Please fill out this form, and give it to your instructor or mail it to USYRU, Box 209, Newport, RI 02840. Thanks for your help!

Name_____ ☐ Female ☐ Male _____/_____/_____
                                                                        Date of Birth

Address _____

City_____State_____Zip_____

Location of course: _____

Instructor _____

Please use the scale below to rate this course:

	Poor	Fair	Good	Very Good	Excellent
Facilities	_____	_____	_____	_____	_____
Condition of boats	_____	_____	_____	_____	_____
Textbook *(Start Sailing Right)*	_____	_____	_____	_____	_____
Video tapes *(Learn-to-Sail Videos)*	_____	_____	_____	_____	_____
Instructors	_____	_____	_____	_____	_____
Emphasis on safety	_____	_____	_____	_____	_____
Overall course rating	_____	_____	_____	_____	_____

If we could make **one** change to improve the quality of the course, what would it be?_____
_____

Was this course fun?   Yes _____ No _____
Would you recommend this course to your friends?   Yes _____ No _____
What is your primary sailing interest after completing this course?
☐ Racing   ☐ Day Sailing   ☐ Cruising   ☐ Boardsailing   ☐ Multihull Sailing

- -

SPECIAL OFFER! Congratulations on completing the best
learn-to-sail course in the country. As you begin sailing on your own, you may want to join America's foremost family of sailors, and enjoy low-cost boat loans, travel savings, discounts on the best sailing books and videos, a free racing rulebook, USYRU's monthly newsmagazine AMERICAN SAILOR — and more!

Check the box below to receive a free copy of AMERICAN SAILOR and more information about USYRU. Or join now! Your completion of this course entitles you to membership at the **special first-year rate of $25** (a $15.00 savings!).

[ ] Please send my free copy of AMERICAN SAILOR and more information on the
     benefits I can enjoy as a USYRU member.

[ ] Sign me up now!

     [ ] My $25 check or money order payable to USYRU is enclosed.
     [ ] Charge my credit card (MasterCard, VISA, or American Express):

MasterCard, Visa or American Express orders please complete the section below:

_____ Circle one: MC   VISA   AMX
Name on credit card

_____ Expiration Date: _____ / _____
Card number

Types of Sailboat Rigs

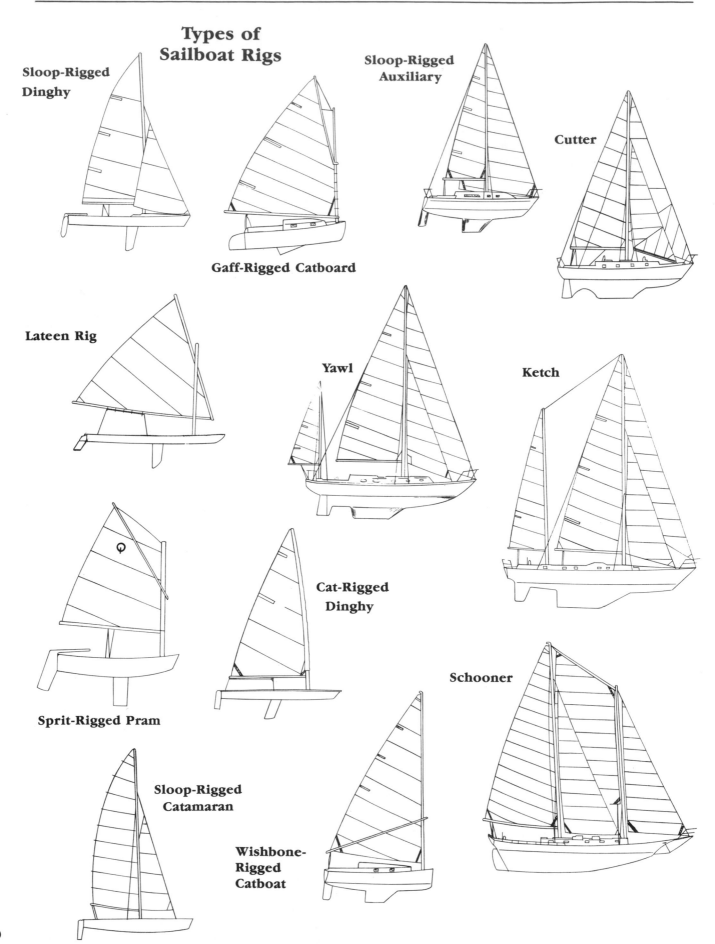

Sloop-Rigged Dinghy

Gaff-Rigged Catboard

Sloop-Rigged Auxiliary

Cutter

Lateen Rig

Yawl

Ketch

Sprit-Rigged Pram

Cat-Rigged Dinghy

Schooner

Sloop-Rigged Catamaran

Wishbone-Rigged Catboat

Examples of Sailing Dinghies

Definitions:

Length — The maximum length of hull, not including rudder.

Beam — Width at widest point.

Draft — The depth of the boat below the water's surface, measured with the centerboard and rudder in the down position.

Centerboard — An underwater appendage in the middle of the boat that pivots as it is raised and lowered.

Daggerboard — An underwater appendage in the middle of the boat that is raised and lowered vertically.

Leeboard — A pivoting underwater appendage that is attached to one side of the boat.

Weight — The total weight of the boat, including rig and sails.

Self-Rescuing — Design features that allow a capsized boat to be easily re-righted, bailed out and sailed away without outside assistance.

Sailors — Suggested number of people (adult or youth) for optimum performance.

Blue Jay

Length: 13'6" Board Type: centerboard
Beam: 5'2" Weight: 275 lbs.
Draft: 3'9" Self Rescuing: yes
Sailors: 2 adults or 2-3 youths

Butterfly

Length: 12'2" Board Type: daggerboard
Beam: 4'6" Weight: 170 lbs.
Draft: 2'6" Self Rescuing: yes
Sailors: 1 adult or 1-2 youths

Coronado 15

Length: 15'4" Board Type: centerboard
Beam: 5'8" Weight: 385 lbs.
Draft: 3'6" Self Rescuing: yes
Sailors: 2 adults or 2-3 youths

Flying Junior

Length: 13'3" Board Type: centerboard
Beam: 5'3" Weight: 209 lbs.
Draft: 2'6" Self Rescuing: yes
Sailors: 2 adults or 2-3 youths

420

Length: 13'9" Board Type: centerboard
Beam: 5'5" Weight: 220 lbs.
Draft: 3'2" Self Rescuing: yes
Sailors: 2 adults or 2-3 youths

Hobie 16

Length: 16'7" Board Type: no board
Beam: 7'11" Weight: 320 lbs.
Draft: 6" Self Rescuing: yes
Sailors: 2 adults or 2-3 youths

Examples of Sailing Dinghies

Holder Hawk

International Optimist

Length: 7'6"   Board Type: daggerboard
Beam: 3'8"   Weight: 92 lbs.
Draft: 2'8"   Self Rescuing: yes
   Sailors: 1 youth

Length: 9'0"   Board Type: centerboard
Beam: 3'10½" Weight: 95 lbs.
Draft: 2'3½"   Self Rescuing: yes
   Sailors: 1 adult or 1-2 youth

Laser & Laser Radial

Lido 14

Naples Sabot

Length: 13'10½" Board Type: daggerboard
Beam: 4'6"   Weight: 130 lbs.
Draft: 2'6"   Self Rescuing: yes
   Sailors: 1 adult or 1-2 youths

Length: 14'0"   Board Type: centerboard
Beam: 6'0"   Weight: 310 lbs.
Draft: 4'0½"   Self Rescuing: yes
   Sailors: 2 adults or 2-3 youths

Length: 7'11"   Board Type: leeboard
Beam: 3'10"   Weight: 105 lbs.
Draft: 1'6"   Self Rescuing: no
   Sailors: 1 youth

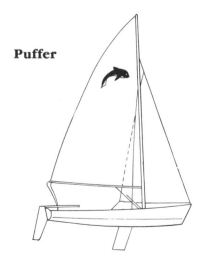
Puffer

Sunfish

X-boat

Length: 13'10"   Board Type: daggerboard
Beam: 4'1"   Weight: 129 lbs.
Draft: 2'7"   Self Rescuing: yes
   Sailors: 1 adult or 1-2 youths

Length: 12'6"   Board Type: daggerboard
Beam: 4'10"   Weight: 160 lbs.
Draft: 2'8½"   Self Rescuing: yes
   Sailors: 2 adults or 2-3 youths

Length: 16'0"   Board Type: centerboard
Beam: 6'1"   Weight: 500 lbs.
Draft: 1'3"   Self Rescuing: yes
   Sailors: 2 adults or 2-3 youths

Glossary of Important Sailing Terms and Expressions

This glossary is a comprehensive list of sailing vocabulary and terms used in this book and elsewhere. Words having the same or similar meaning (*synonyms*) are also included to assist in word association and account for regional differences in the sailing language.

A

Abeam   A direction off the side of a boat, at right angles to a line from bow to stern. Syn. *On the Beam*.

Aerobic Exercises   Activity such as bicycling, jogging, or swimming which stimulates the cardiovascular system.

Aft   1. Towards, near, or at the back end of a boat. Syn. *Astern*. 2. A direction behind the stern of a boat. Syn. *Astern*.

Amidships   The middle of a boat.

Anaerobic Exercises   Activity such as lifting weights which helps promote strength, flexibility, and muscle development.

Anchoring   Stationary positioning of a boat in the water by a weight connected to the boat by a rope and/or chain.

Anemometer   A device used to indicate wind speed.

Apparent Wind   The wind that flows over a moving boat, which is the result of the "true wind" affected by the movement of the boat.

Appendage   An underwater fin, such as a centerboard, daggerboard, leeboard, keel, or rudder.

Astern   See **Aft.**

Athwartships   A sideways direction on a boat that is at a right angle to the line from bow to stern.

B

Back   To push a sail out against the wind to help turn the boat, or move it backwards.

Backwind   The wind flowing off the jib or mainsail. Sometimes, backwind from the jib can cause the forward edge (luff) of the mainsail to luff or flap.

Bailers   Openings in the bottom or transom of a boat to remove water when sailing. Syn. *Self-Bailers*.

Ballast   Weight used to give a boat stability. On large boats, ballast in the keel (usually lead) provides stability. On smaller boats, stability is usually provided by the weight of the sailors.

Barometer   A device used to indicate atmospheric pressure.

Batten   A thin wooden or plastic strip inserted into a pocket on the back part (leech) of a sail.

Beam   The width of a boat.

Beam Reach   Sailing at approximately 90 degrees to the wind source with the wind coming from abeam and the sails let out about half way. (One of the points of sail.)

Bear Away   See **Head Down.**

Bear Off   See **Head Down.**

Bear Up   See **Head Up.**

Beating   Sailing toward the wind source, or against the wind, with the sails pulled in all the way, tacking as you go, to reach a destination upwind. Syn. *Close-Hauled, On the Wind, Sailing to Weather, Sailing to Windward, Sailing Upwind*.

Bilge   The lowest part of a boat inside the hull.

Block   The nautical term for a pulley. It can have one or more sheaves, or wheels.

Bolt Rope   The rope sewn into the forward (luff) and bottom (foot) edges of the mainsail.

Boom   A spar used to hold out or anchor the bottom of a sail.

Boom Vang   A control line, usually a multi-purchase tackle, secured to the boom to prevent it lifting. Syn. *Vang*.

Glossary continued

Bow The forward end of a boat.

Breeze Wind.

Broad Reach Sailing with the wind coming over the rear corner of the boat, or with the bow approximately 135 degrees to the wind source. (One of the points of sail.)

By the Lee Sailing downwind with the wind blowing over the leeward side of the boat, increasing the possibility of an unexpected jibe.

C

Capsize A boat turned over on its side or upside down.

Cast Off To untie a line and let it go, or to remove a line from a cleat and let it go.

Cat See **Catamaran.**

Catamaran A boat with two parallel hulls. Syn. *Cat.*

Catboat A boat that has only a mainsail, with the mast located at the bow.

Centerboard A pivoting plate of wood, fiberglass, or metal, projecting below the bottom of a sailboat to help prevent the boat from sliding sideways.

Centerline An imaginary line that runs down the center of the boat from the bow to the stern.

Chart A nautical map showing water depths, obstructions, restricted areas, markers and buoys.

C-Jibe The boat is steered through a downwind turn which results in the mainsail suddenly crossing from one side to the other side uncontrollably. The path of the boat makes a "C." Syn. *Slam Jibe, Flying Jibe.*

Class A category into which boats of similar design are grouped.

Cleat A wooden, plastic, or metal device which is used to hold or secure lines.

Clew The lower back corner of a mainsail or jib.

Close-Hauled Describes a boat sailing as close to the wind as possible with its sails pulled in all the way. Syn. *Beating, On the Wind, Sailing to Weather, Sailing to Windward, Sailing Upwind.*

Close Reach Sailing with the wind just forward of abeam, or with the bow approximately 70 degrees to the wind source. (One of the points of sail.)

Cockpit The open well in a boat where the helmsman and/or crew sit or put their feet.

Come About To turn the bow of a sailboat through the wind, or no-go zone, so that the sails fill on the opposite side. Syn. *Tack.*

Come Down See **Head Down.**

Come Up See **Head Up.**

Coming About See **Tacking** and **"Hard-a-Lee."**

Compass An instrument used to determine the direction that a boat is headed, or to take a bearing (sight) on an object.

Constant Angle to the Wind The correct angle of the wind to a sail, which remains the same when the sail is correctly trimmed (positioned) for all points of sail, except when the wind is blowing from behind the stern.

Control Line A rope used to adjust and trim a sail, such as a sheet, outhaul, downhaul, cunningham or boom vang. Syn. *Running Rigging, Sail Controls.*

Control Signals Hand signs used between instructors and sailors to communicate while on the water.

Course The direction that a boat is steered to reach a destination.

Crabbing (to Weather) See **Feathering.**

Crew The people who help the helmsman sail a boat.

Cunningham A control line that tensions the forward edge (luff) of a sail.

Cunningham Hole A hole in the tack of a sail through which the cunningham line runs to tension the forward edge (luff) of the sail.

Current The horizontal movement of water caused by tides, wind, or change in elevation.

D

Daggerboard A movable plate of wood, fiberglass, or metal let down below the bottom of a boat to help prevent the boat from sliding sideways. Similar to the centerboard, except it is raised and lowered vertically rather than pivoted.

Deck The top (horizontal) surface of the hull.

De-Rigging Removing and stowing sails and equipment.

Displacement The weight of water displaced by a floating boat. The weight of water is equal to the weight of the boat; therefore, a boat's weight is often called its displacement.

Downhaul A control line that adjusts and tensions the luff of a sail by moving the end of the boom at the mast. The movable fitting joining the mast and boom is called the "gooseneck."

Downwind 1. Sailing away from the wind source with the sails let out all the way. (One of the points of sail.) Syn. *Run, With the Wind.*
2. In the opposite direction from the wind source, or where the wind is blowing to. Syn. *Leeward.*

Downwind Side See **Leeward Side.**

E

Ease To let out a line or sail. The opposite of pull. Syn. *Let Off, Sheet Out.*

Electrical Hazards Overhead power lines, electrical cables, electrical power tools and equipment used near the water, or near launching and boat storage areas.

Environmental Awareness The continuous monitoring of wind, weather, sea conditions, current, and distance from the shore.

F

Fairlead A fitting, such as a ring, eye, block or loop which guides a rope in the direction required.

Fall Off See **Head Down.**

Feathering Sailing upwind so close to the wind that the forward edge of the sail is stalling or luffing, reducing the power generated by the sail and the angle of heel. Syn. *Crabbing (to Weather), High, Light, Pinching, Sailing Thin.*

Fly See **Telltale.**

Flying Jibe See **C-Jibe.**

Foot The bottom edge of a sail.

Fore Towards, near, or at the bow.

Fore and Aft Towards, near, or at both ends of a boat.

Fore-and-Aft Line An imaginary line that runs lengthwise on a boat.

Forestay A support wire connecting the mast to the bow. Part of the standing rigging.

Furling Folding or rolling a sail and securing it.

G

Glide Zone The distance a sailboat takes to coast to a stop after turning into the no-go zone or letting out the sails.

Go Up See **Head Up.**

Gooseneck The joint fitting that connects the boom to the mast.

Gunwale The edge of a sailboat where the deck and hull meet.

Gust See **Puff.**

Gybe See **Jibe.**

Gybing See **Jibing.**

H

Halliard See **Halyard.**

Halyard A line used to raise or lower a sail. Syn. *Halliard.*

"Hard-a-Lee" A command made by the helmsman when the tiller is moved to leeward to tack a sailboat. Syn. *"Coming About," "Helms-a-Lee," "Tacking."*

Harden Up See **Head Up.**

Head The top corner of a sail where the halyard is attached.

Head Down To turn the boat away from the wind. Syn. *Bear Away, Bear Off, Come Down, Fall Off, Head Off.*

Head Off See **Head Down.**

Head Up To turn the boat toward the wind. Syn. *Bear Up, Come Up, Go Up, Harden Up, Luff Up.*

Heading The direction in which a boat is pointing.

Head-to-Wind When the bow of a boat is pointing directly into the wind, or in the middle of the no-go zone.

Heat Emergencies See **Hyperpyrexia.**

Heel 1. When a boat leans over or tips to one side. 2. The lower end of the mast.

Helm 1. The tiller or wheel of a boat. 2. The tendency of a sailboat to turn towards or away from the wind on its own. The helmsman compensates by pushing or pulling the tiller. If the boat wants to turn toward the wind (to weather), it has a **weather helm**, or if it wants to turn away from the wind (to leeward), it has a **lee helm.**

Glossary continued

"Helms-a-Lee" See **"Hard-a-Lee."**

Helmsman The person who steers or drives a boat. Syn. *Skipper.*

High Pressure Higher atmospheric pressure generally associated with fair skies and good weather.

High Side The side of a sailboat nearest to the wind source. Syn. *Weather Side, Windward Side, Upwind Side.*

Hiking When a person leans over the side of a boat to counteract heel.

Hiking Stick See **Tiller Extension.**

Hole (in the Wind) See **Lull.**

Hull The body of a boat, excluding rig and sails.

Hull Speed The maximum speed that a boat can achieve without planing.

Hyperpyrexia Increase in body temperature caused by prolonged exposure to the sun, heat, and humidity. Syn. **Heat Emergencies.**

Hypothermia Reduction in body temperature caused by prolonged exposure to cold temperatures or cold water.

I

In Irons When a boat is pointed into the wind and has stopped or is moving backwards through the water, and is temporarily unable to turn onto either tack. Syn. *In Stays.*

In Stays See **In Irons.**

In the Groove When a sailboat is moving well with proper balance and sail trim, and is steered so the sails are working at their best with the telltales flowing properly.

J

Jet Stream A snakelike river of air at about 35,000 feet in the atmosphere which affects the positions and movement of high and low pressure systems.

Jib The smaller triangular sail in front of the mast.

Jibe Changing from one tack to the other when sailing downwind. The mainsail swings across the boat, which can be a controlled maneuver or can happen unexpectedly as the wind crosses the stern. Syn. *Gybe, Jibing, Gybing.*

"Jibe Ho" A command made by the helmsman as he or she starts to jibe. Syn. *"Jibing."*

Jibing 1. The maneuver of changing from one tack to the other when sailing downwind. Syn. *Gybing, Jibe, Gybe.* 2. A command made by the helmsman as he or she starts to jibe. Syn. *"Jibe Ho."*

Jury Rig A temporary fix or replacement to damaged equipment which enables a boat to be sailed.

K

Keel The fixed underwater fin on a sailboat hull which helps provide stability and prevents the boat from slipping sideways.

Knot One nautical mile per hour. 1 knot equals 1.2 miles per hour.

L

Land Breeze See **Offshore Wind.**

Leech The back edge of a sail (between the head and clew) where the battens are located.

Leeward In the opposite direction from the wind source, or where the wind is blowing to. Syn. *Downwind*

Leeward Side The side of a sailboat or sail away from the wind source. Syn. *Downwind Side, Low Side.*

Leeway The distance a boat is pushed to leeward of its course by the action of the wind or current.

Lift 1. The aerodynamic or hydrodynamic force that results from air passing by a sail, or water flowing past a centerboard or rudder. 2. A change in wind direction which lets the boat head up.

Light 1. When only the forward edge of a sail is stalling or luffing. Syn. *Feathering, High, Luffing, Pinching, Soft.* 2. Description for low wind speed. Syn. *Soft.*

Line A rope used for a function on a boat, such as a sheet, halyard, cunningham or painter.

Low Pressure Lower atmospheric pressure generally associated with clouds, rain, and inclement weather.

Low Side The side of a sailboat away from the wind source. Syn. *Downwind Side, Leeward Side.*

Luff 1. The forward edge of a sail. 2. To stall or flap the sail at its forward edge, or over the entire sail.

Luff Rope The rope sewn into the forward edge (luff) of the mainsail, which is usually attached to the groove or track on the mast. Syn. *Bolt Rope.*

Luff Up See **Head Up.**

Luffing When the sail is stalling or flapping at its forward edge, or the entire sail is flapping. Syn. *Feathering, High, Light, Pinching, Soft.*

Lull A decrease in wind speed for a short duration. Syn. *Hole.*

M

Main See **Mainsail.**

Mainsail The sail which is attached to the mast and boom. Syn. *Main.*

Mast A spar placed vertically in a boat to hold up the sails.

Masthead The top of a mast.

Masthead Fly A wind direction indicator at the top of the mast.

MOB A person who has fallen overboard (man-overboard).

Monohull A boat with only one hull.

Moor To fasten a boat to a mooring.

Mooring A permanent anchor connected to a buoy by a rope and/or chain, to which a boat may be fastened.

Multihull A boat with more than one hull, such as a catamaran or trimaran.

N

No-Go Zone The area into the wind where a sailboat cannot sail, even with the sails pulled in all the way. The zone covers the direction pointing directly into the wind source and extending to about 45 degrees on either side of it. Syn. *No-Sail Zone.*

No-Sail Zone See **No-Go Zone.**

O

Off the Wind Any of the points of sail, except sailing upwind.

Offshore Away from the shore.

Offshore Wind Wind blowing away from the shore to the water. Syn. *Land Breeze.*

On the Beam See **Abeam.**

On the Wind See **Upwind.**

One-Design Any boat built to conform to rules so that it is identical to all others in the same class.

Onshore Toward the shore.

Onshore Wind Wind blowing from the water to the shore. Syn. *Sea Breeze.*

Outhaul A control line that is attached to the clew of the mainsail that adjusts tension along the bottom (foot) of the sail.

P

Painter A rope attached to the bow of a small boat, which is used to fasten the boat to a dock or mooring.

PFD A personal flotation device. Syn. *Life Jacket, Life Vest.*

Pinching See **Feathering.**

Planing When a boat accelerates enough to break loose from its bow wave and ride on top of the water.

Points of Sail The headings of a sailboat in relation to the wind, i.e., upwind, close reach, reach, broad reach, downwind.

Port The left side of a boat (when looking forward).

"Prepare to Tack" See **"Ready About."**

Pterygium An eye disease caused by the prolonged exposure to sun and salt water.

Puff A sudden increase in wind speed.

Push-Pull Principle The way a sail generates power to propel a boat through the water. The wind acts to push **or** pull the boat.

R

Reach Sailing with the wind coming over the side, or abeam. (One of the points of sail.)

"Ready About" A command made before tacking to ensure everyone is ready to tack. Syn. *"Prepare to Tack," "Ready to Tack."*

"Ready To Tack" See **"Ready About."**

Reef To reduce the area of a sail.

Glossary continued

Rig 1. The spars, standing rigging, sails, or their configuration, which determines the type of sailboat, such as a catboat, sloop, yawl or schooner. 2. To prepare the boat for sailing.

Right-of-Way A right-of-way boat has precedence over others on conflicting courses and has the right to maintain its course.

Roller Furling A way of stowing a sail by rolling it up around its front edge (luff), like a window shade.

Rudder An appendage in the water, which is used to steer or scull the boat.

"Rules of the Road" Laws establishing right-of-way in different situations that are intended to prevent collisions on the water.

Run Sailing away from the wind source with the sails let out all the way. Syn. *Downwind, With the Wind.*

Running Rigging The lines and associated fittings used to adjust and trim the sails, such as halyards, sheets, outhaul, downhaul, cunningham or boom vang. Syn. *Control Lines, Sail Controls.*

S

Safety Position When a boat is stopped with the sails eased and flapping with the wind coming from the side.

Sail Controls Ropes used to adjust and trim the sails, such as sheets, outhaul, downhaul, cunningham, boom vang. Syn. *Control Lines, Running Rigging.*

Sail Trim The positioning and shape of the sails to the wind. Syn. *Set.*

Sailor's Code Standards of behavior and courtesy demonstrated by sailors to other boaters.

Scoop Recovery Method The method of righting a capsized boat while "scooping" a person(s) into the cockpit as the boat rights.

Scope The ratio of the length of anchor rope let out to the depth of the water.

Scull 1. To propel a sailboat forward by moving the rudder and tiller side to side repeatedly. 2. To propel a boat forward by using an oar or paddle in a figure eight motion at the stern of the boat.

Sea Breeze Wind resulting from cooler air over the water moving in to replace the warm air that rises over the land. Syn. *Onshore Wind.*

Sea Conditions The size, shape, and frequency of the waves.

Self-Bailers See **Bailers.**

Self-Bailing The automatic draining of water from a boat through openings in the bottom or transom when sailing.

Self-Reliance The ability to sail and react to changing conditions by oneself without needing outside assistance.

Self-Rescue 1. The maneuver of righting a capsized boat and removing any water quickly without outside assistance. 2. An important design characteristic of a sailboat which allows it to be righted and bailed out quickly after a capsize without outside assistance.

Set 1. To raise and trim a sail. 2. The direction in which a current flows. Syn. *Drift.*

Shackle A U-shaped fitting closed with a pin and used to secure sails to lines or fittings, and lines to fittings.

Sheet 1. The rope which pulls in or lets out a sail. Syn. *Line.* 2. To adjust a sail by using the sheet. Syn. *Set, Trim.*

Sheet In To pull in a sail. Syn. *Take In, Trim.*

Sheet Out To let out a sail. Syn. *Ease, Let Off.*

Sheeting Pulling in or letting out the sail. Syn. *Setting, Trimming.*

Shrouds Wires which support the mast on either side. Syn. *Standing Rigging.*

Side to Side Balance Using body weight to achieve proper angle of heel for the boat.

S-Jibe A preferred method of jibing a sailboat which results in the mainsail crossing the boat under control. The path of the boat makes an "S."

Skipper See **Helmsman**

Slam Jibe See **C-Jibe.**

Soft See **Light.**

Spar A wooden or metal pole used to support a sail, such as a mast or boom.

Spinnaker A lightweight, three-cornered balloon type sail used when sailing downwind.

Squall A strong wind of short duration, usually appearing suddenly and accompanied by rain.

Standing Rigging The fixed wires and associated fittings used to support the mast.

Starboard The right side of a boat (when looking forward).

Stern The back end of a boat.

Stowing Putting away and securing sails and equipment.

T

Tack 1. To turn the bow of a sailboat through the wind or no-go zone so that the sails fill on the opposite side. Syn. *Come About.* 2. When the wind is blowing on a side of a sailboat on any of the points of sail (does not include the no-go zone), i.e., starboard tack, port tack. 3. The forward lower corner of a mainsail or jib.

Tacking 1. The maneuver of turning a sailboat through the no-go zone so the sails fill on the opposite tack. Syn. *Coming About.* 2. A command made by the helmsman when the tiller is moved to leeward to tack the boat. Syn. *"Coming About," "Hard-a-Lee," "Helms-a-Lee."*

Telltales 1. Short pieces of yarn, ribbon, thread, or tape attached to the sail which are used to show the air flow over the sail. 2. Short pieces of yarn, ribbon, thread, or tape attached to the shrouds to indicate the apparent wind direction. Syn. *Fly.*

Tidal Current The horizontal movement of water caused by tides.

Tide The vertical rise and fall of water caused by the gravitational forces of the moon and sun.

Tiller The stick or tube which is attached to the top of a rudder that is used to turn it.

Tiller Extension A stick or tube which is attached to the tiller that allows the helmsman to sit further out on the side of the boat. Syn. *Hiking Stick.*

To Weather See **Upwind.**

Topsides The sides of the hull above the waterline.

Towing Pulling a sailboat with a powerboat.

Transom The back end of a boat which is vertical to the water.

Traveller A track or bridle that controls sideways (athwartships) movement of the boom and mainsail.

Trim To adjust a sail by using the sheet. Syn. *Sheet, Set.*

Trimaran A boat with three parallel hulls, the center hull usually being the longest.

True Wind The actual speed and direction of the wind felt when standing still.

Turnbuckle A fitting used to adjust the length and tension of a shroud or forestay.

Turtling A capsize position with the boat turned upside down with the mast pointing down to the sea bottom.

U

Upwind 1. Sailing toward the wind source, or against the wind, with the sails pulled in all the way, tacking as you go. Syn. *Beating, Close-Hauled, On the Wind, Sailing to Weather, Sailing to Windward.* 2. In the direction of the wind source or where the wind is blowing from. Syn. *Windward, To Weather.*

Upwind Side See **Windward Side.**

V

Vang See **Boom Vang.**

W

Walkover Recovery Method A capsize recovery method where the helmsman climbs over the windward gunwale when re-righting the boat.

Water Reading Observing and assessing the wind blowing on the water surface.

Waterline The line where the water surface meets the hull when the boat is floating at rest.

Weather Helm The natural tendency of a sailboat to turn toward the wind (to weather), which the helmsman feels as the tiller tries to turn to leeward.

Weather Side See **Windward Side.**

Wind Sensing Determining wind direction and velocity using feel, sight, and hearing.

Windward In the direction toward the wind source, or where the wind is blowing from. Syn. *To Weather, Upwind.*

Windward Side The side of the sailboat or sail toward the wind source. Syn. *High Side, Weather Side, Upwind Side.*

Wing and Wing Sailing directly downwind with the jib and mainsail set on opposite sides of the boat to capture more wind.

With the Wind See **Run.**

A Typical Chart: Roadmap for the Water

A quick look at a nautical chart of your sailing area can be entertaining *and* informative. The small numbers in the water areas **(A)** indicate water depth at low tide, with light blue tints **(B)** showing the shallowest water depth and white showing the deepest. Navigational buoys marking channels, shallow water and rocks **(C)** are designated by different colors and numbers to correspond with the actual colors and numbers of the buoys. Prominent landmarks on shore **(D)** are also indicated, such as towers, smokestacks and large buildings, which can serve as valuable reference points.

The face of a compass — called a "compass rose" **(E)** — is usually overlaid on the chart at several locations, allowing sailors to establish, or "chart," a compass course between various locations on the chart. The sailor then knows what direction to match on his boat's compass to head for a certain destination. Most dinghy sailors are close enough to land, however, that compass navigation is not necessary.

Studying a chart is not only fun, it will make you a safer and more confident sailor.

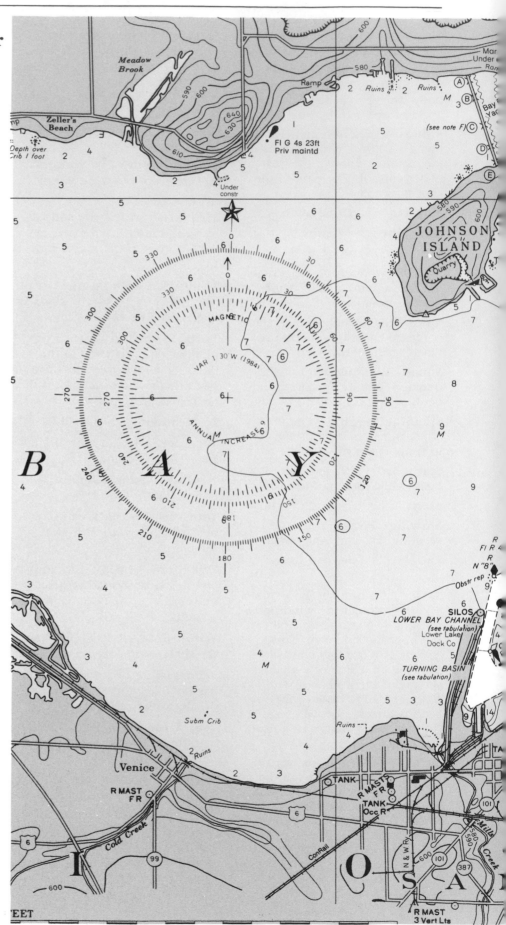

Car-topping and Trailering

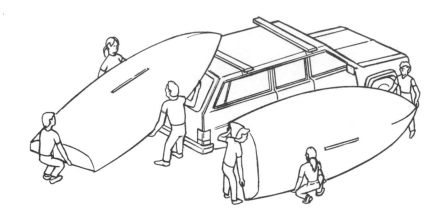

When car-topping a boat, it can be loaded from the rear of the car or the side. Be sure to have enough people to lift the boat comfortably to avoid possible injury or damage.

Tie-down boat securely on car top with straps or lines across boat and lines from bow and stern to forward and rear bumpers — preferably to each corner.

Trailering is necessary for larger boats. Trailer designs and features vary. Remember proper trailer maintenance will help prevent breakdowns on the road.

Mast support and tie-down

Bow socket

Mast tied down

Ball & socket

Safety chain and brake light wires

Padding on end of mast

Straps for hull

Brake lights

Hoists and Safety

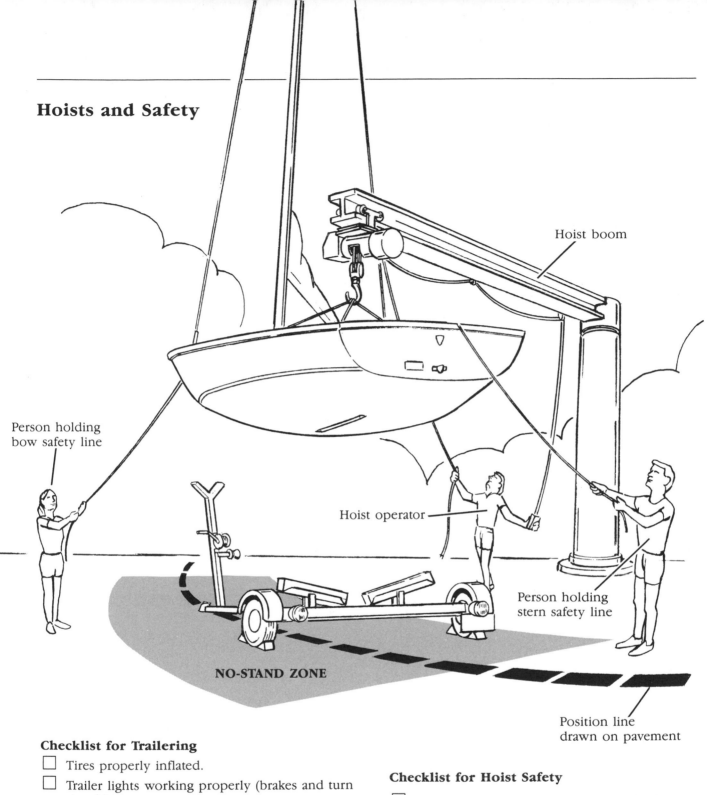

Hoist boom

Person holding bow safety line

Hoist operator

Person holding stern safety line

NO-STAND ZONE

Position line drawn on pavement

Checklist for Trailering

☐ Tires properly inflated.

☐ Trailer lights working properly (brakes and turn signals).

☐ Ball on hitch and trailer socket matched and secure.

☐ About 10-15% weight on trailer tongue.
(If boat is too far back, trailer will "fishtail.")

☐ Axle and wheel bearings well greased.

☐ Boat centered on trailer.

☐ Tiedowns securely fastened (check frequently).

☐ Safety chain connected to car frame (not bumper).

☐ Check state trailering laws for states you're traveling through.

Checklist for Hoist Safety

☐ Hoist area clear of overhead power lines.

☐ Bailers and drain plugs in hull closed.

☐ Centerboard secured in "up" position.

☐ Safety line attached to bow and stern.

☐ Bridle or straps securely fastened.

☐ All persons clear of area under boat and boat's path during launch.

☐ No one in boat when boat is on hoist.

Land Drills for Improving Sailing Skills

*Trapping Mainsheet - To transfer mainsheet to the tiller, pass it behind you and firmly grab tiller and mainsheet.

Walking Tacking Drill

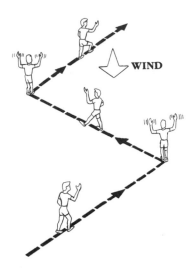

WIND

Walking Jibing Drill

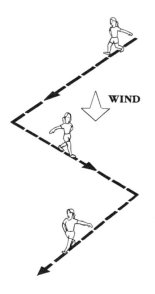

WIND

Right-of-Way Walking Drill

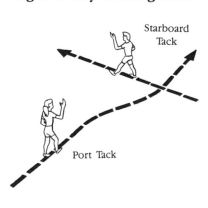

Starboard Tack

Port Tack

Tacking Drill (Helmsman)

To practice ashore, three stools, a broom handle and length of rope represent the boat as shown in 1.

1. Push tiller away from you. Facing forward, step across boat, crouch to avoid boom, shift body to opposite side.

2. Trapping mainsheet in sheet hand* reach sheet hand behind you to grab tiller.

3. Sit down on opposite side. Front hand reaches across chest to pick up sheet from tiller hand.

Jibing Drill (Helmsman)

1. Preparing to Jibe. . .grab mainsheet parts, pull tiller toward you, step across boat and crouch to avoid boom as you guide it across.

2. As boat shifts, center yourself and, facing forward, reach sheet arm behind and grasp tiller and sheet — freeing other hand.

3. Sit down on opposite side. With new front arm, reach across chest to take sheet. Adjust sheet to retain speed on new course.

Capsize Recovery Land Drill
(for boats under 150 lbs.)

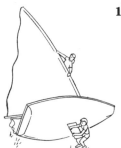  

WIND

1. Two people carefully capsize boat on grass.

2. Student leans on daggerboard and starts to re-right boat.

3. Student climbs into boat. Sheet should be all the way out with sail luffing.

Water Drills for Improving Sailing Skills

Stop and Start Solo Drill

Safety Position Solo Drill

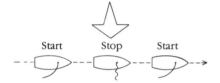

Circling Solo Drill

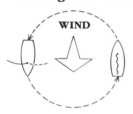

Glide Zone Solo Drill

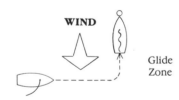

Leaving and Returning Drill

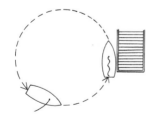

Man-Overboard (MOB) Drill

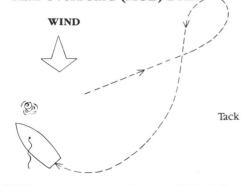

Oval Upwind - Downwind Drill

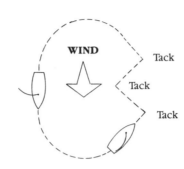

Oval Tacking & Jibing Drill

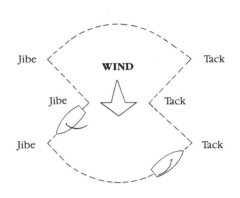

Group Practice

Stop and Start Group Drill

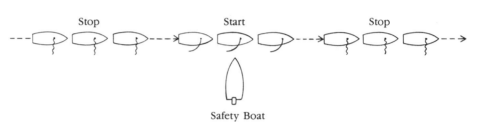

Safety Position Group Drill

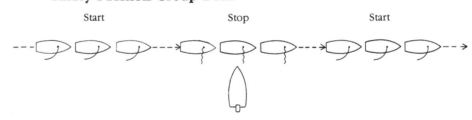

Follow-the-Leader Drill

Crosswind Figure-8 Drill

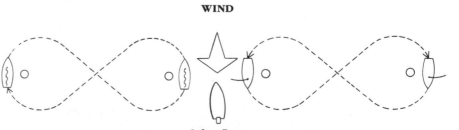

Group Drills continued

Circle Safety Boat Drill

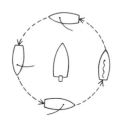

Crosswind Loop Drill

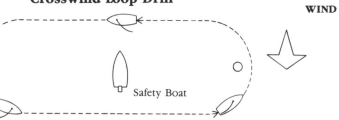

Safety Boat

WIND

Oval Upwind - Downwind Drill

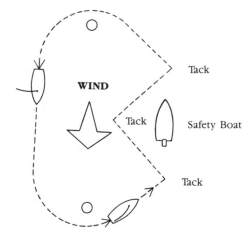

WIND

Tack

Tack

Safety Boat

Tack

Oval Tacking - Jibing Drill

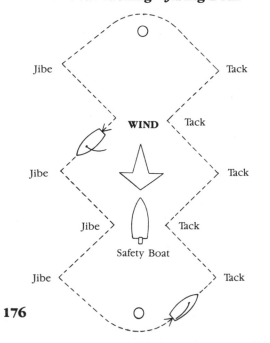

Jibe   Tack

Jibe   Tack

WIND

Jibe   Tack

Jibe   Tack

Safety Boat

Jibe   Tack

Rectangular Course Drill

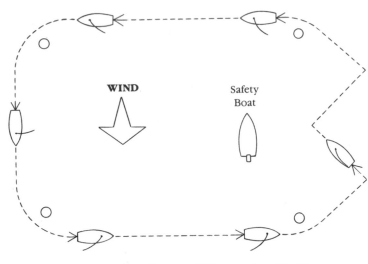

WIND   Safety Boat

Leaving and Returning Drill

WIND

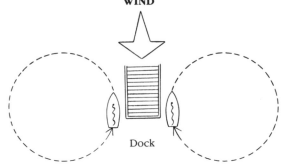

Dock

Coming Alongside Drill

WIND

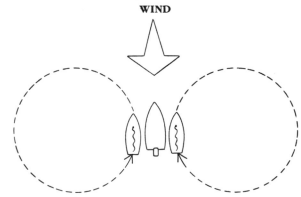

Confined Sailing Area Drill

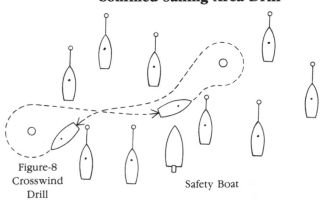

Figure-8 Crosswind Drill   Safety Boat

Helpful Books and Videos

BOOKS

The Annapolis Book of Seamanship — by John Rousmaniere. Published by Simon & Schuster, New York, NY. This book covers basic to intermediate sailing and seamanship, and is particularly suitable for anyone who intends to sail a cruising boat with family and friends. Includes extensive sections on navigation, weather, modern electronics, maintenance, safety and design theory.

Sail Power: The Complete Guide to Sails & Sail Handling — by Wallace Ross. Published by Alfred Knopf, New York, NY. All you ever wanted to know about sail theory, design and proper trim.

Weather for the Mariner — by Rear Admiral William J. Kotsch, USN (Retired). Published by Naval Institute Press, Annapolis, MD. This classic textbook provides a thorough and intelligent explanation of weather for the sailor, ranging from basic principles of meteorology to forecasting techniques. Interesting and valuable for both weekend sailors and oceangoing salts. It is not a quick read.

Knots and Lines Illustrated — by Paul and Arthur Snyder. Published by John deGraff, Inc., Clinton Corners, NY. An excellent introduction to basic knots and how to use them onboard a boat. Includes the handling of cleats and winches as well as heaving and stowing lines—all shown in step-by-step detail.

Dinghies and Daysailers— by Butch and Rita Wilcox. Published by Barca De Vela Publishing, Phoenix, AZ. A catalog of nearly 200 daysailers and one-design classes from six to 38 feet. Complete with specifications, photos, drawings and descriptions of each boat.

VIDEOS

Learn to Sail Videos— produced by McNamara Video, Inc. The award-winning three-tape instructor/student series is distributed by American Red Cross, Washington, DC and USYRU, Newport, RI. A two-tape student series is also available from Sea TV, Ltd., New Haven, CT. *Start Sailing Right* has been designed and produced as a companion to the *Learn to Sail* video tapes.

Annapolis Book of Seamanship — produced by Creative Programming, Inc., New York, NY. Available through numerous marine outlets. Three-tape series: *Cruising Under Sail, Heavy Weather Sailing* and *Safety at Sea*. Narrated by John Rousmaniere, author of the book of the same name, with an emphasis on auxiliary cruising sailboats.

For More Help and Information

USYRU — Training Office
Box 209
Newport, RI 02840
(401) 849-5200

For information concerning basic sailing, intermediate and racing courses, instructional manuals and videos, basic sailing certificates, and certified instructors.

USYRU — Inshore Office
Box 209
Newport, RI 02840
(401) 849-5200

For information concerning boats, class associations, boat manufacturers and power-line safety.

American Red Cross
National Headquarters
17th and D Streets NW
Washington, DC 20006
(202) 737-8300

For information concerning basic sailing, canoeing, kayaking, swimming, lifeguarding, first aid, CPR, instructional manuals, videos and certificates.

United States Coast Guard
Commandant (G-BEL-4)
2100 2nd Street SW
Washington, DC 20593-0001
(202) 267-2229

For information concerning national laws and regulations for water safety, boating and equipment requirements.

National Oceanic & Atmospheric Administration (NOAA)
National Ocean Service
Distribution Branch, N-CG33
Riverdale, MD 20737
(301) 436-6990

For information concerning weather, water, charts, and NOAA weather reporting stations.

Appendix

Answer Key for Review Exercises (Chapters 1-20)

Chapter 1

I. Multiple Choice

1.b, 2.a, 3.b

II. Matching

1.d, 2.a, 3.e, 4.b, 5.c

III. Exploring Sailing

1. Problems for your sailing site might include electrical hazards, overhead wires, current, group instruction limitations, confined sailing areas, freighter traffic, shallow water, little wind in the morning hours, and launching/docking.
2. Exercise and nutrition contribute to both the mental and physical skills of a sailor to be more successful in sailing. Nutrition helps with both physical and mental readiness, and exercise assists strength, endurance, and reduces the chance of injury.
3. Examples might include extra drinking water, towlines, special clothing, extra small sails, specialized medical supplies, launching equipment.

Chapter 2

I. True or False

1.F, 2.F, 3.T, 4.F, 5.T, 6.T, 7.T

II. Exploring Sailing

1. Control signals are a very effective way to communicate on the water. Voice commands are often difficult because of the noise from wind and sails. Control signals increase safety on the water by the use of signals that can be easily understood on the water.
2. Paddle, first aid kit, extra PFD's, anchor with line, bailer, horn, compass, tools, supply of water, regional or local requirements such as boat registration.
3. Examples might be overhead wires and cables, electrical outlets, non-grounded outlets, lights, power tools, submerged cables, etc.

Chapter 3

I. True or False

1.F, 2.F, 3.T, 4.F, 5.T, 6.F, 7.F

II. Matching

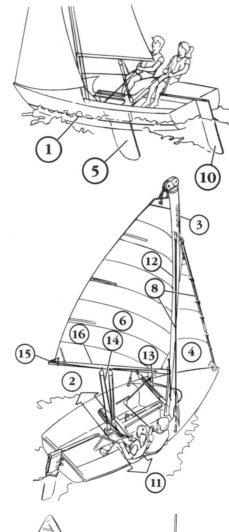

III. Fill in the Blanks

1. lead or iron
2. multihull/catamaran
3. port
4. tiller/tiller extension
5. standing
6. running

Chapter 4

I. Matching

1.f, 2.b, 3.a, 4.c, 5.d, 6.g, 7.h, 8.e

II. True or False

1.F, 2.T, 3.T, 4.T, 5.T

Chapter 5

I. True or False

1.T, 2.T, 3.T, 4.F, 5.F

II. Matching

1.c, 2.a, 3.g, 4.b, 5.f, 6.d, 7.e

Chapter 6

I. True or False

1.T, 2.T, 3.F, 4.T, 5.F, 6.T

II. Exploring Sailing

1. Steps for raising the main: locate the three corners of the sail, then insert head into mast track. Attach halyard to head, tighten and secure halyard. Attach the tack to gooseneck fitting. Uncleat outhaul line, then pull the clew along boom track to back end of boom, and attach the outhaul. Tighten and cleat outhaul, free main sheet and boom vang. Raise mainsail by pulling the halyard while feeding sail in mast track. Tighten and secure halyard.

Chapter 7

I. Multiple Choice

1.c, 2.b, 3.a, 4.b

II. Matching

1.b, 2.c, 3.d, 4.a

III. Exploring Sailing

1. The helmsman and crew must always work together to keep the boat balanced. The helmsman always sits on the windward side — opposite the boom. The crew position depends on the speed of the wind and will change from the windward side, to the middle of the cockpit or the leeward side. When sailing upwind the boat should be heeled to leeward a small amount. At other times, the boat should be nearly level.
2. By sheeting out the sails, or turning the boat into the no-go zone.
3. The crew performs these important tasks on a sailboat: lookout observer, boat balance, sail controls, jib trim, launching or docking, picking up a tow, picking up a mooring and maintaining environmental awareness.

Chapter 8

I. True or False

1.T, 2.F, 3.T, 4.T

II. Multiple Choice

1.b, 2.b, 3.c

III. Matching

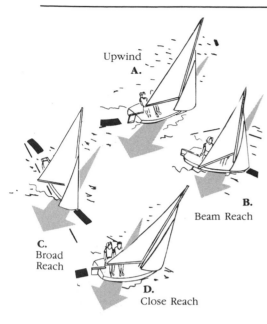

Upwind
A.

B.
Beam Reach

C.
Broad Reach

D.
Close Reach

IV. Exploring Sailing

1. Turn the boat into the no-go zone.
2. When sailing upwind the boat's sail trim, steering, and boat balance all must be working smoothly to make progress toward your destination. It is easy to under or over steer the boat, or to sheet the sails incorrectly. Coordination of all these factors requires time and practice.

Chapter 9

I. Fill in the Blanks

1. "Tacking"/"Hard-a-Lee"
2. upwind
3. 45
4. no-go
5. 5 to 7

II. Multiple Choice

1.b, 2.c, 3.a

III. Exploring Sailing

1. Yes. However, this is not recommended. Keeping the main sheet cleated increases the chance of capsize, and limits the boat's maneuverability especially in medium air or more.
2. The stronger winds make it more difficult for the boat to turn through the no-go zone. This increases the chances of getting in irons or making unsuccessful attempts at tacking. To tack properly in heavier air the tack must be done more quickly.

Chapter 10

I. True or False

1.T, 2.T, 3.T, 4.F, 5.T, 6.F, 7.T, 8.F, 9.F, 10.T

II. Exploring Sailing

1. See "Jibing Steps" in Chapter 10.
2. Also see "Tips for Easier Jibing" in Chapter 10. Be careful not to sail by the lee. Maintain wind sensing and look for wind on the water that is coming from behind and slightly to leeward of the boat. Also, watch the boom. When it starts to rise slightly, an accidental jibe is possible. The boom will not rise, however, if the vang is pulled tight.

Chapter 11

I. Matching

1.b, 2.d, 3.c, 4.a

II. Fill in the Blanks

1. natural/normal
2. wind/no-go zone
3. stronger
4. flotation

III. Exploring Sailing

1. Sudden gust of wind, poor jibe or tack, broken equipment, letting go of the tiller, quick turns in heavy air or failure to sheet out sails.
2. Bringing a person into a boat should occur at the windward side of the transom. At the same time the person in the water is kicking, the person in the boat should pull him/her over the transom. Once the chest is over the transom a leg can be swung over and into the boat. The PFD helps to cushion the body on the transom.
3. Capsize safety rules: 1. Always stay with the boat, 2. Don't swim under the hull, 3. Always stay calm — don't panic, 4. Don't remove your PFD.

Chapter 12

I. True or False

1.T, 2.T, 3.T

II. Multiple Choice

1.b, 2.c, 3.b

III. Exploring Sailing

1. Associated MOB skills: sailing on all points of sail, entering a boat, luffing and safety position, communication and environmental awareness, stopping and starting, tacking or jibing.
2.

Tack

Chapter 13

I. Matching

1.b, 2.c, 3.a, 4.e, 5.d

II. Exploring Sailing

1. For all types of mooring and docking situations, determining the gliding distance of the boat is the key for doing these maneuvers successfully. The glide zone is the safest way to stop a boat by turning it into the no-go zone. Each boat will have a slightly different glide zone factor. If the glide zone is not determined correctly, it can be modified by sculling or paddling, or by backing the sails.

2. At times, when leaving a dock you may get in irons. You can also leave the leeward side of a dock by backing the boat away from it and using the same techniques for getting out of irons. When the boat has started to drift backwards from the dock, push the tiller and the boom in the same direction that you wish to turn the boat (see Chapter 9).
3. The type of beach, the amount of water depth, and the wind direction will affect some of the maneuvers, but the general steps for leaving and returning to a beach are as follows.

Leaving:
a. Helmsman and crew walk boat into water until there is enough water to lower or attach the rudder.
b. Helmsman gets into boat and lowers the centerboard about half way.
c. The crew turns the boat until the bow is pointed in the right direction.
d. The crew gets into the boat, and helmsman and crew sheet in the sails.
e. When the water is deep enough, the crew lowers the centerboard to the correct position for the point of sail.

Returning:
a. The crew raises the centerboard to about half way.
b. The helmsman turns the boat into the no-go zone to stop the boat.
c. The crew gets out of the boat and keeps it pointed into the wind.
d. The helmsman raises or removes the rudder, and then gets out of the boat.
e. The helmsman and crew bring the boat onto the beach with the bow pointing into the wind.
f. The sails are lowered.

Chapter 14

I. Matching

1.b, 2.c, 3.e, 4.d, 5.a

II. True or False

1.T, 2.T, 3.F, 4.F

III. Exploring Sailing

1. To help de-power the sails. This keeps the boat more stable and allows it to go upwind more efficiently.
2. For safety reasons it is best to set a maximum wind speed range. The limit will change as your sailing skills improve. Your instructor is the best person to help you in setting this wind limit.

Chapter 15

I. True or False

1.F, 2.T, 3.T, 4.T, 5.F

II. Exploring Sailing

1. The best way to avoid a collision is through environmental awareness and anticipation of problems. Looking ahead and planning your course is a good method to sail free of trouble situations. Most learn-to-sail students wait too long before making a decision to avoid other boats.

Answer Key for (Chapters 1-20)

2. The crew plays an important role in helping the helmsman steer a safe course. In particular, when sailing on a reach or upwind, the helmsman's view is blocked by the jib. The crew can easily look behind the jib or through the window in the jib. Along with sail trim and boat balance the crew should also provide continuous environmental awareness.

3. Five basic right-of-way rules: 1. Starboard tack boat has right-of-way over the boat on port tack. 2. Leeward boat has right-of-way over the windward boat. 3. If one boat is tacking or jibing, the other boat on a tack has right-of-way. 4. If one boat is overtaking another, the slower boat has right-of-way. 5. Sailboats have right-of-way over most powerboats.

Chapter 16

I. Multiple Choice

1.a, 2.a, 3.b, 4.a, 5.c

II. Matching

1.b, 2.a, 3.c, 4.d

III. Exploring Sailing

1. Steps for anchoring are: make sure the anchor and its line are free and clear of entanglements, then turn the boat into the no-go zone. After the boat has stopped, drop the anchor by lowering it slowly into the water. Give a sharp pull on the line to make the anchor dig (set) into the bottom. Secure the line to the bow of the boat and lead it through a chock, if possible. Then, drop the sails and stow them if needed.

2. The best method of coming alongside another boat is to use the glide factor and coast to a stop by sailing into the no-go zone. Make sure fingers and hands don't get caught between the two boats. An alternative method is to sail on a beam reach and slowly sheet out the sails while the boat coasts to a stop at the transom of the other boat.

Chapter 17

I. Multiple Choice

1.b, 2.a, 3.c

II. Matching

1.d, 2.c, 3.f, 4.b, 5.e, 6.a

III. Exploring Sailing

1. In the mid-latitudes of the northern hemisphere most prevailing winds are from the west. This is the result of the Earth's rotational forces combined with the heating and cooling forces between the tropical and arctic areas.

2. This is a regional decision.

3. Poor weather signs are: increase in cloud cover and darkening skies, sudden increase or decrease in wind speed, change in wind direction, lightning, thunder on the horizon, gusty wind conditions and/or falling barometer.

Chapter 18

I. Matching

1.e, 2.f, 3.d, 4.b, 5.c, 6.a

II. Exploring Sailing

1. Rope types and their uses: *Dacron* — used for halyards and sheets because it has low stretch. *Nylon* — used for anchors and dock lines because it stretches. *Polypropylene* — used for pickup lines for moorings and towing because it floats.

2. Steps for tying a bowline. Step 1: Make a loop at least a foot from the end of the line by crossing the short end over the long end. Step 2: Bring the short end through the loop from underneath. Step 3: Pass it behind the long end and back down through the same loop. Step 4: Pull it tight.

3. The low stretch and soft texture make dacron ideal for sheets.

Answer Key for Sailing Fundamentals Review

Review Question #1

a. no change, b. sheet in, c. sheet out

Review Question #2

a. no change, b. pull tiller away from sail, c. push tiller toward sail

Review Question #3

a. move the tiller to the right, b. move the tiller to the left

Review Question #4

a. sheet out, b. turn toward the wind

Review Question #5

a. push the tiller toward the sail

Review Question #6

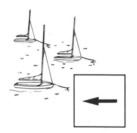

Review Question #7

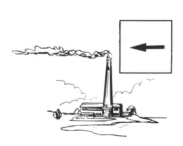

Review Question #8

Upwind

Reach

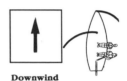

Downwind

Review Question #9

1. D, 2. B/H, 3. A/F, 4. E, 5. A/F, 6. C

Review Question #10

a. no, b. one person holds onto the inside of the cockpit and kicks, and the other puts his or her weight on the centerboard, c: no

Heather Colston (213) 596-1960

Coast Guard Classes:
Safety

Russ Ward
213 498-6702

Answer Key for Additional Sailing Skills Review

Review Question #1

a. more wind speed, b. the boat will heel more, c. sheet out the sail a little, d. turn the boat toward the wind a little

Review Question #2

a. course 2, b. A) tacking, B) tacking, C) turning away from the wind (heading off), D) turning toward the wind (heading up) onto a close reach, E) jibing, F) turning toward the wind (heading up) onto a close reach

Review Question #3

a. tighten it, b. tighten it

Review Question #4

a. all the way down, b. all the way down, c. half up, d. three-quarters up, e. three-quarters up

Review Question #5

a. B, b. course 1, c. course 2

Review Question #6

a. course 1, b. before you have picked up the tow

Review Question #7

a.

b. course 3

Review Question #8

1. a, 2. b/e 3. a, 4. c, 5. d, 6. a.

Review Question #9

a. B, b. A, c. Z
d.

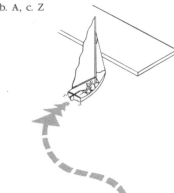

e. *C* — turning away from the wind (heading off), *D* — turning into no-go zone and entering glide zone, f. *E* — sheeting out sails, g. *F* — turning into no-go zone, *G* — lowering sails, and then turning for the dock

Review Question #10

a. and b. see diagram (below)

c. A - downwind sailing, B - beam reach, C - upwind sailing d. jibe, e. sail a straight course, f. tack, g. sheeted out all the way, h. sheeted in half way, i. sheeted in all the way

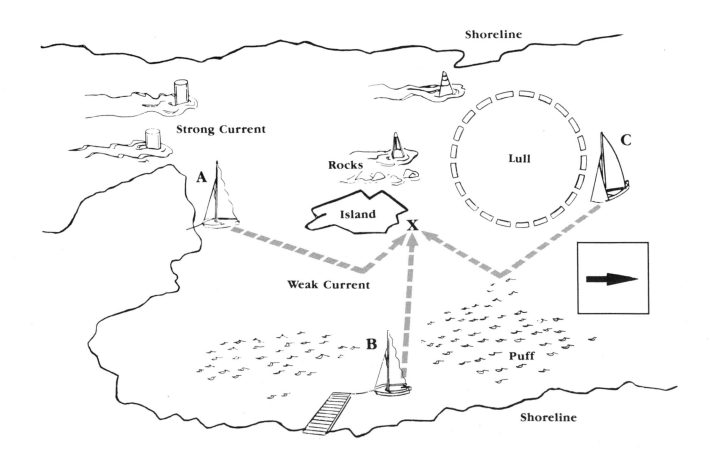